Governing Cross-Border Higher Education

D1614939

Governing Cross-Border Higher Education examines the role of governments in relation to three key aspects of international education: student mobility; migration of international students; and transnational provision through collaboration or branch campuses. The research for this book is informed by interviews with key stakeholders in ten countries and extensive engagement with policy makers and international agencies. It analyses the ways in which governments are able to direct or at least influence these cross-border movements in higher education.

The book explores key issues that national governments are invariably required to contend with in an increasingly globalized higher education market, as well as the policy options available to them in such a climate. Alongside this, there is analysis into why states adopt particular approaches, with critical assessment of their varying success. Key topics include:

- the political economy of international higher education;
- recruiting students;
- promoting and regulating transnational provision;
- student migration;
- governing educational imports;
- managing the outflow of students;
- the regulated market.

This book will be a valuable and insightful resource for those involved in higher education policy and interested in the globalization of the higher education market.

Christopher Ziguras is Deputy Dean, International in the School of Global, Urban and Social Studies at RMIT University, Melbourne, Australia.

Grant McBurnie is an Associate in the School of Global, Urban and Social Studies at RMIT University, Melbourne, Australia.

Internationalization in Higher Education
Series Editor: Elspeth Jones

This series addresses key themes in the development of internationalization within Higher Education. Up to the minute and international in both appeal and scope, books in the series focus on delivering contributions from a wide range of contexts and provide both theoretical perspectives and practical examples. Written by some of the leading experts in the field, they are vital guides that discuss and build upon evidence-based practice and provide a clear evaluation of outcomes.

Titles in the series:

Tools for Teaching in an Educationally Mobile World
Jude Carroll

Developing the Global Student
Higher education in an era of globalisation
David Killick

Governing Cross-Border Higher Education
Christopher Ziguras and Grant McBurnie

Governing Cross-Border Higher Education

RT

Christopher Ziguras and Grant McBurnie

Routledge
Taylor & Francis Group

LONDON AND NEW YORK

First published 2015
by Routledge
2 Park Square, Milton Park, Abingdon, Oxon OX14 4RN

and by Routledge
711 Third Avenue, New York, NY 10017

Routledge is an imprint of the Taylor & Francis Group, an informa business

British Library Cataloguing in Publication Data
A catalogue record for this book is available from the British Library

Library of Congress Cataloging in Publication Data
Ziguras, Christopher.
Governing cross-border higher education / Christopher Ziguras and
Grant McBurnie.
    pages cm.—(Internationalization in higher education series)
1. Transnational education—Government policy. 2. Education and
globalization. I. McBurnie, Grant, 1960– II. Title.
LC1095.Z54 2014
378.1'75—dc23   2014010147

ISBN: 978-0-415-73487-5 (hbk)
ISBN: 978-0-415-73488-2 (pbk)
ISBN: 978-1-315-76401-6 (ebk)

Typeset in Galliard
by Book Now Ltd, London

Printed and bound in Great Britain by
TJ International Ltd, Padstow, Cornwall

Contents

Tables

Series editor's foreword

This series addresses the rapidly changing and highly topical field of internationalization in higher education. Arising from the notion of international education, which had essentially a curricular focus on international themes such as development studies and comparative education, use of the term 'internationalization' began more recently, during the latter part of the twentieth century. Since that time attention to the international dimension of higher education has become increasingly visible in institutional strategies as well as national and international agendas. Early distinctions were established between, on the one hand, market-driven interests in the recruitment of international students and, on the other, practitioners who see transformational potential through internationalization activities as a means of enhancing personal and professional development.

While those themes continue to be of importance, the intervening years have seen a more nuanced range of interests bridging that divide. Informed by diverse disciplines including anthropology, languages & communication, business & marketing, environmental studies, strategic leadership and pedagogy, internationalization is now high on the priority list for universities around the world. This is, in part, as a response to changing global environments but also in reaction to globalization itself with its potential for homogenization if taken to extremes. The many dimensions of contemporary internationalization require institutions to adjust and define the concept for their own purposes, adding to the richness of our understanding of the 'meta-discipline' in practice. This is perhaps most evident in countries where institutional and curricular internationalization is a more recent development, and traditional 'western' internationalization practice requires further exploration for appropriacy in local contexts. Development and implementation of the concept in such new environments will add to our understanding of the benefits and challenges of internationalization practice over the coming years.

The answer to the question 'what is internationalization?' will thus vary from one university to another and indeed by subject discipline within that institution. Reframing the question as 'what is internationalization for this university, in this particular context, and for this discipline within it?' begins to reflect more accurately the diversity and complexity of this growing field.

Today there are compelling drivers for university leaders to adopt an integrated rather than a unidimensional approach to internationalization. Intensifying competition for talent, changes in global student flows, international branch campuses and growing complexity in cross-border activity, along with the rising influence of institutional rankings, all provide economic impetus and reputational consequences of success or failure. Meanwhile additional incentive is provided by growing awareness that the intercultural competence required for global contexts is equally important for living and working in today's increasingly diverse and multicultural societies. Research indicates a rising demand by employers for university graduates with enhanced global perspectives and intercultural competence, and students themselves are showing increased interest in international and intercultural experience. Internationalization thus has both global and more local intercultural interests at its heart.

Internationalization can facilitate an inclusive, intercultural dimension to the teaching, research, service and the commercial and entrepreneurial pursuits of a contemporary university. It is most successful when seen as an enabling factor in the achievement of wider corporate goals rather than as an aim in itself. Embedding internationalization through changing institutional language, culture and attitudes into standard university practice is more likely to achieve this than if seen as a separate goal in itself.

Internationalization as a powerful force for change is an underlying theme of this series, in contrast to economic or brand-enhancing aspects of international engagement. It seeks to address these complex topics as internationalization matures into its next phase. It aims to reflect contemporary concerns, with volumes geared to the major questions of our time. Written or edited by leading thinkers and authors from around the world, while giving a voice to emerging researchers, the series will offer theoretical perspectives with practical applications, focusing on some of the critical issues in this developing field for higher education leaders and practitioners alike.

Governing Cross-Border Higher Education

This volume examines the role of governments in relation to three key aspects of international education: student mobility; migration of international students; and transnational provision through collaboration or branch campuses. It analyses the ways in which governments are able to direct or at least influence these cross-border movements in higher education.

Challenging the notion that education and commerce are fundamentally incompatible, the book maps cross-border educational flows and government policies towards them. It examines skilled migration policies and the impetus for trans-national education. Inward and outward flows of students are considered along with the positive and negative implications for the home country.

The book goes on to consider different types of regulatory framework for foreign programmes and campuses, and the domestic political factors influencing the ways in which governments frame the regulation of foreign providers. It finds that states are centrally involved in promoting and managing cross-border flows and proposes a reconceptualization of the role of governance to assist stakeholders in engaging with the emerging political landscape of international education.

Key topics include:

- the political economy of international higher education;
- recruiting students;
- promoting and regulating transnational provision;
- student migration;
- governing educational imports;
- managing the outflow of students;
- the regulated market.

The book offers valuable insight for those involved in higher education policy, and the globalization of higher education markets.

Elspeth Jones
Emerita Professor of the Internationalisation of Higher Education,
Leeds Metropolitan University

Acknowledgements

This book has been many years in the making, and the over that time we have had the pleasure of working with many who have influenced our thinking. We would like to acknowledge the support of Tony Adams, Elspeth Jones, Jane Knight, Kurt Larsen, Betty Leask, Simon Marginson, Dean Neubauer, Julia Nielson, the late Marjorie Peace Lenn, Madeleine Green, Eva Egron-Polak, Tony Pollock, Fazal Rizvi, Karel Reus, Antony Stella, Andree Sursock, Stamenka Uvalic-Trumbic, Zeynep Varoglu, Dirk Van Damme, Stephan Vincent-Lancrin, Peter van der Hijden, Bernd Wachter, Marijk van der Wende, Leo West and David Woodhouse.

In particular we would like to thank Cate Gribble for her support over many years, especially in relation to Vietnam, Singapore and Malaysia. Thanks also to Aramiha Harwood for his research assistance, Kym Holthouse for his work for us in Timor Leste, and Hung Hiep Pham for his valuable feedback.

Chris would like to express appreciation to Hans de Wit, Davina Potts, Edi Mazzoleni and Francesca Finotello at the Center for Higher Education Internationalization at Università Cattolica del Sacro Cuore in Milan. The Tony Adams Visiting Senior Scholar fellowship supported me to spend several months at CHEI in late 2013, a wonderful opportunity to think, write, discuss and learn, in the company of an impressive band of international educators. And very special thanks to my family – Ilana Werba and Willow and Zoe Ziguras – who have been eternally supportive through this shared journey. They lived international education wholeheartedly in Milan while I simply wrote about it, and their enthusiasm and insightfulness was inspiring to me and to many others.

Special thanks from Grant to Kerry Lee, my B1.

We gratefully acknowledge the support we have received from the Australian Research Council without which this book would not have been possible.

Introduction

The world has become indifferent to tradition and past reputations, unforgiving of frailty and ignorant of custom or practice. Success will go to those individuals, institutions and countries which are swift to adapt, slow to complain and open to change. And the task for governments is to help citizens rise to this challenge.

Andreas Schleicher (2013), OECD Deputy Director for Education and Skills, responding to claims that PISA results were flawed

Hours after the OECD released the results from the latest Programme for International Student Assessment (PISA) which showed Shanghai's school system leading the field, *Time* magazine, without having read the technical report on the testing process, published an article alleging that the Chinese must have cheated. The magazine's unwillingness to believe the data and Schleicher's terse defence represent two polar responses to the effects of globalization on education policy. PISA has globalized a relatively old technology of governance, testing outcomes, to render certain forms of learning comparable globally, and has generated a wealth of discussion about the effects of various policies and practices on students' learning. The OECD's Assessment of Higher Education Learning Outcomes (AHELO) proposes to do the same for higher education, in a more student-focused manner than existing university rankings, which focus heavily on research and reputation (OECD, 2013a, 2013b; Tremblay, Lalancette & Roseveare, 2012).

The globalization of standardized assessments is one of many developments that are transforming the global education landscape, placing educational systems, institutions and students around the world in an increasingly unified field. Similarly, the growing ease of international mobility for students and education providers is allowing both the consumers and producers of higher education to move across that global field more readily. Like testing, mobility is not new. Higher education systems around the world have been developed from a small set of models originating in Europe, scholars have moved as long as universities have existed, and disciplinary knowledge in every field has always transcended the nation. But higher education mobility has changed in recent decades. The volume of information available to students about foreign educational options has been dramatically expanded by the Internet and by global networks of student recruitment agents. The affordability and convenience of international travel have improved steadily, allowing both students and educators to relocate more easily. And economic globalization has both expanded the global pool of students with the means to pursue higher education, and fuelled labour market demand for advanced qualifications. Much has been written on the globalization of higher education, and we do not intend to dwell on these developments in this book. Instead, we take globalization for granted and ask instead how governments respond to the changing context in which higher education is more readily offered across national borders.

This book focuses on the ways in which national governments seek to steer students and higher education providers within an increasingly globalized higher education market and the extent to which they are effective in doing so. At the most fundamental level, this is a study of how states are able to manipulate their differential control over (and responsibility for) organizations and individuals on either side of their borders to shape the conditions of both national and transnational markets in education.

Our interest in is the ways in which governments attempt to influence forms of cross-border education that are neither totally directed by the state nor free of state interference, but are rather subject to a range of regulatory interventions that attempt to steer students and providers in ways that meet the aims of various governments. The analysis is thematic, focusing on three issues that appear to be assuming growing importance to governments around the world: how to balance expanded access to international education with equitable and socially useful distribution; how to manage the tendency of international student mobility to lead to skilled migration; and how to regulate the provision of education by transnational institutions operating outside their home country.

This book is primarily concerned with cross-border provision of whole programmes through the cross-border movement of students or providers. This is, of course, a small part of the internationalization of higher education, but an important component. Governments' higher education internationalization strategies are increasingly broad, moving towards what Hudzik (2011) terms 'comprehensive internationalisation', involving also the adoption of international curriculum and pedagogies, increasing inter-institutional linkages, boosting research profiles, and various other means of improving the international standing of national systems. In recent years there have been many studies of such policy approaches at the national level, particularly in Asia where governments have been very proactive (Gopinathan & Lee, 2011; Lo, 2009; Luijten-Lub, Van der Wende & Huisman, 2005; Yamada, 2012). We begin, however, from a different point. Rather than examining governance of internationalization from the standpoint of particular national strategies, we begin with the observation that governments are rarely the drivers of change in this field. In an increasingly open global higher education environment in which most cross-border study is self-funded, students and educational institutions make their own choices. These choices, as we will demonstrate, are shaped in many respects by the ways in which governments regulate, but the patterns of cross-border education that arise from the actions of millions of individual actors are often those that governments desire.

The social-theoretical literature has tended in recent years to understand these developments as caused either by neoliberal forms of governmentality that emphasize individual responsibility and market solutions, or else by the increasingly rapacious activities of commercially motivated providers. We avoid such reductionist accounts, and instead focus on the ways in which an intrinsically inter-related set of fundamental changes in the dominant forms of production, exchange, communication and enquiry in different places are transforming the social conditions that frame international education markets. In relation to governance, we consider that it is fruitless to ask whether such developments make nation states more or less powerful, since the nature of the social relations that states seek to govern, and the mechanisms at their disposal to engage in such governance, have changed dramatically.

Most simply, to 'govern' means both to 'steer' and to 'rule', and we use the term governance in the broadest sense to allow us to consider a range of approaches adopted by different governments. In some settings, the term 'regulation' is appropriate to describe the ways in which states act in relation to cross-border education flows, and we use the term throughout the book. However, some other means that governments use to affect cross-border flows are not captured by the term, such as funding selected students or providers, promotional activities such as national branding, market research, and diplomatic initiatives in bilateral and multilateral forums. That is to say that governments do not simply regulate the activities of independent students and providers of education; governments are also purchasers and providers, advocates and lobbyists.

There has been much written in recent years on the tendency since the 1980s for some Western governments to shift from direct control over institutions to steering at a distance (King, 2009; Marginson, Nyland, Sawir & Forbes-Mewett, 2010). Such 'new governance' or new public management reforms in the public sector have sought to facilitate 'a shift from a hierarchical bureaucracy towards a greater use of markets, quasi-markets and networks' in the delivery of government services (Bevir, 2007, p. 3). We observe the ways in which such approaches have informed the advice provided by international institutions and Anglophone governments concerning global education markets. However, such 'new governance' is far from universally accepted, and throughout this book we illustrate wide divergence still in the varieties of governance of cross-border higher education, with efforts to directly command and control students and providers still evident in many jurisdictions.

We have found the work of Braithwaite and Drahos (2000) on global business regulation particularly helpful. They chart the development of globally convergent principles underpinning governance of distinct industry sectors, and we have sought to identify the consolidation of such principles in each chapter of this book, though considerable diversity is still evident. Where possible, we endeavour to uncover the mechanisms through which these principles become globalized by being accepted as legitimate by a wide range of governments, and the actors that play key roles in the diffusion of such regulatory principles.

The work of Gita Steiner-Khamsi (2012) on educational policy transfer has been useful in this regard, stressing the two different processes involved in policy diffusion, that are variously referred to as borrowing and lending, import and export, reception and diffusion. Her work emphasizes the partial and selective adoption of policy models, and highlights ongoing diversity. Critical of forms of neoinstitutionalism that overstate the degree of convergence based on a superficial analysis of official pronouncements, she reminds us to look for the 'local meaning, adaptation, and recontextualization of reforms that had been transferred or imported' (p. 4). As well as looking for the shared principles that underpin global policy diffusion, we need to be alert to the selectivity of adoption and implementation that may result in similar principles having quite diverse effects in practice when applied by different governments to different contexts. Early policy transfer research tended to use bilateral frames of reference, in which one government borrowed a policy from another, but this approach is no longer particularly useful in a more globalized era in which similar policy approaches are invariably adopted and promoted by a range of states and international agencies. Some policies are able to be identified, at least initially, with a particular national origin, but deterritorialization occurs over the lifespan of a policy, and as several states adopt and adapt a similar approach its origins are often forgotten or irrelevant.

We focus in this book on the actions of national governments, aware that these are by no means unitary actors. Cross-border education is significantly impacted by the actions of departments of education, immigration, labour, economic development, foreign affairs, and trade, as well as agencies with varying levels of autonomy to which some governments delegate responsibility for quality assurance, international promotion and marketing. In federal systems some of these roles are devolved to sub-national units. When one examines international education policies from the top down, beginning with public pronouncements of governmental intentions, the actions of these diverse arms of government tend to be presented as acting cooperatively and coherently to achieve an overarching national strategy. However, when examined from the bottom up, as we prefer, we see that mobile students and institutions are often rarely the subject of a whole-of-government approach. Given the wide range of actors involved, policy incoherence, in the form of inconsistent drivers emanating from different governmental units, is often evident.

Transnational actors are clearly also important in this field. Within Europe in particular, regional governance plays a significant role in shaping cross-border education, for example by extending national treatment and market access principles to students and education providers across EU member states. Among intergovernmental bodies, the OECD, UNESCO, the WTO and APEC have been influential in promoting particular policy approaches, and we consider the impact of these in some detail in Chapter 1. Less easy to identify are those informal networks of policy professionals that Braithwaite and Drahos (2000) refer to as 'epistemic communities', by which they mean those 'loose collections of knowledge-based experts who share certain attitudes and values and substantive knowledge, as well as ways of thinking about how to use that knowledge' (p. 501). Given the nature of cross-border higher education policy, experts in this field tend to be very well aware of policy developments in other countries, and act as conduits for global policy convergence. Braithwaite and Drahos observe that, 'if regulations and procedural rules are the hardware of international regimes, the knowledge and discourses of epistemic communities of actors are its software' (p. 501). For example, the epistemic community of professionals and stakeholders with an interest and expertise in international quality assurance has been developing rapidly, as is evidenced by a proliferation of models, guidelines, resources, approaches and discussions addressing cross-border education in general and programme mobility in particular. This has taken place at global, regional, national and institutional levels (McBurnie & Ziguras, 2011).

The research

This book draws on research we conducted over the past decade on cross-border higher education policy in a range of countries, participation on policy forums, and our professional experience in international education administration. The most significant fieldwork we have undertaken was funded by the Australian Research Council, and involved over 150 interviews between 2006 and 2009 in 10 countries: Australia, Singapore, Malaysia, Canada, Greece, Norway, Japan, Vietnam, Timor-Leste and China. In each country, interviews were conducted with between 10 and 20 participants whom we had identified as having a detailed knowledge of that country's policy and regulatory frameworks, including government officials dealing with international higher education, senior managers in both domestic and foreign education providers, higher education policy researchers, education counsellors of foreign governments, and representatives of domestic and international student associations or international alumni groups. Our approach followed what Rubin and Rubin (2012) call 'responsive interviewing'. Interviews were in-depth conversations that were relatively unstructured but clearly focused on the ways in which policy problems had been characterized, and on identifying ways in which government had responded. Interview participants were usually familiar with some of the policy responses considered in this book but not others. These interviews were effective in shaping our access to and interpretation of information about each country, and detailed accounts of particular issues from each feature in various chapters.

Then, in 2008–09 we led a group of researchers on a project funded by Education New Zealand that involved detailing regulatory frameworks in seven countries: India, China, Malaysia, South Korea, Vietnam, Oman and Thailand. Drawing on policy documents, scholarly research, market research reports and discussions with in-country staff of New Zealand's Department of Trade and Enterprise, we produced accounts of each country's regulatory environment for New Zealand education providers seeking to engage in those countries. This study provided us with fascinating insights into the practical issues faced by educational institutions seeking to operate abroad, which are very often hampered more by lack of detail and clarity in published regulations and unpredictable implementation than by the actual content of published rules.

As well as drawing on this research on national policy frameworks, the book is also significantly informed by our participation in many focused discussions of cross-border higher education policy issues at international forums that have brought together policy researchers, government officials and senior managers from internationally focused higher education providers. Such events provide significant opportunities for cross-fertilization and participants are often very candid in discussing the competing policy objectives, concerns and practical experiences they encounter both at home and abroad. We are thankful to the organizations that have hosted the events we have attended, including the OECD, UNESCO, APEC, the East-West Center, the Observatory on Borderless Higher Education, the British Council, the Malaysian Ministry of Higher Education, the Mexican National Association of Universities and Higher Education Institutions, Australian Education International and the Australian Department of Foreign Affairs and Trade.

In writing this book we have also drawn on our professional experience as agents of internationalization. We have recruited international students, initiated and managed offshore programmes, worked with international branch campuses, conducted quality assurance visits to offshore partner institutions, negotiated international articulation agreements, served as panellists on internationalization audits conducted by the International Association of Universities and the European Universities Association, and attended numerous international education industry conferences in Europe (EAIE) and North America (NAFSA), Australia (AIEC) and New Zealand (NZIEC). We have observed that those who we have worked alongside usually maintain a keen interest in policy developments in the countries in which they operate. Like our colleagues in international education worldwide, we have been interested in how changes to scholarship programmes and loans schemes in source countries will influence demand for international programmes, how changes to student visa conditions and immigration policies conditions in other destinations will influence where students choose to study, and how regulations for foreign programmes will influence where new programmes are offered. We have been fortunate to have access to much high-quality research conducted by institutions themselves, professional associations and government, most of which is sadly not publicly available. As industry insiders we have an appreciation for the ways in which governments shape every aspect of cross-border higher education, sometimes knowingly but often inadvertently, and we see how governments' actions tend to be interpreted within different types of educational institutions in different countries. But as social scientists we are interested in understanding not just how governments affect cross-border education but why, and we hope that in this book we are to make a contribution to both types of questions.

The approach

We begin this book with a discussion of three competing sets of policy prescriptions, each of which presents a relatively coherent form of advice to governments concerning the governance of cross-border higher education. First we consider calls from market liberals and exporting nations for governments to liberalize trade in education services, whose influence perhaps peaked in the early 2000s. Then we consider the policy advice emanating from those who argue that governments should harness cross-border education to increase the competitiveness of their workforce. Finally we consider those who see cross-border higher education as a threat to public education, equity and cultural diversity, and advocate policies that would preserve the integrity of national systems.

The bulk of the book comprises three pairs of chapters that examine the role of governments in relation to key aspects of cross border higher education – student mobility, the migration of international students, and transnational provision. The first chapter in each pair considers the challenges facing governments of education exporting countries, and the second in the pair considers the perspective of education importing countries. We emphasize that many countries are both importer and exporter, though usually with a preponderance of one or the other, and that several are on a trajectory from net importer to net exporter. In this way we hope to illustrate that the choices available to students or education providers that cross borders are shaped by governments in both countries. We analyse the ways in which governments – and other key players – are able to direct or at least influence these cross-border movements. We explore key issues that governments invariably are required to contend with, including the policy options that are available to states, an analysis of why particular approaches have been adopted, and an assessment of their success in managing the issue.

Chapter 2 examines the shift from aid to trade approaches in key exporting countries – and their student 'clients' – from the 1980s to the present day, and the growing treatment of higher education as an internationally traded service, reflected in the architecture of GATS and international trade agreements. We outline the role of governments in the development of user-pays international education, including the establishment of national branding, regulation of providers, funding mechanisms and the establishment of promotional agencies abroad. In the case of public universities in particular, there can be tensions between the domestic responsibilities of the institution and its international entrepreneurial activities. We consider a range of potential effects on the domestic system. Will local students be displaced if they are less 'profitable' than international students? What implications are there for the discipline mix? For example, will subjects popular with international students, such as business studies, dominate entrepreneurial universities, while less commercial offerings such as the arts wither on the vine? What is a suitable balance between international and local student numbers – how many is too many? Can the institution become over-reliant on international student fee income, and over-exposed to non-education factors such as currency fluctuations? While proponents laud the success of the international education 'industry', critics and supporters alike acknowledge that the treatment of education as an export has led to friction between the role of student as learner and as client, and the threat that the quality of education can be undermined (or at least perceived to be undermined) by a concentration on the pursuit of profit at the expense of traditional educational values. Problems in the education field – such as poor quality of provision, ineffective regulation of providers, poor treatment of students – can become flashpoints that fray international relations. As traditional education-importer countries in the region seek to become major education-exporters and regional education hubs, they too will be obliged to deal with these tensions.

Chapter 3, focusing on student mobility from the importer perspective, explores the role of governments in students' home countries in relation to outward mobility. In the past, governments tended to either be uninvolved or to try to restrict outward mobility of their citizens. Now, many governments actively support students to study abroad by offering loan schemes or purchasing places at foreign institutions for their citizens. In addition, governments of countries with large student populations abroad are playing a more significant role in advising/influencing student choice and providing consular support for those students. Sending countries are concerned with the reliability and quality of education in the host nations, as well as the safety and welfare of their mobile citizens. We focus on three sending countries: China, India and Norway. The Chinese government brings to bear several powerful instruments. In order to 'help self-funded students choose appropriate institutions' the Ministry of Education (MoE) publishes lists of some 15,000 'qualified' providers across 33 countries and points students to the relevant host country websites listing registered institutions. Perhaps the greatest impact is via the Ministry's periodic 'Study Abroad Alerts', advising students on problems (such as college closures) and developments (including changes in regulations) in host countries, and – most importantly – advising which providers and indeed in some instances *countries* that Chinese students should avoid. The Alerts are published on the MoE website and are widely reported in the Chinese media – especially in the more colourful cases of college collapses. Mindful that the intention of some of its citizens is to work in and migrate to the country of study, China monitors and publicizes developments in migration regulations as they affect student visas and migration applicants. When Australia's Department of Immigration and Citizenship reduced the list of preferential skilled occupations (discussed in Chapter 4) the MoE issued a Study Abroad Alert warning that many young hopefuls should reconsider their plans, and should not be misled by the blandishments of misguided or unscrupulous agents.

From the Norwegian government perspective, there is not a strong incentive to prevent or reduce student outflow. It is probably cheaper to subsidize study abroad than to greatly expand local infrastructure, particularly as the domestic system is free of fees. Exporting students is also a more flexible strategy for addressing student preferences as they mutate over time. Study abroad is encouraged both ideologically and financially. Students receive a combination of government grants and subsidized loans that can be applied to carrying out degrees abroad. There is close government engagement with mobile students. Recent developments demonstrate that students are strongly influenced by perceptions or publicity about the prestige of study destinations and employer preferences – as most students return it is important for them to take on board the signals as to which foreign degrees may best be received in the Norwegian labour market. Students are also sensitive to funding levers: in this case, changes in the relative proportions of the loan (repayable) and grant (non-repayable) components of their government support.

One of the chief criticisms made by sending countries is that too many of their mobile student-citizens are concentrated in one location. In that situation, students are less likely to get the full benefit of international education. Rather, they will be in an enclave of their fellow-nationals, speaking the home language rather than the host language, mixing with their compatriots rather than locals and, in some cases, will find that their teachers are also fellow-nationals, recently graduated and wheeled in to help deal with the expanding student numbers. (Indeed, one of the authors interviewed international students at an Australian university as part of a quality assurance review – chief amongst the complaints by Indian and Chinese students were that: 'there are so many of us here that it seems like my whole street from back home is sitting in class with me', 'my teacher is from my country and his English is worse than mine'.) There is also the implication that, if there is a preponderance of international students, then the course is being specifically provided for them, rather than being a mainstream offering of the host institution (and perhaps watered down, or unduly resembling a factory production line rather than the higher intellectual calling of an educational institution). In the case of private colleges recently created to meet the demand for international students using education as a means to migrate, several commentators – including the Chinese government – caution students to beware.

Personal security and safety is a key issue. We explore the concerns about robberies and assaults committed on Indian students in Australia. What is perhaps most notable is the key role of non-government actors: international students and the media. Sending and host governments were both criticized for being slow to react, and in both cases opposition parties were able to gain political mileage lambasting governments for dealing poorly with the situation. It is notable that the perpetrators may not be local. Another high-profile case was Chinese government concerns about their student-citizens falling victim to criminal gangs (run by their fellow Chinese) in New Zealand. We conclude the chapter by exploring several approaches that might be taken by sending countries to further benefit their mobile student-citizens.

Chapters 4 and 5 deal with the relationship between the market in international education and a parallel international market for skilled labour. Several (mainly) developed countries are vying with each other to attract international students and retain them as migrants. There are several expressions for the phenomenon, such as the race for talent (Shachar, 2006), the great brain race (Wildavsky, 2010) and, depending on whether you are a sending, receiving or transit country, brain drain, brain gain, or brain circulation. There are also various expressions for the governmental response, for example Brain Competition Policy (Reiner, 2010) and competitive migration regimes (Shachar, 2009). An important – and in the future possibly vital – source of such population is in the form of international students, particularly those already studying in the host country. It is, at least in theory, an efficient method: the student is already in the country; has sufficient academic ability and facility with the domestic language to engage in postsecondary study (presumably a good indicator for future employability); is acculturated or currently becoming acculturated to local ways (and therefore more likely to successfully integrate); will bear a host-country qualification, thereby avoiding the need to assess its provenance or equivalence; and will be well-motivated to get a job to recoup the cost of study fees (and therefore less likely to be a burden on the welfare system); they will generally be in their twenties or thirties (and therefore demographically desirable).

Neoliberal economic orthodoxy and left-liberal cosmopolitanism are generally united in their support for migration. The argument contains several components. First, there is an ageing demographic in developed countries – migration (especially of the skilled young) is necessary to boost the ratio of working-age population to the retired population. Second, the growth in migration is economically beneficial for the host economy, as it boosts GDP by expanding the number of producers and consumers. Third, the vibrancy of high-migrant cities attracts further migration as well as investment (one of the key arguments in the influential writings of Richard Florida), and cultural and lifestyle benefits for the host population. Fourth, attracting skilled migrants is a rapid, cost-effective way of meeting the growing needs of the knowledge economy. More specifically, two-step migration (first step is entering the country as a student, second step is applying for migrant status at the end of the study period) is a strategy that makes transition easier both for the migrant and the host nation.

In recent years, however, there has been growing criticism of the fundamentals of the pro-migration position. First, critics argue that the demographic/pensions rationale is misguided. Massive immigration, whilst a short-term buffer, will in the longer run exacerbate the problem as the 'new citizens' in turn retire and collect their entitlements. A more effective and economically sustainable solution is to strategically raise the age at which citizens can retire or collect superannuation, and to provide more modest benefits. A second argument is that the economic benefits of migration are negligible – or indeed negative – for the receiving country population. In cases where migration caused population to rise at a greater rate than GDP, it could be concluded that the pre-migration population were in fact worse off. (That is, the cake is bigger, but you get a smaller slice than before because it needs to be divided among more people.) Third, the 'vibrancy' argument is offset by public concerns about overstressed infrastructure (such as congested roads, crowded public transport, overcrowded public hospital emergency rooms and so on) and the rising cost of housing. Fourth, there are concerns about the effectiveness of current approaches to addressing skills shortages through the migration route. Studies in Australia have shown that the student-migrant pathway has attracted significant numbers of poor-quality students, who are not working (and indeed are unemployable) in the skilled fields for which they were granted migrant status. Further, the influx of foreign labour may be seen to disadvantage local labour, by increasing competition for jobs and potentially driving wages down. The quick-fix skilled labour-importation approach can be seen as a squib – giving employers and governments an opportunity not to meet their responsibility for ensuring the nation's citizens are properly educated and trained to meet society's needs.

The governance of migration is a key issue, intersecting directly with the governance of trade in higher education services. There are several levers that countries can use to increase or reduce the flow of international student-migrants, including: level of requisite language standards; requiring student-visa applicants to have a specified sum of money in the bank; student work rights; whether family members can accompany (and in turn whether they have work rights); what courses/occupations qualify; the duration of post-graduation stay before employment must be secured; and manipulating points systems for migration status. These can be eased or tightened in response to economic conditions, policy priorities and in response to public opinion. In this chapter we explore the fortunes of student-migration policy, drawing on examples from Australia, the UK, Canada and Singapore.

The following chapter considers the impact of such policies on students' home countries, examining the consequences of large-scale emigration of outbound students who might otherwise play a vital role in national development. Avoiding abstracted claims that student migration is inherently detrimental or necessarily beneficial, we consider instead whether governments have identified student emigration as a policy problem and if so, what measures they have put in place to address the issue. We examine in this chapter the particular priorities of seven quite different sending countries – China, Greece, India, Malaysia, Singapore, Timor Leste and Vietnam. Each of these faces a unique set of challenges and has interpreted the actual and potential positive and negative effects of outmigration of mobile students in its own way.

Chapter 6 analyses the role of governments in relation to their national providers operating programmes and campuses abroad, both in encouraging and facilitating their overseas expansion and in regulating quality. Providers based in the UK, the USA and Australia enrol hundreds of thousands of students in

transnational programmes and campuses around the world. For critics of the commercialization of higher education, transnational education (TNE) is the most
egregious/blatant example of the unbridled pursuit of profit. It exemplifies
the separation of education from traditional academic values: classroom based,
face-to-face teaching (including pastoral and mentoring roles), by well-qualified
research academics, with a commitment to community service. Further, it would
seem likely that almost none of the students are disadvantaged aid-recipients
(who tend to receive scholarships to study in the donor country). The worst-
case picture is of low-ability students (those not accepted into regular, reputable
institutions), using pre-packaged cookie-cutter foreign lecture notes, in cramped
office premises under the supervision of poorly qualified locals, supplemented by
occasional visits by jet-lagged fly-in fly-out (FIFO) academics. The local partners
are suspected to be of dubious repute: private operators, unreliable and prone
to financial collapse, treating education as just any other business, and happy to
rapidly shift their footloose capital and entrepreneurial cunning/skill to exploit
the next money-making opportunity that arises. The counter image propounded
by champions of TNE is of high-quality education (underpinned by carefully
modularized curriculum materials and pedagogically road-tested learning strategies) being delivered to where the demand (and need) is highest, saving students
the cost and disruption of studying abroad, building capacity in the host country,
strengthening relations between the provider and host countries, and enhancing the exporter country's international reputation and competitiveness. The rewards
and risks are the obverse of each other: if financial gain is one of the rewards
sought for by successful entrepreneurial activities of universities, financial loss is
the flipside. By extension, exporter governments and their domestic publics gain
if successful enterprise helps to fund the educational mission; conversely, they
lose if such activities eat into taxpayer funded resources and reduce the ability of
institutions to carry out their domestic responsibilities. Similarly, there is the perceived effect of enhanced international reputation for the successful exporter, and
reputational damage if a country's offerings are seen to be substandard or prone
to collapse or sudden withdrawal.

In Chapter 7 we examine the types of regulatory frameworks that have
been implemented, and the domestic political factors that influence the ways
in which governments frame regulation of foreign providers. We explore the
potential risks for nations in hosting TNE. These include: imported education may be poor quality or culturally inappropriate, thereby undermining
the employability and future study options of graduates; it can reduce the
host government's ability to regulate the discipline mix and other factors in
the interests of nation-building; staff and students may be drawn away from the
domestic system to the detriment of taxpayer-funded institutions; if the foreign operation collapses or withdraws, students will be affected financially and
their studies may be wasted; the host faces reputational damage if it is perceived to be unable to adequately regulate foreign provision. Host nations
have deployed several strategies, ranging from strict protectionism (allowing

no foreign provision) to attracting prestigious providers through subsidies and other favourable treatment.

References

Bevir, M. (Ed.). (2007). *Encyclopedia of Governance*. Thousand Oaks, CA: Sage Publications.

Braithwaite, J., & Drahos, P. (2000). *Global Business Regulation*. Cambridge: Cambridge University Press.

Gopinathan, S., & Lee, M. H. (2011). Challenging and co-opting globalisation: Singapore's strategies in higher education. *Journal of Higher Education Policy and Management, 33*(3), 287–299. doi: 10.1080/1360080x.2011.565001.

Hudzik, J. K. (2011). *Comprehensive Internationalization: From Concept to Action*. Washington DC: NAFSA Association of International Educators.

King, R. P. (2009). *Governing Universities Globally: Organizations, Regulation and Rankings*. Cheltenham, England and Northampton, MA: Edward Elgar.

Lo, W. (2009). Reflections on internationalisation of higher education in Taiwan: perspectives and prospects. *Higher Education, 58*(6), 733–745.

Luijten-Lub, A., Van der Wende, M., & Huisman, J. (2005). On cooperation and competition: A comparative analysis of national policies for internationalisation of higher education in seven western European countries. *Journal of Studies in International Education, 9*(2), 147–163. doi: 10.1177/1028315305276092.

Marginson, S., Nyland, C., Sawir, E., & Forbes-Mewett, H. (2010). *International Student Security*. Cambridge: Cambridge University Press.

McBurnie, G., & Ziguras, C. (2011). Global trends in quality assurance for transnational education. In A. Stella & S. Bhushan (Eds.), *Quality Assurance of Transnational Higher Education: The Experiences of Australia and India* (pp. 19–32). Australian Universities Quality Agency and the National University of Educational Planning and Administration.

OECD. (2013a). *Assessment of Higher Education Learning Outcomes. Feasibility Study Report: Volume 2 – Data Analysis and National Experiences*. Paris: Organisation for Economic Cooperation and Development.

OECD. (2013b). *Assessment of Higher Education Learning Outcomes. Feasibility Study Report: Volume 3 – Further Insights*. Paris: Organisation for Economic Cooperation and Development.

Reiner, C. (2010). Brain competition policy as a new paradigm of regional policy: A European perspective. *Papers in Regional Science, 89*(2), 449–461.

Rubin, H. J., & Rubin, I. S. (2012). *Qualitative Interviewing: The Art of Hearing Data* (3rd ed.). Thousand Oaks, CA: Sage.

Schleicher, A. (2013). Are the Chinese cheating in PISA or are we cheating ourselves? www.oecdinsights.org/2013/12/10/are-the-chinese-cheating-in-pisa-or-are-we-cheating-ourselves

Shachar, A. (2006). The race for talent: highly skilled migrants and competitive immigration regimes. *NYU Law Review, 81*, 148–206.

Shachar, A. (2009). *The Birthright Lottery: Citizenship and Global Inequality*. Cambridge, MA: Harvard University Press.

Steiner-Khamsi, G. (2012). Understanding policy borrowing and lending: Building comparative policy studies. In G. Steiner-Khamsi & F. Waldow (Eds.), *World

Yearbook of Education 2012: Policy Borrowing and Lending in Education (pp. 3–17). London: Taylor and Francis.

Tremblay, K., Lalancette, D., & Roseveare, D. (2012). *Assessment of Higher Education Learning Outcomes. Feasibility Study Report: Volume 1 – Design and Implementation.* Paris: Organisation for Economic Cooperation and Development.

Wildavsky, B. (2010). *The Great Brain Race: How Global Universities Are Reshaping the World.* Princeton, NJ: Princeton University Press.

Yamada, R. (2012). The changing structure of japanese higher education: Globalization, mobility, and massification. In D. Neubauer & K. Kuroda (Eds.), *Mobility and Migration in Asian Pacific Higher Education.* New York: Palgrave Macmillan.

Chapter 1

Global policy prescriptions
Trade, protection and competitiveness

Most of this book focuses on the actions taken by national or subnational governments in relation to education provided across their borders, and across the next six chapters we examine the wide range of ways in which they can shape cross-border movements and the varied reasons they might have for doing so. First, though, we will consider three prevailing ideological positions that exercise considerable influence on the thinking of governments around the world. We are interested in the ways in which these bodies of thought impact upon regulatory practice, and we do not intend to examine each as a political philosophy as there has been much already written on the broader political responses to globalization.

We consider three contemporary political positions that have been influential over the past decade, but which of course have much deeper historical roots. The first is the liberal commitment to free trade in education, by limiting state-imposed restrictions on the cross-border activities of students and education providers. We do not use the term 'neoliberal' in this book as the term is commonly used to describe a much broader group of political views than we are concerned with here. The second broadly Left political grouping we consider is concerned not with the freedom of the mobile but in protecting the vulnerable from the negative consequences of educational mobility, such as brain drain, increasing inequality in access, and exploitation of students. The third view we consider is a more centrist and pragmatic position that encourages governments to play an active role in regulating cross-border mobility in order to assist in social and economic development.

The dream of open education markets

Economic liberals dream of an open global market for goods and services, and education is no exception. Advocates of free trade in education encourage governments not to place any restrictions on the free flow of students and providers across their borders, and to treat foreign providers the same as domestic providers. As we will see in the chapters that follow, there are fewer obvious barriers to student mobility so most of those advocating for governments to liberalize trade in education services since the mid-1990s have focused on the regulation of transnational providers, arguing that regulation and quality assurance should be transparent and applied fairly to all providers regardless of nationality. In relation to student migration, liberals focus on the outcomes for the individual, asserting the rights of graduates to choose to live and work in the place that suits them, although migration has been a less contentious issue in the past decade than it had been earlier, as we will see in Chapters 4 and 5.

Bashir (2007), in a report for the World Bank, has usefully distinguished between international trade in education (the purchase of education services from a foreign country using domestic resources) and international aid (where the provision of services is financed by the providing country or a multilateral aid agency), estimating that the value of trade in higher education exceeds the value of aid in higher education tenfold (p. 9). The ease with which students and education providers can cross borders is celebrated by market liberals. The growth in student mobility can be seen as a response to market forces, in the sense that unmet demand for education in one place leads students to study elsewhere where the supply is greater. Likewise, the establishment of transnational programmes and campuses can be seen as an alternative means of responding to unmet student demand in other countries, thereby assisting in building educational capacity where the demand exists.

What, then, are trade agreements and what is their effect? Trade agreements are formal contracts between governments setting out the rules and conditions under which trade will be conducted between the signatory parties. Interestingly, the legalization, or codification, of trade in education through the General Agreement on Trade in Services (GATS) and other trade agreements has elicited much greater opposition than the growth of commercial international education ever did. These agreements can be multilateral (such as the GATS, which is administered by the World Trade Organization (WTO)), regional (such as Mercosur in South America) or bilateral (such as the Singapore–New Zealand Free Trade Agreement).

All trade agreements apply the principles of *market access* and *national treatment* to trade in services, and to illustrate what these mean in relation to transnational education we will consider the GATS, which is an extensive multilateral agreement binding all of the WTO's 159 member countries. Each WTO member country voluntarily commits to uphold these principles in relation to particular services. Relatively few countries have made commitments applying to education services, while most have made commitments on financial services and telecommunications where cross-border trade is more extensive.

Unrestricted market access in education services exists when foreign services and service providers are not subject to any quantitative limitations, limitations on forms of legal entity under which educational institutions may be established, or limitations on foreign equity participation. A commitment to national treatment binds governments to 'accord to services and service suppliers of any other Member, in respect of all measures affecting the supply of services, treatment no less favourable than that it accords to its own like services and service suppliers' except where conditions and qualifications are specified in the schedule of commitments (WTO, 1995). Whether foreign services and service providers are subject to 'formally identical treatment or formally different treatment', they must not be treated in such a way as to modify the conditions of competition in favour of domestic providers. This means that foreign education providers may be subject to different requirements than domestic providers but the effect must not be to disadvantage foreign providers over their domestic competitors. In the GATS, education services are distinguished according to level (primary, secondary, higher, adult and other), and governments choose which of these to commit to liberalizing, if any. Like all services, education is also classified according to the 'mode of supply', which relates to the location of the supplier and consumer of the service.

Mode 1, cross-border supply, refers to the supply of a service 'from the territory of one Member into the territory of any other Member' (WTO, 1995). In education this mode includes transnational 'distance', 'correspondence' or 'online' education in which an educational institution from one country is teaching a student who is resident in another country, where teachers and students remain in their own countries and communicate through post, fax, the Internet, etc. Mode 2, consumption abroad, refers to the supply of a service 'in the territory of one Member to the service consumer of any other Member.' This relates to students travelling abroad to study in another country. This is the only mode of supply that does not impact upon transnational education. Mode 3, commercial presence, refers to the supply of a service 'by a service supplier of one Member, through commercial presence in the territory of any other Member.' This relates to the establishment of branch campuses of foreign educational institutions (WTO, 1995 Article I). Mode 4, presence of natural persons, involves provision of a service 'by a service supplier of one Member, through presence of natural persons of a Member in the territory of any other Member'. In education, this refers to teachers, academics, administrators or marketing staff travelling across national borders to provide educational services (including the administration and marketing thereof) in the student's home country. Short courses may be provided purely through the presence of natural persons, but in most cases the movement of natural persons in education is used to complement cross-border supply and/or commercial presence. The distinctions between these modes of supply matter when governments commit to liberalizing some forms but not others. In practice, the implications of commitments to free trade in education are complex and subject to legal interpretation in each country, given the range of regulatory frameworks and types of institutions involved.

Further complicating the impact of trade agreements, is the fact that most countries are in practice much more open to foreign education providers than they commit to being under international treaties. Since the early 1990s, many countries have embarked on 'unilateral' liberalization, meaning that they have opened their systems to private and foreign providers unilaterally and voluntarily, often without binding it in an international agreement. For example, Malaysia is very open to foreign programmes and has been actively recruiting branch campuses for a decade, but it has not 'bound' this open approach legally by enshrining it through the GATS or any bilateral free trade agreements. This means that Malaysia retains the option of closing off some of the rights of foreign providers in the future. When countries make commitments within a trade agreements they very rarely commit to a level of openness that was not already in place. So rather than trade agreements prising open markets and thereby growing the volume of transnational education provision, they instead provide greater certainty to educational institutions that the regulatory environment will not become significantly less open in the future. In this way, trade agreements decrease the level of risk faced by institutions operating transnationally, but they have done little on their own to change governments' policies.

The liberalization agenda was pushed in the stalled Doha Development Round of WTO talks, which commenced in 2001, by the United States, Australia and New Zealand. Each country tabled negotiating proposals to the WTO, and interestingly each in a similar manner reaffirmed the crucial role that the public sector plays and called for greater market access for foreign institutions operating in the private sector (WTO, 2000, 2001a, 2001b). Within the United States, it should be noted, most of the educational establishment are uninterested or opposed to trade liberalization, and the liberalization agenda is being driven by for-profit education providers, the testing industry, and the Department of Commerce (Vlk, 2006). Britain, which is also a major exporter, is constrained in its advocacy for trade liberalization by its membership of the European Union. While flows of students and institutions have been liberalized extensively within the EU, externally the UK is represented by Brussels, which is ambivalent on educational trade matters due to the diversity of views among the EU membership.

While some advocates, usually economists, point to generic benefits of market liberalization while providing little or no detail about education in particular (e.g. LaRocque, 2003), most proponents cite a wide range of educational gains. Australia's negotiating position statement to the WTO, for example, argues that liberalizing trade in education services will promote the broader social, cultural and academic benefits of international education. Australia argues that:

> the liberalisation of trade in education services [is] the most effective way of encouraging the internationalisation of education and enhancing flows of students between countries. The long-term benefits accruing from internationalising education include:
>
> - fostering a knowledge and appreciation of other languages, cultures and societies. The skills and knowledge that are acquired will benefit students both professionally and culturally;
> - facilitating an exchange of people, ideas and experiences. These exchanges add a richness of diversity at the national and international levels, as well as contributing to the international cross-fertilisation of academic knowledge;

- networking relationships among individuals, groups and institutions which can facilitate future economic, political and socio-cultural alliances.

These significant benefits underpin the desirability of facilitating greater cross-border flows of students as well as educational services providers.

(WTO, 2001a)

Perhaps the most prevalent argument put forward in favour of trade liberalization is that allowing students to access foreign education can increase the overall scale of provision where there are supply shortages, usually due to a combination of rapid growth in demand coupled with an inability of the domestic sector to respond. Knight (2002) notes that while the rationales for liberalization put forward by the United States, Australia and New Zealand varied slightly between the three countries, all three focused on the aggregate economic benefits (primarily improved competitiveness) resulting from greater integration into to the global knowledge economy. Of the intergovernmental institutions, the OECD has most emphasized the ways in which cross-border higher education can contribute to capacity building in low- and middle-income countries, and the Australian government worked closely with the OECD during the early 2000s to promote such benefits through publications and events (Vincent-Lancrin, 2007; Ziguras, Reinke & McBurnie, 2003). The exporters at each opportunity have explained to the importing nations that freeing up transnational education will expand access to foreign education to a wider range of students, as the United States Trade Representative explained in 2003:

> Each year, thousands of students travel to the United States to study. They take home knowledge of engineering, science, mathematics, management, medicine, economics, and other disciplines essential to their country's development – as well as some experience in democracy … . Traveling to the United States, however, is far beyond the reach of most people in developing countries. Education and training could be provided at lower cost in the countries where they are needed. Yet many countries continue to block U.S. companies from operating training programs or providing for-profit education. In our multilateral and bilateral trade negotiations, we respect each country's choices concerning public education, yet private educational and training opportunities can complement public schools.
>
> (Zoellick, 2003)

Cross-border education not only expands scale but expands diversity of providers and programmes, thereby providing students with a wider range of choices. Similarly, when countries allow foreign providers to operate on their soil, the host government will declare that this is for the benefit of its citizens, in terms of widening choice and educational opportunity. The United States' negotiation proposal to the WTO, for example, asserts that the presence of foreign education providers 'increases the variety and amount of education services available to WTO members'

(WTO, 1998, p. 1). Accordingly, the USA has argued that countries' policies relating to transnational education should 'be reviewed and the restrictions liberalized to the greatest extent possible' (WTO, 1998, p. 2). New Zealand's proposal to the WTO argues that 'increased access for Members to education where it has previously been limited is a vital component in the development of human capital' (WTO, 2001b). Such proposals to ease restrictions in order to expand the scale of private and/or foreign education provision may appear benign from Washington or Wellington, but they can easily cause alarm to established providers, and the organizations representing established institutions and their staff were not slow to mobilize to resist such suggestions, as we will see below.

After expansion of supply of education, a second common argument is that liberalization leads to systemic reform arising from greater competition, but advocates of liberalization have to tread a fine line in relation to the claimed benefits of competition from foreign entrants. Clearly, in classical economics the competition between providers fostered by open markets generates incentives for providers to respond to consumer demand and to lower costs. That some providers will lose out to others is a necessary condition of effective market mechanisms, which are the best way to ensure that providers are responsive to the demands of users of the system, primarily students and employers. This type of argument was attractive to ministries concerned with trade, investment and economic development in both importing and exporting countries. As a report produced by Australia and New Zealand governments for Asia-Pacific Economic Cooperation (APEC) explained, 'The process of competition which foreign entry facilitates is also an important mechanism through which the benefits of reform are transmitted to the rest of the community – consumers in particular' (APEC, 2001, p. 11). In its negotiating proposal to the WTO, Australia noted that trade liberalization would have the effect of 'facilitating access to education and training courses that in qualitative and quantitative terms are not otherwise available in the country of origin' and that 'education services negotiations should aim to give consumers (students) in all countries access to the best education services wherever they are provided and through whatever mode of supply they are provided' (WTO, 2001a, p. 3). The Australian statement refers to 'providing a competitive stimulus to institutions with flow-on benefits to all students' (WTO, 2001b, p. 1). These are 'demonstration effects', which may result from foreign provision exposing the local system to other curriculum, pedagogical styles, administrative and managerial systems, and research approaches.

So governments are encouraged to embrace competition as a means of reforming existing institutions for the sake of consumers. However, such an argument is not at all appealing to ministries of education, which in many countries constitute the major provider. So the exporters tended to focus on less confronting effects of foreign providers on domestic institutions, such as those put forward in New Zealand's negotiating proposal to the WTO, which speaks of the benefits generated 'through academic exchange, increased cross-cultural linkages and technology transfer' (WTO, 2001b, p. 1).

The promotion of market liberalism as a basis for regulation of transnational education receded as it became clear during the mid-2000s that opposition to expansion of the GATS from developing countries would stall the progress of the Doha Development Round. Equally influential was the strident opposition to the liberalization of education markets by established education providers in the major exporting countries. Developed countries baulked at making further commitments to opening their education services markets because of public opposition from university associations, education unions and students groups (e.g. AUCC, ACE, EUA & CHEA, 2001; Education International & Public Services International, 2000). Many of the criticisms of the WTO and GATS are, in fact, criticisms of trade in education or criticisms of the growth of private provision and funding rather than criticisms of the trade agreement per se, but the codification of the global trade system in the form of the WTO and the GATS has provided a visible and tangible target for groups opposed to commercialization of education on a national and international scale (Mundy & Ika, 2003).

Now, nearly two decades since the GATS came into effect, and with hundreds of bilateral trade agreements also having been implemented, it is difficult to escape the conclusion that trade agreements have achieved less in relation to cross-border education than anyone expected. They have not caused wholesale privatization of education systems, eroded national quality assurance systems or led to an influx of low-quality global education brands, but neither have they prised open markets previously closed to transnational providers. But, while these international legal agreements have proved relatively insignificant, the principles on which they are based have been adopted widely by governments. The principle that new institutions, whether privately owned, publicly listed or religious, for-profit or not-for-profit, should be allowed to enter education markets and compete for students with established providers has become more accepted over the past two decades. Similarly, the notion that governments should not discriminate between local and foreign providers is becoming gradually more widely accepted. Liberalization based on these principles has occurred more extensively in other service industries, to the extent that in most economically advanced economies it is difficult to remember a time in which governments protected a small number of domestic providers against new domestic and foreign entrants to their markets. Now we accept and benefit from the deregulation and global integration of banking, telecommunications, transportation and media. The education sector has moved more slowly in most countries, but the same principles of economic liberalization have assisted the growth of transnational education in many countries in which supply of tertiary education was previously highly restricted.

From 'trade liberalization' to 'exchange and cooperation' in APEC

Although the GATS negotiations broke down, efforts to further liberalize trade in education services have continued in other forums, including bilateral agreements and various regional groupings. The history of deliberations on education within the APEC forum show how interest in trade liberalization has evolved, but not disappeared. Between May and September 2012, during Russia's chairmanship of APEC, the organization's leaders initiated the boldest foray into the higher education sector in APEC's history. The Leaders' Meeting in Vladivostok committed APEC to promoting cross-border educational cooperation, collaboration and networking, particularly in higher education and technical and vocational education.

As far back as 1996, APEC's Human Resources Development Working Group had been tasked with working towards 'provision of better opportunities for cross-member investment in the delivery of educational services and skills training' (APEC, 1996) and APEC's Group on Services has also had an interest in liberalization of trade in education services. There has for over a decade been a steady flow of work on this topic, led by several countries, but without much traction at senior levels until recently.

Australia, a key provider of cross-border higher education in the region, was the driving force behind early APEC international education projects, while at the same playing a similar role promoting education services liberalization within the WTO and OECD. In 2001 it sponsored with New Zealand a Group on Services project, *Measures Affecting Trade and Investment in Education Services in the Asia-Pacific Region* (APEC, 2001), and in the following year Australia sponsored an APEC Education Network 'Thematic Dialogue on Trade in Education Services' in Hanoi. Several years later it sponsored two reports, *APEC and International Education* (Centre for International Economics, 2008) and *Measures Affecting Cross Border Exchange and Investment in Higher Education in the APEC Region* (APEC, 2009). As well as these overtly trade-related projects, Australia also sponsored regional collaboration for capacity building in quality assurance, and as well as several bilateral projects commissioned the Australian Universities Quality Agency (2006) to produce a report for APEC, *Enhancement of Quality Assurance Systems in Higher Education in APEC Member Economies.*

China has been very active on this issue also, and after the implementation of its new national policies governing cross-border programme delivery in 2003, it sponsored a research project, *Improving the Institutional Capacity of Higher Education Under Globalization: Joint Schools Among APEC* (Shanghai Institute of Higher Education, 2004), which involved collaboration with Australia and New Zealand. Then, in 2011 China led another, larger, project on *Capacity Building for Policies and Monitoring of Cross-Border Education in the APEC Region*, which involved a seminar in Shanghai followed by a report that describes regulatory approaches across the region (Zhu & Zhu, 2011). China's decision to sponsor such a project perhaps reflects its desire to grow the number of incoming students it receives and to encourage its universities to establish themselves abroad. In the same year the USA led a project, *Quality in Higher Education: Identifying, Developing, and Sustaining Best Practices in the APEC Region* (Neubauer & Hawkins, 2011).

These various initiatives provided opportunities for information sharing between officials across the region but did not appear to be a high priority for

APEC. In fact, there was no mention of higher education in the statements of earlier Education Ministerial Meetings, which were held in 2008, 2004, 2000 and 1992, apart from some encouragement in 2008 for members to make more efforts to facilitate international educational exchanges. Education ministers were evidently focused on building capacity and quality in compulsory education, which are understandably more pressing issues for most governments.

The May 2012 Education Ministerial Meeting in Gyeongju, Korea marked a significant turning point for APEC. Ministers agreed on the need to explore ways of expanding education cooperation and supported the development of multi-year projects in facilitating and evaluating regional collaborative projects, the 'Gyeongju Initiative'. The Russian Federation proposed an initiative on higher education cooperation and announced that they would hold a conference on this topic later in the year.

The following month, the meeting of APEC Ministers Responsible for Trade took up the education ministers' lead and their contribution was to recognize the importance of both 'cross-border *trade* in education services and deepening educational *cooperation* in the Asia-Pacific' (my emphasis). They asked officials to examine ways to 'better facilitate mobility of students, researchers and providers in the region taking into consideration circumstances of individual economies and to report on progress by September 2012' (APEC, 2012a).

The conference sponsored by Russia one month later in July 2012, 'Shaping Education within APEC', brought to Vladivostok education and trade officials, academics and private sector representatives from across the region to discuss ways to enhance higher education cooperation. To the trade ministers' list of priorities they added points on collaboration between institutions and data collection. So the priorities for future work to enhance APEC higher education cooperation became:

1   enhancing the mobility of students;
2   enhancing the mobility of researchers;
3   enhancing the mobility of education providers;
4   increasing the interaction between higher education institutions;
5   increasing data collection on trade in education services.

The summary of the Russian conference was then endorsed by the APEC Economic Leaders' Meeting held two months later also in Vladivostok (APEC, 2012b). Russia has since sponsored a second APEC Conference on Cooperation in Higher Education in the Asia-Pacific Region, in Vladivostok in February 2013.

So Russia seems to have very successfully put cross-border higher education on the top of the APEC agenda. But why? Russia does host a large number of international degree students, 129,690 in 2010 according to UNESCO figures, but a small proportion of these are from APEC member economies with the vast majority coming from former Soviet states. And Russia has not previously been active in this space within APEC.

The location may provide some clues. The Leaders' Summit took place on the newly built island campus of the Far Eastern Federal University, which was specially constructed in time to host the summit and will then provide facilities for the university. The university's website states that 'The main target of the FEFU Strategic Program for 2010–2019, supported by extensive federal funding, is to make FEFU a world-class university, integrated into the education, research and innovation environment of the Asia-Pacific region' (FEFU, 2013). So the city of Vladivostok, and this very international university in particular, appear central to Russia's efforts to expand its educational engagement with the region.

So APEC is committing to both 'educational cooperation and promoting cross-border exchange in education services'. These are in fact two quite different agendas, but at times overlapping. Educational cooperation can mean many things, but all involve institutions (ministries, universities, quality assurance agencies, etc.) in different countries working together with partners in other countries. Rarely is anyone opposed to such a notion, but developing viable and sustainable collaborative projects is often challenging, given the resources required. Cross-border exchange in education services, on the other hand, generally involves students from one country undertaking programmes of study in another country, or the movement of scholars from one country to another. The ability of students and scholars to move freely and to engage with foreign educational institutions as easily as they do with domestic institutions is clearly in line with APEC's mission to champion free and open trade and investment and to promote and accelerate regional economic integration. However, institutions in less well-developed higher education systems often see the resulting international competition for students and scholars as a threat rather than an opportunity.

In August 2013 the Australian Department of Foreign Affairs and Trade sponsored an event held in Kuala Lumpur and entitled 'Facilitating Good Regulatory Practices for Trade and Investment in Higher Education Services in the APEC Region'. The forum brought together regulators, trade and education officials, scholars and industry representatives from most APEC member economies. It very quickly became apparent that across the member economies represented there is a keen interest in the internationalization of education systems. Increasingly, governments and institutions in a wider range of APEC economies are interested in international engagement, whether it be recruiting international degree students, engaging in exchange relationships, collaborating with foreign institutions to deliver international programmes, internationalizing research or teaching. However, there is limited institutional capacity and experience in many institutions. There was considerable discussion of the practical steps that are needed to enable broader international engagement, such as funding schemes, improved immigration procedures for exchange students and staff, practical guides for staff, professional development seminar programmes, and cooperation between international education professional associations.

However, when discussion turned to further opening education systems to allow more mobility for students, scholars and providers, there are still clearly significant differences of opinion between and within countries. Several participants argued that because of the different stages of development of national systems there is not a level playing field, and that introducing greater international competition for domestic providers would undermine their national development strategies. It is not uncommon for incumbents in any protected industry sector to oppose measures that would allow competitors to enter their markets, and in some ways universities behave no differently to the way other service providers, such as banks or airlines, might. But the education sector plays a unique role, and is of critical importance in fostering social and economic development, so governments are very wary of introducing changes that key institutions see as weakening their position, especially if those institutions are operated by the ministry of education.

Protecting national education from predatory commercialism

Meanwhile, critics of trade liberalization point out that increased reliance on private and foreign providers will exacerbate social inequalities in access, particularly in low-income countries. We have often heard the metaphor of the level playing field employed by officials and university leaders from middle-income countries who feel that their institutions need to be protected from more powerful actors from high-income countries. If there was a level playing field, the argument goes, then equal treatment for domestic and foreign providers would be reasonable, but until universities in lower-income countries attain similar standards to those in the education-exporting countries, discriminatory treatment against foreign providers is required. Altbach's work on cross-border higher education (Altbach, 1980, 1998, 2006; Altbach & Knight, 2007) foregrounds the challenges posed by ongoing inequality and the dependency of the academic periphery on the core, which makes the development of reciprocal relationships difficult, especially when combined with the rise of market mechanisms in higher education worldwide:

> The landscape of international higher education is characterized by inequalities and is increasingly focused on commercial and market concerns. These inequalities are especially stark in the context of relations between developing and developed countries, but market concerns are central to academe worldwide. This, of course, creates serious problems for international academic relations based on cooperation and on traditional academic norms and values.
>
> (Altbach, 2005, p. 14)

While the education exporters argue that liberalization of services will lead to the transfer of new skills and technology, amongst a host of other claimed benefits, education-importing countries fear more that their institutions will lose staff and students to their wealthier, and more commercially driven foreign competitors.

The GATS agreement provided a focal point for critique of student-funded cross-border education, and especially transnational provision. As we saw in earlier chapters, Left criticism of the development of an international education industry serving fee-paying students had been simmering since the mid-1980s, but after 2000 the GATS also focused the Left's attention on transnational education. Here we will not focus on the many criticisms of the treatment of education in the WTO system, but rather on the ways in which critics of liberalization have over time advocated restrictive forms of regulation of cross-border higher education.

Here we will draw on several key actors that shaped the critique of student-funded cross-border higher education – higher education peak bodies from North America and Europe, UNESCO and the affiliated International Association of Universities (IAU), Education International which represents education unions around the world, and scholars such as Philip Altbach, who gives voice to sentiments we have encountered frequently over the past decade. In response to negotiating proposals from the United States, Australia and New Zealand, the peak bodies representing universities in the United States, Canada and Europe issued their own statement, the Joint Declaration on Higher Education and the General Agreement on Trade in Services, which set out their opposition to the liberalization agenda (AUCC et al., 2001). While governments of the education-exporting countries were working with the OECD to promote liberalization, the developing countries were mobilizing UNESCO three kilometres away on the other side of the Seine.

As Altbach (2005) notes, those in favour of trade liberalization in the United States during the GATS negotiations were the for-profit education providers, the testing industry and the U.S. Department of Commerce, while the higher education community was 'skeptical or opposed'. This pattern was repeated the world over, and is unsurprising; domestically focused firms (as universities usually are) in any industry will normally resist efforts to open their markets to foreign competitors. What made this opposition particularly effective in many low- and middle-income countries was the very close relationship between higher education providers and the ministries of education that oversee them. This is a very different role for governments compared with those service sectors that have been more opened to international trade through the GATS and other reforms. In other services sectors, governments in most countries have been gradually privatizing the provision of services, while taking on the role of industry regulator rather than service provider. This trend has been slower in the education sector, where governments in many countries continue to own, operate and closely manage public institutions. Even in those countries with extensive private higher education sectors, the power of elite private institutions to influence policy is significant.

If the pro-market advocates pointed to vague and abstract benefits arising from the growth of transnational education, anti-market campaigners pointed to vague and abstract risks. The tone of the IAU's (2012) statement, *Affirming Academic Values in Internationalization of Higher Education*, illustrates this approach well. It questions some of the claimed benefits of transnational education, then points to several threats:

The growth of transnational programs and creation of branch campuses raises a number of questions including how these enhance the educational capacity of host nations over the long-term, and how able they are to deliver on the promise of an education comparable to that delivered by the sponsoring institution in its home country. A foreign educational presence, with its perceived prestige, has the potential to disadvantage local higher education institutions striving to respond to national needs. Some host nations experience difficulty regulating the presence, activity and quality of foreign programs.

(IAU, 2012, p. 4)

A decade ago, La Rocque (2003) observed that much of the concern expressed about trade liberalization in New Zealand was not based on real consequences that would necessarily flow from such policies, but on hypothetical scenarios couched in loose phrases such as 'may also come into question', 'could generate complaints', 'there are dangers that' and 'there might well be pressure to recognise' (p.2). Such a lack of clarity about consequences was perhaps understandable in the early 2000s, but the continued reliance on such rhetorical devices a decade later, now that much more is known about transnational education, suggests to us that posing such questions is sometimes a more effective polemical strategy than presenting evidence based on experience.

The only instance we are aware of in which a trade agreement dramatically challenged a government's approach to transnational providers is Greece's dispute with the European Commission within the context of the European common market which represents the most intensive form of economic integration. Greece's case is unusual, and arises because of a clash between the EU's free trade principles and Greece's constitutional prohibition of private higher education, as we discuss in Chapter 7. Despite the millions of words of warning written about the harmful effects of the GATS and bilateral free trade agreements on education, similar clashes over a nation's right to regulate are difficult to locate.

Let us then consider the substance of the critiques to cross-border education, which we will categorize as concerns with commercialism, inequality, and cultural imperialism. Much student-funded cross-border higher education is characterized as a simple commercial transaction between cash-strapped universities and second-rate students who miss out on a place in local institutions. It is viewed as a profit-driven activity that exploits deficiencies in the supply of education in developing countries without making a valuable contribution to national development. Altbach (2000) argued over a decade ago that transnational higher education, 'does not really contribute to the internationalization of higher education worldwide. Knowledge products are being sold across borders, but there is little mutual exchange of ideas, long-term scientific collaboration, exchange of students or faculty, and the like' (p. 5). In our experience, such views are widely held. One reason for this perception is that students in transnational education typically do not receive government funding so foreign programmes and campuses are usually funded entirely from tuition fees.

Many transnational providers are therefore offering no-frills international degrees, incorporating only those fields of study and non-teaching activities that can be provided inexpensively.

However, in the early 2000s there was a rapid growth in the number of international branch campuses being established, especially in Singapore, Malaysia and the Gulf States (Lawton & Katsomitros, 2011). Altbach, writing with Jane Knight, has more recently acknowledged the growing diversity of provision, stating that, 'The market for international higher education initiatives thus ranges from students who cannot obtain access at home and seek almost any means to study to carefully targeted elite students in small, high-quality programs' (Altbach & Knight, 2007, p. 295). However, the largest proportion of the transnational education markets, they argue, are '"demand-absorbing" programs that provide access to students who could not otherwise attend a postsecondary institution' (Altbach & Knight, 2007, p. 294). By serving only students with the capacity to pay fees, even though they may not be eligible to enter local institutions, transnational providers exacerbate domestic inequality and undermine efforts to develop merit-based access to higher education.

That education is 'not a commodity' but is a 'public good' is frequently asserted at the outset of declarations issued by UNESCO and is echoed from time to time by industry associations. For example, the peak bodies representing universities in North America and Europe proclaim this 'fact', when arguing that trade agreements have no right to include the regulation of education: 'Higher education exists to serve the public interest and is not a 'commodity', a fact which WTO Member States have recognized through UNESCO and other international or multilateral bodies, conventions, and declarations' (AUCC et al., 2001, p. 1). To say, as many critics of trade liberalization do, that education is not a commodity and therefore cannot be traded, clearly flies in the face of facts. Nothing is inherently a commodity, but rather a thing becomes a commodity when it is exchanged for money. While an objection to the treatment of education as a commodity is an understandable ideological position, it is incorrect to say that education *cannot* be treated as a commodity because it possesses some innate quality that cannot be the subject of commercial exchange. To say, in the context of GATS, that education is a complex service that *should not* be treated the same as cars and bananas, is another matter. Similarly, the absence of a trade agreement does not mean that trade is not taking place, nor will the signing of a trade agreement necessarily lead to an increase in the volume of international trade of any one service or good.

Similarly, Education International (2008) argues that 'international exchange and cooperation should be fair, should be sensitive to local needs, and should be based on educational values, not commercial imperatives' (p. 2). These many declarations suggest that transnational programmes that serve the interests of fee-paying students but do not otherwise contribute to the public good are not legitimate forms of higher education. What is more, there is often a conflation of the terms 'public good', 'publicly funded' and 'not-for-profit'. The question of the public good that results from the provision of education is a very real one, but it is a mistake to equate public good with public or not-for-profit provision. Such assertions serve a political, rather than analytical, purpose. Cross-border higher education is regularly accused of being motivated by profit seeking, even when undertaken by public or private not-for-profit institutions.

It is not only education providers and exporting governments that are accused of commercial instrumentalism; international students too are criticized for seeking an international education for the wrong reasons, such as attaining a competitive advantage over their peers. Often this is portrayed as a recent change:

> Traditionally, students studied abroad mainly to acquire cultural and language skills. Students perceived a stay at a foreign university mainly in terms of gaining so-called 'soft skills': experiencing a different country, improving language ability, living out cultural diplomacy, etc. Today, however, students increasingly view studying abroad not only as a cultural experience, but as a means for high-ranking qualifications (or at least higher ranking qualifications than those offered by domestic institutions) and subsequently better access to a wider job market.
>
> (Martens & Starke, 2008, p. 5)

It is true, as we will see in the following chapters, that the proportion of self-funded international students has increased since the 1980s, but we suspect that those 'traditional' students who had access to funded international programmes were also very interested in qualifications and employment prospects. If we look back to the early origins of the modern university, we can see that the students who would travel from across Christendom to study at the University of Paris in the thirteenth century were motivated by a desire to gain prestigious and portable qualifications that would launch their careers as preachers or officials in the ecclesiastical or secular bureaucracies (Wei, 2012). For that matter, we are also not convinced the factors that motivate students' choices of domestic study options are so much different.

After commercialism, a second criticism is that of exploitation. Exporting countries are accused of taking unfair advantage of structural inequalities in ways that further undermine development efforts. Altbach and Knight (2007) argue that, 'Globalization tends to concentrate wealth, knowledge, and power in those already possessing these elements. International academic mobility similarly favors well-developed education systems and institutions, thereby compounding existing inequalities' (p. 291).

While market liberals aim at formal equality of treatment by regulatory agencies for domestic and foreign institutions, critics focus on the inequalities of opportunity which they argue result in vulnerabilities in developing countries. Removing barriers to trade, they argue, does not create a level playing field, it actually exacerbates existing inequalities by providing more opportunities for powerful systems to exploit weaker ones. Given these inequalities, the ability of strong institutions to insert themselves into a developing country with relatively weak institutions is likely to undermine efforts at national development. The joint declaration from North American and European peak bodies demanded that 'education exports must complement, not undermine, the efforts of developing countries to develop and enhance their own domestic higher education systems' (AUCC et al., 2001, p. 2). The IAU statement, *Affirming Academic Values in Internationalization of Higher Education*, explains that 'The asymmetry of relations between institutions, based on access to resources for the development and implementation of internationalization strategies, can lead to the pursuit of goals that advantage the better–resourced institutions and can result in unevenly shared benefits' (IAU, 2012, p. 4).

Transnational education providers are sometimes accused of taking advantage of the inability of host countries to effectively regulate higher education. Sometimes a lack of quality assurance and accreditation processes allow any provider to operate, allowing both bona fide and rogue foreign providers to enter an unregulated market in which students and their families can be easily exploited. In some cases, colleges that do not have degree awarding powers partner with foreign universities to offer their degrees instead, a loophole that flouts a government's efforts to restrict degree provision to qualified institutions.

Transnational providers may undermine domestic institutions by poaching both students and staff. The president of the Canadian Bureau for International Education told the Observatory on Borderless Higher Education (OBHE) that transnational education could create an 'internal brain drain' by syphoning off the best and wealthiest students, thereby reducing the capacity for indigenous higher education development (Lawton et al., 2013, p. 19). The president of the New Zealand Post Primary Teachers' Association raised the same concerns in 2003, worrying that teachers may be lured to work for high-quality foreign providers that pay higher salaries and have better quality facilities than local institutions (LaRocque, 2003). This does not, on the face of it, sound like a bad outcome for the Association's members, but clearly opposition to private provision runs deep in the education union movement.

A third major concern is cultural imperialism, in particular the dominance in transnational education of Western, Anglophone universities who impose their cultural values on non-Western students. For example, the president of the European Association for International Education told the OBHE that transnational education 'can be conceived as a "form of neo-colonialism" if it consists only of international qualifications delivered in Asia with local teachers and without any significant differentiation in the curriculum' (Lawton et al., 2013, p. 19). Institutions on the one hand achieve economies of scale by providing the same programmes in many locations, but also have to balance this with the educational imperative to tailor teaching to suit the needs of particular student cohorts (Shams & Huisman, 2012). This is not only a concern for transnational education, but reflects a deep current of concern about the extent of Western, and particularly, American influence on the internationalization of higher education (Choi, 2010; Mok, 2007). The effects of the widespread usage of English in transnational programmes contributes to cultural homogenization, which is seen as a possible adverse consequence of internationalization of education by the IAU (IAU, 2012). Education International (2008) advocates that in order to 'ensure the relevance of VET content and to promote linguistic and cultural diversity ... governments, institutions and relevant authorities should retain the ability to adopt policies and practices which favour or accord preferences to domestic VET providers' (p. 3).

These organizations and scholars advocate for the right of governments to be able to regulate to mitigate the negative consequences of cross-border education, and are opposed to any international agreements which limit the policy options available to national governments. While the policy prescriptions of market liberals is quite clear – allow access to new providers and do not discriminate against foreign entrants – there is less detail forthcoming from critics of commercialism in transnational education. More clear are the policy objectives that are prioritized, which involve governments regulating in ways that ensure equality of access to education for students, and ensure that foreign providers do not threaten domestic institutions or challenge cultural or social values, and that partnerships must be based on equality between providers in each country.

In the education-exporting countries too, there are frequent warnings about the vulnerability of education providers to international markets (Knight, 2008). Often the concern is focused on institutions' dependency on revenue from international students, although they are typically more dependent upon revenue from local students and national governments, which can also be volatile (Nelson, 2003). Usually the remedy proposed by those who seek to protect institutions from such international vulnerabilities is increased government funding and fewer international students. Concerns are also expressed that international students are displacing local students, that international students with language difficulties may lower the quality of the classroom experience for locals, and that international students may command a disproportionate amount of academics' time. In the major education-exporting countries, a key question is at what point academic programmes, institutions, local communities and even cities reach a 'saturation' level of international students. There is a possibility of a backlash from local communities and stakeholders if institutions appear to be putting international students, whether fee-paying or government funded, ahead of their domestic teaching, research and community service responsibilities. The most common measure proposed to protect local communities from the competitive pressures posed by international students is to impose a quota on their numbers.

Harnessing cross-border education to enhance competitiveness

The liberalization debate in the early 2000s focused much attention on the growth of transnational education and the need for governments to regulate, but due to the high degree of polarization there was little practical discussion of effective policy measures. Proponents of liberalization were not inclined to advocate measures that would give credence to fears of negative impacts that they believed were unfounded, while opponents of liberalization were not inclined to propose regulatory measures that would legitimize commercial transnational programmes and campuses.

In 2004 the IAU collaborated with US and Canadian peak bodies to produce a joint statement on quality cross-border provision which, as well as opposing participation in GATS, actually did provide some constructive advice for governments (IAU, AUCC, ACE, & CHEA, 2005). As well as advocating that governments provide more support for higher education capacity building in developing countries and for qualified international students with financial need, it advocated that host governments should 'ensure that foreign higher education providers operating within their countries are appropriately authorized and monitored' and 'make widely available accurate, timely, and user-friendly information on the country's higher education institutions and quality assurance and accreditation practices' (p. 5). However, it was the OECD that became the leading international institution to move beyond this stand-off, by shifting its focus away from trade liberalization to instead focus on the positive contribution that cross-border educational exchanges can make to the development of national higher education systems.

The notion that a quality higher education sector is a necessary prerequisite for national competitiveness has come to be universally accepted by governments. But rather than deregulating their higher education sectors and allowing the market to shape national systems, as free trade advocates had hoped, governments have continued to be closely involved in regulating markets of all kinds (Braithwaite, 2005) and especially higher education. King (2009) observes that despite differences of emphasis and the mechanisms by which systems are managed, most Western governments and the major international institutions involved in higher education (the OECD, World Bank and UNESCO) advocate a consistent policy template that incorporates features of new public management and advocates systemic diversity (King, 2009). They promote a regulatory environment that fosters institutional autonomy, devolving management wherever possible to the institutional level, while government sets the broad parameters within which institutions operate and establishes rewards and incentives for performance. While in practice, governments can often not help themselves from meddling in the affairs of institutions, support for such a model of governance is widespread. Altbach and Salmi (2011), for example, share a belief that such regulatory environments allow research universities to thrive, despite the fact that the former is an academic critic of Western educational neo-imperialism and the latter a World Bank technocrat. Similarly, a recent ranking of higher education regulatory environments sponsored by the Universitas 21 network of research-intensive universities advocates the same qualities (Williams, de Rassenfosse, Jensen & Marginson, 2013). The regulatory characteristics they chose to rate as desirable include:

the existence of national monitoring agencies, especially the ones that make public their findings; academics are not government employees and are free to move institutions; the chief executive officer (CEO) is chosen by the university; and there is complete flexibility to appoint foreign academics.

(p. 601)

Another feature of the standard global policy template, King (2009) argues, is the notion that a mix of different types of institutions is beneficial, including both public and private, vocational and research-focused, comprehensive and niche, and even a mix of domestic and foreign providers.

The OECD's approach was premised on a belief that cross-border education, when well regulated, can benefit both sending and receiving countries. In particular, the OECD argues that transnational education, which is most restricted by government policies, helps to meet local student demand through the provision of additional places. It provides students with an option to earn a foreign degree at a lower cost than studying abroad; students studying in their home country usually have a lower cost of living, save on air fares and have greater opportunity to engage in paid work while studying (i.e. without visa restrictions limiting employment hours). Frequently, tuition fees are lower than at the home base of the foreign provider. By reducing the outflow of funds that accompany students studying abroad, transnational education can assist importer countries with their balance of payments. Furthermore, the user-pays approach to meeting student-demand frees up public funds that can be spent on other government priorities. The presence of foreign providers can create local employment opportunities for academic and managerial staff. In the case of full branch campuses, there is an expansion of local infrastructure (libraries, laboratories, IT facilities, classroom space), as well as expanded curriculum material, and administrative systems. The effect of competition and collegiality with foreign providers may have beneficial impacts on local academic and managerial practices.

Increasing the capacity of education systems is a key precondition for many types of economic and social development and so has been a major focus of development assistance. As Vincent-Lancrin (2005) points out, countries with few tertiary education graduates face major difficulties in increasing the number of graduates, but increasing the supply of graduates is often a critical precondition both for improving the competitiveness of domestic firms and attracting foreign direct investment. Even with adequate finances, shortages of suitably qualified teaching staff are common, exacerbated by the flow of the highly trained to more lucrative positions overseas. Some countries with large higher education systems may nevertheless face supply constraints in certain disciplines, such as business administration, agriculture or engineering, if local institutions have been unable to respond to student, government or employer demand in some fields.

Vincent-Lancrin (2005) goes on to argue that growing numbers of students travelling overseas to study often do little to build capacity in the student's home country. In addition, student mobility has several drawbacks. First, overseas study is expensive and therefore not available to most of the population. The cost of studying in a transnational programme or institution is usually higher than local institutions but much lower than studying abroad, because of lower tuition fees, and lower living and travel expenses. Transnational programmes are therefore accessible to a much larger number of students than is study abroad. Second, overseas study is inconvenient for people already in the workforce, which explains why a high proportion of transnational programmes are delivered at postgraduate level. Third, many students who study overseas seek residency in the country in which they study, causing some governments to be concerned about the resulting brain drain of the highly educated to education-exporting nations. Students in transnational programmes are less likely to emigrate than students who study abroad, and the teaching positions created in transnational programmes and institutions create local employment. Vincent-Lancrin (2005) also argues that encouraging transnational provision can lead to quality improvement in host countries:

> Foreign programmes delivered at local institutions or foreign institutions operating in the country can in specific fields offer students a better education or training than some domestic institutions are able to. At their best, such programmes are able to link developing countries with cutting-edge knowledge and in this way assist in training an effective workforce as well as a high quality faculty for the domestic system. Finally, partnerships or foreign programmes may also help develop the infrastructure to undertake more efficient teaching and research and ultimately create a more effective and cost-efficient organisation of the higher education institutions and sector.
>
> (p. 10)

The three international forums on trade education that the OECD had sponsored (in Washington in 2002, Trondheim in 2003 and Sydney in 2004) had made little headway in terms of commitments to liberalized trade, but did focus attention on the need for practical advice for governments on how they could effectively regulate transnational education. The governments of Australia, Japan and Norway sponsored the development of *Guidelines for Quality Provision in Cross-border Higher Education* (OECD & UNESCO, 2005). The OECD decided to collaborate with UNESCO to develop and publish the guidelines in an effort to broaden their acceptance among developing countries, who represented the major host countries for transnational education and the major opponents of liberalization. Consultation meetings were chaired by a Norwegian with representatives of South Africa and India as vice-chairs, an additional effort to elicit cooperation from countries traditionally antipathetic to the expansion of cross-border higher education. This move was not so successful, however, with the South African education minister publicly castigating Norway and other countries for making requests within the GATS framework for South Africa to provide greater market access to foreign providers (Sørensen, 2005).

The OECD & UNESCO guidelines urged governments to take responsibility for ensuring that students have access to clear information about providers and are protected from sub-standard providers, that qualifications recognition processes are transparent and that quality assurance agencies collaborate with those in other countries (OECD & UNESCO, 2005). In short, the emphasis is not on persuading governments to reduce trade barriers, but on persuading them to ensure the quality of cross-border higher education provided by institutions from their country and from other countries. The major exporting governments have also adopted a similar focus on the benefits of international exchange since the mid-2000s since it became clear that the language of free trade was achieving very little.

Conclusion

GATS provided the forum for discussion of regulation in general, and the arguments really can be seen as commentary both on the role of the WTO, and on the proper role of national governments. In a highly polarized debate during the 2000s, the proponents included the WTO, U.S. Trade Representative, U.S. Department of Commerce, European Services Forum, the EU Directorate-General for Trade, the Government of Australia and the Government of New Zealand. The key opponents included education unions, associations of higher education institutions, student organizations and anti-globalization groups (Vlk, 2006). The hyperbole about the potential impact of the GATS turned out to be overblown on both sides, but the debates have been influential in shaping debate on cross-border higher education policy since that time. For example, Maldonado-Maldonado and Verger (2010) have recounted long-winded debates that played out during the drafting of the text of the communiqué at UNESCO's higher education conference, with the USA on one side battling several Latin American states and India on the other, over whether education should be defined as a public good, whether GATS should be condemned and whether international rankings should be supported. These polarized pro-market and anti-market ideologies continue to colour various aspects of the governance of cross-border higher education, as we shall see in the following chapters. In between these two poles, governments are busily going about the task of trying to steer the flows of students and providers in productive directions across their borders, in a global market that is neither free nor equal.

References

Altbach, P. G. (1980). The university as centre and periphery. In I. J. Spitzberg (Ed.), *Universities and the International Distribution of Knowledge*. New York: Praeger.
Altbach, P. G. (1998). Twisted roots: The western impact on Asian higher education. In P. G. Altbach (Ed.), *Comparative Higher Education: Knowledge, the University and Development* (pp. 55–77). Hong Kong: Comparative Education Research Centre, The University of Hong Kong.

Altbach, P. G. (2000). The crisis in multinational higher education. *International Higher Education, 21*(Fall), 3–5.

Altbach, P. G. (2005). The political economy of international higher education cooperation: Structural realities and global inequalities. Paper presented at the NUFFIC Conference: 'A Changing Landscape', The Hague. www.nuffic.nl/ nederlandse-organisaties/nieuws-evenementen/evenementen-archief/past-event-1/Downloads

Altbach, P. G. (2006). Globalization and the university: Realities in an unequal world. In J. J. F. Forest & P. G. Altbach (Eds.), *International Handbook of Higher Education* (pp. 121–139). Dordrecht, Netherlands: Springer.

Altbach, P. G., & Knight, J. (2007). The internationalization of higher education: Motivations and realities. *Journal of Studies in International Education, 11*(3–4), 290–305. doi: 10.1177/1028315307303542.

Altbach, P. G., & Salmi, J. (Eds.). (2011). *The Road to Academic Excellence: The Making of World-Class Research Universities.* Washington, DC: The World Bank.

APEC. (1996). Joint statement – from vision to action. Eighth APEC Ministerial Meeting, Manila, Philippines. Singapore: Asia Pacific Economic Cooperation.

APEC. (2001). *Measures Affecting Trade and Investment in Education Services in the Asia-Pacific Region: A Report to the APEC Group on Services 2000.* Singapore: Asia Pacific Economic Cooperation.

APEC. (2009). *Measures Affecting Cross Border Exchange and Investment in Higher Education in the APEC Region.* Singapore: APEC Human Resources Development Working Group.

APEC. (2012a). *Statement – 2012 Meeting of APEC Ministers Responsible for Trade, Kazan, Russia.* Singapore: Asia Pacific Economic Cooperation.

APEC. (2012b). *Vladivostok Declaration: Integrate to Grow, Innovate to Prosper.* Vladivostok: APEC.

AUCC, ACE, EUA, & CHEA. (2001, 28 September). Joint declaration on higher education and the general agreement on trade in services. Retrieved 15 May, 2002, from www.unige.ch/eua/En/Activities/WTO/declaration-final1.pdf

Australian Universities Quality Agency. (2006). *Enhancement of Quality Assurance Systems in Higher Education in APEC Member Economies.* Canberra: Department of Education, Science and Training.

Bashir, S. (2007). *Trends in International Trade in Higher Education: Implications and Options for Developing Countries.* Washington DC: The World Bank.

Braithwaite, J. (2005). *Neoliberalism or Regulatory Capitalism.* RegNet Occasional Paper No 5. Canberra: Regulatory Institutions Network Research School of Social Sciences, Australian National University.

Centre for International Economics. (2008). *APEC and International Education.* Canberra: Department of Education Employment and Workplace Relations.

Choi, P. K. (2010). 'Weep for Chinese university': a case study of English hegemony and academic capitalism in higher education in Hong Kong. *Journal of Education Policy, 25*(2), 233–252.

Education International. (2008). *Guidelines on the Cross-Border Provision of Vocational Education and Training.* Brussels: Education International.

Education International & Public Services International. (2000). *The WTO and the Millennium Round: What is at Stake for Public Education.* Brussels: Education International.

FEFU. (2013). Internationalization. From: www.dvfu.ru/web/fefu/internationalization1

IAU. (2012). *Affirming Academic Values in Internationalization of Higher Education: A Call for Action*. Paris: International Association of Universities.

IAU, AUCC, ACE, & CHEA. (2005). *Sharing Quality Higher Education Across Borders: A Statement on Behalf of Higher Education Institutions Worldwide*. Paris: International Association of Universities, Association of Universities and Colleges of Canada, American Council on Education, Council for Higher Education Accreditation.

King, R. P. (2009). *Governing Universities Globally: Organizations, Regulation and Rankings*. Cheltenham, England and Northampton, MA: Edward Elgar.

Knight, J. (2002). *Trade in Higher Education Services: The Implications of GATS*. London: Oberservatory on Borderless Higher Education.

Knight, J. (2008). *Higher Education in Turmoil: The Changing World of Internationalization*. Rotterdam and Taipei: Sense.

LaRocque, N. (2003). Serving everybody's interests: GATS and New Zealand education. Paper presented at the 12th New Zealand International Education Conference, Wellington, New Zealand.

Lawton, W., Ahmed, M., Angulo, T., Axel-Berg, A., Burrows, A., & Katsomitros, A. (2013). *Horizon Scanning: What Will Higher Education Look Like in 2020?* London: UK Higher Education International Unit and the Leadership Foundation for Higher Education.

Lawton, W., & Katsomitros, A. (2011). *International Branch Campuses: Data And Developments*. London: Observatory on Borderless Higher Education.

Maldonado-Maldonado, A., & Verger, A. (2010). Politics, UNESCO, and higher education: A case study. *International Higher Education* (58).

Martens, K., & Starke, P. (2008). Small country, big business? New Zealand as education exporter. *Comparative Education, 44*(1), 3–19.

Mok, K. H. (2007). Questing for internationalization of universities in Asia: Critical reflections. *Journal of Studies in International Education, 11*(3–4), 433–454.

Mundy, K., & Ika, M. (2003). Hegemonic exceptionalism and legitimating bet-hedging: Paradoxes and lessons from the US and Japanese approaches to education services under the GATS. *Globalisation, Societies and Education, 1*(3), 281–319.

Nelson, B. (2003). *Engaging the World Through Education: Ministerial Statement on the Internationalisation of Australian Education and Training*. Canberra: Commonwealth of Australia.

Neubauer, D. E., & Hawkins, J. N. (Eds.). (2011). *Quality in Higher Education: Identifying, Developing and Sustaining Best Practices in the APEC Region*. Singapore: APEC Human Resource Development Working Group.

OECD & UNESCO. (2005). *Guidelines for Quality Provision in Cross-Border Higher Education*. Paris: United Nations Educational, Scientific and Cultural Organization and the Organisation for Economic Co-operation and Development.

Shams, F., & Huisman, J. (2012). Managing offshore branch campuses: an analytical framework for institutional strategies. *Journal of Studies in International Education, 16*(2), 106–127.

Shanghai Institute of Higher Education. (2004). *Improving the Institutional Capacity of Higher Education Under Globalizaion: Joint Schools Among APEC*. Singapore: APEC Human Resources Development Working Group.

Sørensen, O. (2005). GATS and higher education's role in development. *International Higher Education* (40), 6–8.

Vincent-Lancrin, S. (2005). *Building Capacity Through Cross-Border Tertiary Education*. London: Observatory on Borderless Higher Education.

Vincent-Lancrin, S. (2007). *Cross-Border Tertiary Education: A Way Towards Capacity Development*. Paris and Washington, DC: Organisation for Economic Cooperation and Development and The World Bank.

Vlk, A. (2006). *Higher Education and GATS: Regulatory Consequences and Stakeholders' Responses*. Enschede, Netherlands: Center for Higher Education Policy Studies, University of Twente.

Wei, I. P. (2012). Medieval universities and their aspirations. In A. R. Nelson & I. P. Wei (Eds.), *The Global University: Past, Present, and Future Prospects* (pp. 133–152). New York: Palgrave Macmillan.

Williams, R., de Rassenfosse, G., Jensen, P., & Marginson, S. (2013). The determinants of quality national higher education systems. *Journal of Higher Education Policy and Management, 35*(6), 599–611. doi: 10.1080/1360080x.2013.854288.

WTO. (1995). *General Agreement on Trade in Services*. Geneva: World Trade Organization.

WTO. (1998). *Communication from the United States: Education Services*. World Trade Organization Council for Trade in Services.

WTO. (2000). *Communication from the United States – Higher (Tertiary) Education, Adult Education and Training*. Geneva: World Trade Organization Council for Trade in Services.

WTO. (2001a). *Communication from Australia: Negotiating Proposal for Education Services (S/CSS/W/110)*. Geneva: World Trade Organization.

WTO. (2001b). *Communication from New Zealand: Negotiating Proposal for Education Services (S/CSS/W/93)*. Geneva: World Trade Organization.

Zhu, X., & Zhu, Y. (2011). *Capacity Building for Policies and Monitoring of Cross-Border Education in the APEC Region*. Singapore: APEC Human Resource Development Working Group.

Ziguras, C., Reinke, L., & McBurnie, G. (2003). 'Hardly neutral players': Australia's role in liberalizing trade in education services. *Globalisation, Societies and Education, 1*(3), 359–374.

Zoellick, R. B. (2003). Freeing the intangible economy: Services in international trade. Speech to the Coalition of Service Industries Dinner. Retrieved from http://iipdigital.usembassy.gov/st/english/texttrans/2003/12/20031203114646yessedo0.2135736.html

Chapter 2

The entrepreneurial state
Recruiting students

The movement of students is the most visible and most thoroughly regulated feature of the globalization of education. The number of students travelling abroad to undertake degrees has risen at a fairly consistent rate for as long as data has been collected, and by 2011 they constituted around 4.3 million people (OECD, 2013). In addition, countless numbers travel for shorter periods of study including exchange, study tours, intensive short courses, language studies and work placements. They come from every country (even from North Korea, which has over 2,000 students studying abroad), and they study in almost every country (although some do not provide data on the number of incoming students, so we cannot be sure).

In this chapter we consider the ways in which governments regulate the inward movement of students, and in the following chapter we consider the regulation of outbound student mobility. One notable feature of the frameworks considered in this chapter is the extensive regulatory frameworks in place in those countries that are the most active in recruiting full-fee-paying students, such as the United States, the United Kingdom, Australia and Canada. In these countries the state does not usually fund or directly provide education to foreign students, but a dense web of regulatory measures is in place to govern a market in which relatively autonomous providers engage with and recruit independently mobile students. In other places in which host governments are able to control the flow of students more directly by funding and/or providing education, such extensive regulatory frameworks are not as evident. In neither case do we observe a diminished role for the state, as many had predicted in the 1990s.

We must also bear in mind first that international students are recruited by higher education institutions, not by governments. However, we often hear the casual conflation of nation, government and providers, in statements along the lines of 'country X's international education strategy is commercially motivated', or 'country Y is primarily concerned with cultural enrichment'. Here we are not so much interested in institutional strategies, but the ways in which governments endeavour to constrain, enable and influence the recruitment activities of institutions. The challenge for governments is to create a regulatory environment in which institutional interests align with what the government deems to be in the national interest.

Historical context

The pre-modern antecedents of today's higher education institutions existed in a porous world. In Europe, medieval universities shared a common curriculum (theology, medicine, law), a common language of instruction (Latin), common teaching and research methods, and a common mission to promote a universalizing intellectual transcendence of the cultural and linguistic diversity of the continent across which the network was overlaid. Students and scholars often travelled considerable distances to early universities but they did not cross national borders as we know them (Wei, 2012). Being embedded within the power structure of the church rather than the secular state, they were affected little by the changing fortunes of the empires, kingdoms and principalities on whose lands the campuses were located. Similarly, early leading institutions of higher learning in other parts of the world drew scholars from far and wide. Nalanda, an early centre of Buddhist teaching, at one point had a community of 2,000 teachers and 10,000 scholars who came from lands we now call India, China, Korea, Japan, Tibet, Mongolia, Turkey, Sri Lanka and South East Asia, according to the website of its modern namesake. Al-Azhar University in Cairo, similarly had a religious character, attracting scholars from across the Muslim world.

With the emergence of nation states, the character of the university changed dramatically. Higher education systems became organized nationally, although with varying levels of government involvement in their operations. Distinctive national systems of higher education emerged in the nineteenth century in Europe and North America, and in the twentieth century globally. Colonial powers often dictated the models that would be emulated, but even those countries that escaped colonization such as Thailand modelled their new institutions on those in Europe and the United States (Altbach, 2006).

The massification of higher education, first in the advanced economies and subsequently elsewhere, took place within nation states that had a previously unparalleled command of their citizens, their national economies and their borders, and as a result, modern university systems developed with a very high proportions of students, staff and funding sourced within the nation state. During the twentieth century the ability of governments to regulate cross-border flows increased greatly. Many previously porous borders became tightly controlled by immigration regimes and the expansion of state intervention into daily life meant that travelling informally to another territory without 'papers' became increasingly difficult.

Between the end of the Second World War (1945) and the end of the Cold War (1990), student mobility across borders occurred on a much smaller scale than today and was normally coordinated by governments. Altbach (2006) observes of this period that: 'The goals were political and economic, and higher education was a key battlefield. The rationale was sometimes couched in the ideological jargon of the Cold War but was often obscured by rhetoric about cooperation' (p. 126). In communist states, governments cooperated to foster the movement of students between politically allied states, both to build greater social connections between states but also to facilitate the transfer of knowledge and skills to foster economic and social development. (The last bastion of this model is Cuba, which continues to host significant numbers of international students, particularly in medicine, as part of the nation's efforts to build relationships of solidarity with politically friendly states.) In these states, overseas travel was normally highly restricted and participation in such state-sponsored overseas studies was one of the only means for a young person to travel legitimately. In the West, international travel was less politically restricted, but as in the communist states most extra-national study was government sponsored. The United States and former European colonial powers sponsored students from politically aligned developing countries to study in their universities. In most Western receiving countries a significant proportion of the cost of tuition of international students was borne by the host government, through schemes such as the Fullbright Program in the USA and the Colombo Plan in Australia. As Altbach (2006) notes, the recipients of such schemes, both the individual students and their countries of origin, often benefited greatly from the educational support provided to them, but also tied them into an ongoing relationship with one superpower or the other.

However, alongside the government-sponsored students were growing numbers of self-funded or 'private' students. For example, between 1950 and 1975 the Australian government sponsored around 18,000 students, with the largest numbers of students coming from Indonesia, Malaysia, South Vietnam and Thailand. During the same period, however, Australia hosted an additional 45,000 private international students, with the largest numbers from Malaysia, Hong Kong and Singapore. By 1975, less than a quarter of the 12,500 international students in Australia were in government-sponsored programmes (Cleverley & Jones, 1976, pp. 26-29). During the 1970s and 1980s, in the UK, Australia and New Zealand successive government enquiries debated whether subsidizing the tuition of private international students was an effective way of targeting international development assistance. Private international students tended to be affluent, urban and well connected in business and government circles and were hardly the most-needy recipients for development assistance.

Foreign aid for tertiary education continues today. France, Germany and Japan are currently the world's leading international aid donors in tertiary education, contributing between them US$2.7 billion in 2004, which at that time represented 80 per cent of the global total of official development assistance spending on tertiary education (Bashir, 2007). In 2007, these three countries enrolled 21per cent of the world's internationally mobile students who studied abroad for a year or more (UNESCO, 2009). Most countries where English is not the language of instruction in higher education to some extent subsidize international students' tuition in public institutions, through free-tuition or heavily subsidized places and through scholarships to cover living expenses.

Table 2.1 shows both the 20 largest host countries of internationally mobile degree students and the 20 countries with the highest proportion of international

Table 2.1 Major host countries of internationally mobile degree students, 2011

Country	Number	Country	Percentage
United States of America	709,565	Liechtenstein	79.0
United Kingdom	419,946	China, Macao SAR	44.6
France	268,212	Luxembourg	41.4
Australia	262,597	Qatar	40.3
Germany	207,771	United Arab Emirates	38.0
Japan	151,461	Cyprus	28.0
Canada	106,284	Bahrain	20.5
China	79,638	Singapore	20.2
Italy	73,584	Australia	19.8
Austria	70,558	Austria	19.5
South Africa	70,428	United Kingdom	16.8
Malaysia	64,749	Switzerland	16.2
Republic of Korea	62,675	New Zealand	15.6
Spain	62,636	Lebanon	15.3
Egypt	49,011	Barbados	13.8
Singapore	47,915	France	11.9
Switzerland	41,803	Saint Lucia	11.3
New Zealand	40,854	Ireland	10.7
United Arab Emirates	39,345	Jordan	9.9
Ukraine	38,777	Antigua and Barbuda	9.6

Data source: UNESCO (2013).

students as a percentage of total tertiary enrolment in the host country. We can see that for some host countries, such as the UK, France and Australia, international students are both numerous, and a significant proportion of the student body, while some other major host countries, such as the United States, Germany and Japan host a large number of students but these students represent only a small proportion of the student population. Many of those countries with the highest proportions of international students are small states that receive many students from neighbouring countries.

In 1979 the newly elected Conservative government in the UK removed subsidies completely for all international students commencing from 1980. This resulted in a reduction of government funding to universities, and also a short-term reduction in international student numbers overall (UKCISA, 2008). Within a few years, however, numbers rebounded and continued to grow strongly. Australia and New Zealand also shifted from an 'aid' to a 'trade' orientation within a few years. This involved removing government subsidies for private international students and allowing institutions to autonomously determine tuition fees and enrolment levels for international students, thereby creating a bifurcated student market in these countries. Universities could charge a premium for programmes in which there was significant international demand, and were free to promote these programmes and spend the resulting tuition income as they saw fit. Meanwhile, governments continued to exercise tight control over the domestic student market, with regulated tuition income and enrolment levels. Understandably, many institutions developed an entrepreneurial approach to the international education market. Enrolments in all three countries grew dramatically through the 1990s and 2000s.

In these countries, as in the United States and Canada and more recently in Malaysia and Singapore, most education providers have considerable autonomy to recruit international students. On one level this represents a privatization of education, as governments allow many institutions to charge students the full cost of provision. Often, such institutions are engaged in a privatized global education market while also engaging in a national education system that is subject to much greater levels of direct control over student numbers and fee levels. But even though their international provision is privatized, it is not deregulated. In fact, as Martens and Starke (2008) have observed in the case of New Zealand, governments that have adopted a 'trade-oriented' approach to international education exercise a high degree of intervention, especially through the promotion of the country as a destination, the regulation of their education providers and the filtering of students through visa conditions.

As noted, this book focuses on the provision of whole programmes by institutions based in one country to students from another country. This usually involves extended studies overseas. But intensive short courses, often for language studies or professional development, appear to be increasingly common. Data for short courses is difficult to come by as these students usually travel on tourist visas and enrol in programmes that tend not to be included in national statistics. Several other forms of short-term international student mobility serve to add an international dimension to a national qualification. Study tours are organized as part of the student's programme of studies in their home country and sometimes involve collaboration with an overseas educational institution. Exchange programmes involve students spending one or two semesters at an overseas partner institution for credit to their programme of studies in their home country, while paying their usual tuition fees at the home institution and studying free at the host institution. Study abroad involves students spending one or two semesters at an overseas institution for credit to their programme of studies in their home country, while paying tuition fees at the host institution but none at their home institution. These students are often sometimes referred to as 'free movers' in Europe. These forms of international mobility are popular with students from affluent societies, who prefer to study in local universities but seek to enhance their programme with an overseas experience. Such mobility is usually supported by governments in affluent societies through schemes such as University Mobility in Asia and the Pacific and the European region action scheme for the mobility of university students (ERASMUS), which since 1987 has sponsored the international exchange of 2.2 million students, at more than 4,000 institutions in 33 countries (European Commission, 2010).

There are of course many different motivations for governments, educational institutions, and other actors to promote the internationalization of higher education, which Knight has grouped into four categories: social/cultural, political, academic and economic (Knight, 2004; Knight & de Wit, 1995). When governments consider the recruitment of foreign students, though, they express their motivations in economic and political terms. Here we consider briefly the types of economic and political benefits that they hope to achieve; then we will examine the types of regulatory mechanisms that governments are able to employ in an effort to achieve these outcomes.

Economic benefits: Revenue and competitiveness

Many of the major host countries appear primarily focused on the economic benefits arising from international students. The major English-language host countries, USA, UK, Australia, Canada and New Zealand, routinely report on the export income generated by incoming students, based on estimates of students' spending on tuition fees and living expenses, although methodologies do vary slightly between countries (Lane & Owens, 2012). Some of the rapidly growing new host countries are also motivated by a desire to add education to their list of exports. For example, the Malaysian Ministry of Higher Education aims to 'make education an important export commodity that will generate foreign exchange for the country' (MoHE, 2009). It is important to note that not only full-fee-paying students generate such export earnings; even students who received heavily subsidized tuition and exchange students who do not pay fees to their host institution have an economic impact through their spending while in the host country, and as such contribute to export earnings. Some of the economic benefits are very difficult to quantify, such as the value of investment in real estate by foreign students' families, and the extent to which the presence of foreign students leads to visits by relatives and friends. The most comprehensive accounting on export income and jobs generated is NAFSA's online International Student Economic Value Tool, which provides detailed reports for the USA by region, state and congressional district. For the state of Texas, for example, NAFSA estimates that international students support 18,000 jobs and generate US $1.4 billion in economic benefits.

The degree to which such data influences governments' thinking is dependent not only on the dollar amount of export income but also its significance as a proportion of the economy as a whole. Education New Zealand (Boag, 2008) estimated that expenditure from international students accounted for 1.13 per cent of GDP in New Zealand and 1.06 per cent in Australia, considerably higher than the other leading destinations of self-funded students (0.4 per cent in the UK, 0.25 per cent in Canada and 0.16 per cent in the USA). Considered as a proportion of export income, international education is even more significant for Australasia. Expenditure by international students accounted for 6.9 per cent of export revenues for New Zealand, 5.6 per cent for Australia, 1.49 per cent for the UK, 0.94 per cent for the USA and 0.88 per cent for Canada. Education is among the most valuable export industries in both countries. However, international students are concentrated in key urban centres, and when viewed more locally, educating students from across the Asia Pacific region is a vitally important part of local economies of those cities where international students are concentrated (Sydney, Auckland and Melbourne). Education is now the most valuable export industry for the state of Victoria, Australia's second most populous state, in which Melbourne is located. Consequently, both countries put considerable energy and resources into national branding, industry development, market research and government-to-government relations with key source countries, and in driving initiatives in various international forums to promote growth in education mobility and exchange.

We consider specific types of regulation later in the chapter, but in short, governments that seek to generate export earnings from education pursue expansionary policies that often include allowing institutions to set tuition fees, design their own programmes and choose their language of instruction, rapid student visa processing, national educational branding, openness to foreign programmes and campuses, and robust quality assurance processes for providers hosting international students.

For advanced economies, exporting education makes good sense. Globalization has rendered them uncompetitive in producing many tradable goods due to high labour costs, but they remain competitive in knowledge-intensive activities such as education and research. The policy shift from aid to trade in the UK, Australia and New Zealand in the mid-1980s was a small part of a massive restructuring of those economies that also involved the reduction of policy support, including tariffs and subsidies, for uncompetitive industries. Huge numbers of jobs were lost in coal mining in the UK, and manufacturing in Australia, to name but two examples. Meanwhile, many services sectors were becoming internationalized rapidly, leading to growing exports and the generation of thousands of new jobs, not only in the education sector but also in tourism, banking, insurance and accounting, generating thousands of new jobs. In none of these countries was the development of an education export industry initiated by the education institutions themselves, rather it was the result of economic liberalization policies driven by ministries of finance and trade, and this pattern has been repeated in many countries since.

In no country, however, are the benefits of international education thought of simply in terms of export revenue generation. Even the most export-oriented governments continue to fund scholarship programmes, promote short-term exchange programmes and encourage the study of foreign languages and internationalization of the curriculum. There has been a renewed emphasis on such non-commercial international activities in the major English-speaking destinations in recent years. In the United States, such an approach is often called 'comprehensive internationalization' (Hudzik, 2011) and in Australia the renaissance is referred to as a third phase, or third wave, of higher education internationalization. The country's peak body representing universities explains that:

> This third wave approach emphasises a broader and deeper conception of international education integration extending to faculty and research links, doctoral studies, wider disciplinary representation and Australian student study abroad. The goals here are educational richness and not simple revenue payoff.
>
> (Universities Australia, 2010)

Most governments are attracted to such broad internationalization of higher education because they see it as a necessary means to enhance the country's competitiveness in the global economy. A range of 'indirect' economic benefits might result from recruiting international students. Governments hope that by studying alongside foreigners, local students become familiar with other countries and cultures, better enabling them to work in international and multicultural environments after graduation. Governments also hope that ongoing engagement with their overseas alumni will over time result in increased trade and investment with source countries. Recruiting highly capable students from abroad, especially into advanced programmes, can also strengthen a nation's educational institutions and its strength in research and development. This is most starkly apparent in the United States, where 31 per cent of all doctoral degrees were conferred on foreign students in 2012, up from 14 per cent two decades earlier, and over half of all doctorates in engineering (NSF, 2013). The United States' continued leadership in many fields of research clearly depends upon being able to recruit such students. Such contributions to educational and research strength are intrinsically valued by institutions themselves, and Knight (2004) therefore considers them 'academic' motivations for internationalization. However, governments tend to value such outcomes because of the broader economic benefits that strong educational and research institutions can generate.

Political benefits: Public diplomacy

Most governments value the contribution of students to fostering linkages between nations and encourage inward mobility as a means to deepen the nation's international engagement. Governments often cite such benefits. The then US undersecretary of state for public affairs and public diplomacy, Karen Hughes, captured this sentiment well in 2007:

> I believe our academic exchange programs, our student exchange programs, have been our single most successful public diplomacy tool over the last 50 years. When you bring people here, and they have an opportunity to see America for themselves and make up their own minds, they have a much more positive and long-lasting appreciation and understanding of our country. We're educating the leaders of the world, and I meet them. They are leaders in their own countries; they are leaders in industry; they are leaders in the non-profit sector, and they tell me, 'Oh I studied in such-and-such institution 20 or 30 years ago'.
>
> (Quoted in Olsen, Dodd & Wright, 2009, p. 49)

A wide range of benefits are seen to arise from overseas alumni. Some, such as business linkages and research collaboration, are tangible while others, such as goodwill and an enhanced national reputation, are intangible. Kapur (2010) argues that Western-educated elites, although they constitute a small minority of their country's population, have been a

> key mechanism for the transmission of ideas of modernity, be it political regimes or economic systems ... there is evidence to suggest that they promote democracy in their home country, but only if the foreign education is acquired in democratic countries.
>
> (p. 40)

Another reading of this observation might be that returned students tend to take on the political, economic and cultural values of the country in which they studied, and if in a position of power they can influence the direction of national development in line with the values of the country in which their ideas were formed. The prospect of this type of influence is appealing to any government, and we could expect that those who study in a state capitalist society such as China might adopt many of the values of that country and have just as much influence on their home country but in quite a different direction.

The term 'public diplomacy' was once used narrowly to refer to programmes that governments had sponsored that were intended to inform or influence public opinion in other countries. International study scholarships and subsidized university places provided by host governments are obvious example of such programmes. Over time the term has come to be used to describe a much wider range of engagement with foreign publics by both governmental and non-state actors. Now multinational corporations, media producers, advertisers, celebrities, non-governmental organizations and many other actors are able to influence a foreign public's opinion of a nation. For instance, IKEA has had an enormous impact on global perceptions of Sweden. In the same way, the cumulate effects of a country's education providers' deep engagement with tens or hundreds of thousands of young people constitutes a profound influence on global perceptions of the host nation.

The Chinese government portrays its policy to attract more overseas students into degree courses as primarily a means to promote its cultural soft power. To that end the national, provincial and municipal governments, as well as individual institutions and state-owned firms will provide a large number of scholarships so that China can be a leading provider of higher education to Asian students (Chen, 2010). At the national level, the export income that could be generated by international fee-paying students is inconsequential when considered in relation to the economy overall, so it makes sense that such drivers do not figure prominently in the governments' discourse. But, as Litao (2012) points out, for individual universities this driver may not be so trivial, since international students' fees may be up to four to six times higher than domestic students. Litao argues that the soft-power discourse allows higher education to play a key role in China's 'peaceful rise'. Higher education for international students, he observes, has been governed by the Ministry of Public Security, the Ministry of Foreign Affairs and the Ministry of Education. While the Ministry of Education and Ministry of Foreign Affairs have been keen to expand the number of international students, the Ministry of Public Security has been wary that international students may pose a threat to political and social stability. The soft-power discourse, according to Litao, provided a strong political rationale for inbound students that was able to transcended the concerns held by security agencies.

Government-supported programmes typically have both public diplomacy benefits to the host country and international development assistance benefits to the students' home country. Public funding is often justified on both grounds, but with a different emphasis depending on the audience. At home, governments will focus on the extent to which supporting international students is in the national interest, while abroad the same government will explain that the programme is intended to provide support to the student's home country. In practice, economic and public diplomacy rationales for international students recruitment are rarely clearly distinguishable, as the following explanation of the benefits of the German Academic Exchange Service's scholarship programmes illustrate:

> The DAAD scholarships help launch careers and create lasting ties to Germany. They have created a worldwide network of young academics who continue to collaborate with their German host institutions in higher education and research. By training future university teachers and other executives from developing countries, these scholarships are also the basis for successful initiatives in development cooperation.
>
> (DAAD, 2012, p. 18)

While 'soft power' and diplomacy benefits are less immediately tangible than fee-income and foreign currency spent on living expenses, in the mid to long term they can be a vital part of strategic international relations.

Regulation and promotion

Governments have a range of means at their disposal to shape the flow of incoming international students, some of which regulate the activities of education providers and some of which regulate the activities of students. They are able to determine which institutions can enrol international students, how they are to be funded, how they may promote their programmes, what support services they must provide, and sometimes their language of instruction. Through student visa conditions, governments determine which students are allowed to enter the country and what rights they have to paid employment, health care and public services.

One of the difficulties involved in regulating incoming students is that governments are not unitary entities. Horizontally, they are split into ministries or departments with differing objectives and between which there is not always a close working relationship. We might assume that a national policy framework in relation to student recruitment would result in a high degree of coherence between the measures taken by ministries of immigration, foreign affairs and education, but this is surprisingly often not the case. Vertically, governments in many countries are split into national and sub-national jurisdictions, and responsibility for the types of regulatory measures we consider in this chapter are often distributed between levels of government. For example, in Canada and the United States, provinces and states have primacy over most aspects of education policy, while foreign affairs and immigration are mostly centralized. Because of its weak federal oversight of education and disjointed policy, the US government has not been as effective at supporting student recruitment as other Anglophone exporters, and has experienced a long-term decline in its share of the world's international degree students which does not appear likely to change in the near future.

It is very common for each level of government to have different priorities, and for the relationship between the levels to be affected by changes of political leadership at one level or another. At present, institutions in Melbourne, Australia, the city that we are based in, are subject to a three new policy frameworks, at the national level (Chaney, 2013), the state level (Victoria State Government, 2013) and municipal level (City of Melbourne, 2013). Luckily, there is a high degree of coherence between them, with the differences between them due to the specific areas of responsibility of each level of government. The one point on which there has been most tension is, peculiarly, public transport. The state government has refused to allow international students to purchase concession public transport tickets as domestic students can, despite much lobbying from education providers, the other levels of government, and students' groups.

Another complication is the lack of consistency in defining which students are international and which are domestic. First, long-term or permanent residents of a country who do not have citizenship may have some of the rights of citizens but not others. Second, many countries extend national treatment (the same or similar status as local students) to citizens of certain countries within various economic and/or political unions. Within the EU, for example, students of member states enjoy almost the same rights as locals in other member states. A similar arrangement is in place between Australia and New Zealand, and between member states of the Southern African Development Community. Students from Francophone countries enjoy more favourable treatment in Quebec than those from other Canadian provinces. Complex regulatory issues can arise within such unions, especially concerning subsidies and competition for places, and there has been much discussion of these within the European Union in particular. Here we will confine our discussion to the ways in which governments deal with students from outside such agreements.

Regulating institutions

The most profound decision a government makes is how international students are to be funded. Anglophone countries, as discussed earlier, generally require foreign students to pay the full cost of their studies. In fact, in some Anglophone countries, such as Australia, it is illegal for public universities to charge below the full cost of provision of education to international students, to ensure that international students are not being cross-subsidized by funding intended for domestic students. While fees for local students in Anglophone countries (and in-state students in the USA) are often capped by governments, the fees charged to international or out-of-state students are considerably higher. Governments, acting as purchasers of education on behalf of local students, use their regulatory power to constrain the fees that most institution can charge those they fund, while allowing institutions the freedom to charge non-nationals as much as the market will bear. Therefore, international full-fee paying students are making a higher contribution to the cost of running the institution than are the government-subsidized local students they study alongside.

In those countries in which most students are paying full fees, governments provide a range of meritocratic scholarships to international students, usually focused on postgraduate studies and particularly doctoral students. Bilateral scholarships, open to students from a particular country, are also common and usually form part of a broader political engagement strategy that also includes development assistance and various bilateral treaties. Another way to increase accessibility for international students is to provide students with access to loans to cover their fees and living costs. In the United States, international students are able to obtain loans provided by financial institutions if they have an American guarantor, and in the Netherlands, EU students can access low-interest loans to cover tuition fees.

Countries in which negligible fees charged to local students often also fully subsidize the tuition of foreign students, as is the case in France and Germany for example, making these countries the world's leading international aid donors in higher education if one includes the public funds devoted to educating foreign students (Bashir, 2007). Other countries, such as Japan and China, subsidize the tuition of most international students to varying degrees. Table 2.2 shows that nearly all countries where English is not the language of instruction in higher education subsidize international students tuition to some extent, whereas most countries where English is the language of instruction do not. Most would consider public funding for foreign students an act of generosity, but might argue over whether this is the wisest use of public funds. Free trade advocates could argue that public funding constitutes an 'export-enhancing subsidy', that assists providers from their countries to compete in recruiting international students (Poretti, 2009, p. 79). If we were considering the export of widgets then such complaints would be forthcoming from competing suppliers of widgets on the world market, but we have not heard this complaint made by any advocates of trade liberalization in education, signalling that education is still treated as being quite different from other forms of services trade.

There are obviously limits on the number of foreign students that host governments are able to fund, especially if it is perceived that international students are displacing deserving local students through direct competition for places, and as a result, places for government-funded international students are usually capped. This issue erupted in 2011 in Singapore, where tuition fees for international students in public universities are just 10 per cent above local student rates and subsidized only slightly less than domestic students. In response to public sentiment that international students were displacing locals, the government promised to reduce the proportion of international students, which was at that time 18 per cent of all public university enrolments (Tan, 2011). Across continental Europe and Scandinavia, similar debates are ongoing, with proponents of subsidized education for international students arguing that even though fee income is forgone, the broader economic and political benefits described above justify the public expenditure.

Private universities and sub-degree providers in many countries are less constrained than public universities. In the United States, France, Malaysia and Singapore, private institutions are not subject to the same price controls and quotas as public universities, and those that are internationally focused often have far higher proportions of international students compared with public universities in the same country. Some sub-degree institutions, providing shorter vocational programmes or diploma pathways into university programmes are able to charge significantly lower fees than universities, and these have significantly broadened access to international study to students from poorer backgrounds (Baas, 2006). In the 1990s in New Zealand and the 2000s in the UK and Australia, enrolments in such programmes increased dramatically because students were usually able to earn enough in the host country to cover the tuition fees while obtaining a qualification that might lead to permanent residency. This provided new opportunities for hundreds of thousands of students, many from South Asia, who did not have the means to pay the much higher fees required of university degrees. They paid their

Table 2.2 Tuition fee policies of major education exporters

Heavily subsidized	Partially subsidized	Full-cost fees
France (public)	Japan	USA
Germany	Singapore (public)	UK
Malaysia (public)	Switzerland	Australia
	China	Canada
		Malaysia (private)
		New Zealand
		Singapore (private)
		Netherlands
		France (private)

way through their studies by working in precarious employment, often in convenience stores or fast-food outlets, or driving taxis. However, many were living below the poverty line and exposed to exploitative conditions at the bottom end of the labour market, the housing market and the education sector (Marginson, Nyland, Sawir & Forbes-Mewett, 2010). Inadvertently, allowing large numbers of international students to undertake low-cost short duration programmes had put a large number of students at risk and tarnished the reputation of the education provided in these host countries.

In those countries where institutions are not allowed to charge fees to international students, governments are able to exercise control over which institutions are able to enrol international students through their funding powers. Education providers are usually very reluctant to enrol large numbers of unfunded students. However, in environments where education providers are allowed to set their own fees for international students, and retain the income they receive, enrolling international students can be lucrative, especially in highly sought-after destinations. If any institution is allowed to recruit students then 'visa mills' will appear very quickly. These are bogus institutions that allow students to obtain a student visa in return for the payment of fees but do not require the students to attend. A second problem is low-quality providers who act in many ways like visa mills but provide a minimal educational programme in order to avoid detection by authorities. In many cases the 'students' enrolled in such institutions are complicit in the scam, and such arrangements might be their only way of obtaining a visa that would allow them to work in the host country (Migration Watch, 2012). Visa mills and low-quality providers that target international students can severely damage to the host country's reputation for quality education, and especially tarnish legitimate sub-degree providers, since it is often difficult for prospective international students to distinguish between them. They also undermine the country's migration and student visa programme regimes and can lead to public demands for the tightening of visa conditions that may also screen out legitimate students.

Because of these risks, governments implement licensing schemes to ensure that only quality providers are able to sponsor foreigners to obtain a student visa. This sounds like quite a straightforward process but its effectiveness is dependent upon coordination between immigration authorities that issue student visas and educational agencies that must vouch for the quality of institutions, and the capacity of the latter can be easily overwhelmed by rapid growth in the number of private providers. Developing such regulation also takes time, and is generally implemented in response to serious crises and complaints from the industry itself about rogue providers. Within a few years of the UK deregulation of tuition fees in 1980, new private colleges focused on international students had sprung up. In 1987, the UK Council of Overseas Student Affairs published its first Code of Practice, which it encouraged private colleges to adopt, and in the following year it began to lobby the government to require private colleges to obtain accreditation, which took 20 more years for the government to implement (UKCISA, 2008).

Licensing is also a means by which governments can mandate the level of support services provided to international students, with the threat of negative publicity for breaches or, ultimately, revocation of their ability to recruit students from abroad. The level of student welfare support that institutions are expected to provide varies widely between jurisdictions, but might include: the provision of pre-arrival information and advice; orientation; accommodation; employment; health and wellbeing; financial assistance; and support in case of critical incidents (Ziguras & Harwood, 2011). Here governments must strike a balance. Mandating levels of support services that are too low places international students at risk and allows providers to operate legally while providing a level of care that would appear to be below community expectations. Mandating high levels of support services raises costs for institutions and students, and might discriminate against small and new providers.

In countries in which English is not normally the medium of instruction, governments' policies towards language of instruction can also help or hinder institutions, since most of the growth in international student mobility in the past decade has involved students studying in English. Singapore, Malaysia, the United Arab Emirates and Qatar have become regional international education hubs by developing programmes taught in English, mainly by local private education providers and foreign universities. Universities across Europe and Asia have also developed English-language courses, in an effort to attract foreign students and to provide a more internationalized education to domestic students. Compelling institutions to teach in English can generate much opposition and results in poor outcomes where students and teachers lack the language proficiency required (Byun et al., 2010). The Dutch parliament debated such a measure, but decided leave the decision to the institutions themselves, and today over half of the 1,500 masters programmes in the Netherlands are taught in English, along with around 250 bachelor degrees (Becker & Kolster, 2012). Other European countries are following suit, particularly in the north, with the number of masters programmes taught entirely in English currently increasing very rapidly, with some indications that this growth will reduce the UK's market share within Europe (Brenn-White & Faethe, 2013). Similarly, compelling universities to teach only in the national language severely limits their ability to offer programmes and courses that are attractive to foreign students.

Regulating students

Just as governments determine which institutions are able to participate in cross-border education, they also determine which students are able to participate through the issuance of student visas. Typically, they are concerned to ensure that the prospective student has been offered a place at a licensed institution, has the financial means to be able to support themselves during their studies and has an appropriate level of language proficiency. The screening processes employed by different governments are quite varied, differ according to the source country and are subject to change over time. There is considerable pressure from education providers on governments to streamline visa conditions so that prospective students are not dissuaded. One factor in the rapid rates of growth of international students in Australia and New Zealand in the 1990s and 2000s was the speed and efficiency of their student visa processing, providing a much more welcoming face to prospective students than competitor countries. From time to time though, even those countries have tightened their scrutiny of some types of applicants in response to high rates of document fraud and breaches of visa conditions.

International students are typically required to obtain private health insurance in the host country, to continue to attend their programme and to leave the country within a specified period after graduation. Apart from ease of application, there are two main points on which governments use visa conditions to compete for international students. The first is the period of time in which student visas allow students to stay on after graduation, and we will consider this in Chapter 4 on student migration policy. The second point of competition is international students' ability to undertake paid employment. The number of hours that students are allowed to work during term time varies from zero to 20 hours per week, as shown in Table 2.3, and restrictions are often less rigid during breaks. The most concerted recruiters also offer the most attractive work rights. The UK government, having been elected on a platform of reducing the net migration rate (which also counts those on student visas) removed work rights for students in sub-degree programmes as one part of a very short-sighted suite of measures designed to reduce student inflows. Allowing students to work significantly expands accessibility, especially for students from low-income countries studying in high-income countries. Part-time work not only contributes to covering the cost of studies, it also provides work experience in the host economy and the opportunity to engage socially and professionally with locals in ways that may not be possible on campus.

Table 2.3 Work rights for international students in selected host countries

Country	Permitted number of working hours per week
UK universities	20
Australia	20
Canada	20
USA	20 (only on campus)
France	18
Switzerland	15
Germany	14
Netherlands	10
UK sub-degree studies	0
Singapore	0
Malaysia	0
China	0

Data sources: Becker & Kolster (2012) and government websites. Students can work in Malaysia in exceptional circumstances but both government agencies and educational institutions advise against it.

The UK government has, since 2010, focused attention on 'bogus students', a term it has used to refer to foreigners admitted on student visas but whose 'real' purpose is to work rather than study. International students were able work for 20 hours during term time, full-time during breaks, and most were entitled to stay on and work in the UK for two years after graduation. The UK Immigration minister argued that the generous work rights had meant 'too many come to do courses below degree level as a cover for staying and working' and competition from these international students was 'putting an unnecessary extra strain on our own graduates' (minister Damian Green quoted in *Guardian*, 2011). The position was stated even more forcefully by think-tank Migration Watch, which gained headlines with its claim that more than 30,000 'bogus students' annually were working illegally in the UK, and the cost to the taxpayer of supporting unemployed British workers who had been displaced could approach £500 million. Migration Watch chairman Sir Andrew Green argued that, 'the 2.5 million who are now unemployed have a right to expect that the government will clamp down on bogus students who are taking jobs that should be available to them' (quoted in Whitehead, 2011). Even though the students were legally entitled to work, the government's rhetoric frequently painted working students as 'bogus students' and suggested that many were working more than they were entitled to, therefore labelling a whole class of students 'illegal workers'.

The government was primarily motivated by the need to reduce net migration rates to meet its election commitments, and as we discuss at length in Chapter 4, international students bore the brunt of these measures. Private college students were singled out as particularly undesirable; their work rights were ceased, accreditation requirements for private colleges were tightened and English-language requirements for sub-degree programmes were raised. Additionally, for all students the two-year period of work rights following completion of studies was ended (UK Border Agency, 2010; Travis, 2011).

Export promotion

The types of regulation described above are in line with the way governments have come to regulate many other sectors of the economy, and many of the differences in approach can be explained by the relative strength of different varieties of regulatory capitalism (Levi-Faur, 2005; Mok, 2008). But in the education sector, governments are not only regulators, they are also a major provider in most countries and are closely involved in export promotion and marketing. The most active governments fund and manage national education branding campaigns designed to recruit students; these often comprise websites, social media, print publications, media advertising in target countries and a visible presence at student recruitment fairs. These campaigns are based on detailed market research which is shared with providers, often comprising enrolment statistics, surveys of prospective students and employers, and intelligence on educational, regulatory and funding developments in key markets. Providers in countries with such levels of government support are able to recruit much more effectively. These promotion activities are conducted by government agencies such as DBIS in the UK, AEI and AusTrade in Australia, CampusFrance, DAAD in Germany and NUFFIC in the Netherlands, as well as by QANGOs such as the British Council, the IIE in the USA and Education New Zealand.

Dependency on international students

A common critique of government policies in education-exporting states has been that institutions have been forced to be overly dependent upon international students. We will consider the nature of this concern in some detail, since it is not clear why international students should present a problem. Would some have similarly lamented the fact that universities were dependent on female students after they started allowing female students to enrol in the early Twentieth Century? We do not hear such complaints either about universities being dependent on domestic students, or on government funding. Clearly, if there were dramatic reductions in support from any of these groups an institution would be in trouble, and would need to find additional students from other groups to replace them. The fable of the goose (or sometimes hen) that laid the golden eggs, attributed to Aesop, is often invoked by commentators concerned by the success of Anglophone universities in attracting international students. Because this is such a common theme, it is worth recounting the fable here for those who may be unfamiliar:

> A man had a hen that laid a golden egg for him each and every day. The man was not satisfied with this daily profit, and instead he foolishly grasped for more. Expecting to find a treasure inside, the man slaughtered the hen. When he found that the hen did not have a treasure inside her after all, he remarked to himself, 'While chasing after hopes of a treasure, I lost the profit I held in my hands!'
>
> (Gibbs, 2002)

The critique, espoused by higher education researchers such as Marginson (2007a, 2007b) and widely evident in popular media discourse (Benson, 2006), suggests that the attractiveness of universities in these countries results from long-term public investment in infrastructure, education for the public good and research. The commercial full-fee provision of education to international students creates pressures to standardize quality and mass-market programmes, and these pressures often conflict with and undermine the non-profit teaching and research activities. If the commercial pressures become too dominant, the reputation of the university and indeed the national system can be undermined. Universities have become over-reliant on income from international students' tuition fees, and the solution is for governments to increase the level of funding for domestic students and research so that the value of these universities in the international marketplace is not eroded:

Universities are rarely credited for good teaching on a comparative basis, and in building a positive global reputation it is research outcomes that count. For Australia, the worst case scenario is that it becomes locked into the role of global polytechnic by its fiscal settings and business culture, its position-taking strategy becomes a downward spiral, its strong quantity position in the cross-border market is eroded, and the material resource base of Australian higher education is further eroded with it. The way out is public reinvestment at scale and especially in research infrastructure.

(Marginson, 2007a)

The construction of international education as a business activity has led to regarding students as 'clients' or 'customers'. A recent Australian example helps to illustrate the risks involved for educational institutions heading down this road. In early 2006, international students at the Melbourne and Sydney campuses of Central Queensland University staged banner-waving protests and threatened a hunger strike. It was reported that the students were disgruntled by failure rates of up to 80 per cent in their final taxation law exam, accusing the University of treating them as a 'cash cow' and providing poor education services. (Colloquially, a 'cash cow' is a part of a business that generates unusually high profit margins.) Central Queensland University countered that its services were high quality, and that the course was 'notoriously a tough one' with high standards expected (*Sydney Morning Herald*, 17 March 2006, p. 4; *Brisbane Courier Mail*, 17 March 2006, p. 21; *The Age* (Melbourne), 14 March 2006, p. 21). Commenting on the protests, Central Queensland University Professor Paul Rodan underlined the propensity for some students to seek to negotiate a better result:

[T]here is the constant danger that 'customers' will see everything, including academic standards, as negotiable. All too often, students with borderline fail marks seek a pass, not on any academic grounds, but on the same basis as one might haggle over a price in an eastern bazaar. Given a cultural orientation to regard 'no' as merely the start of negotiations, institutions will pay a price if they fail to emphasise that negotiation stops at the classroom door.

(Rodan, 2007, p. 5)

Rodan characterized some of the protesting students as 'opportunistic types who had attended few classes and done minimal work, but who hoped to manipulate their way to a cheap pass' (p. 2). Responding to the protests, CQU agreed to reassess disputed results, and noted that students could in any case have requested a re-mark.

We are not in a position to comment on the merits of either case. The general issue, however, has important implications for student mobility in a higher education market. What is the nature of the relationship between the provider and the client in an educational setting? There is a tension inherent in trying to simultaneously embrace two qualitatively different types of relationship: that between service provider and paying customer (where the old adage is that the 'customer is always right'); and that between teacher and learner (in which the teacher is the one with the knowledge/expertise, and the student is the empty vessel there to gather the pearls of wisdom). What is the nature of the service the student/client is engaging? A university would normally argue that the student is entitled access to specified resources (such as library materials, lecture and tutorial attendance, and so on) which, combined with successful study on the student's part, can result in the award of a qualification. Failure to reach a common understanding can lead to accusations that inadequate students are passed (so as to not upset the client or potential clients) or, conversely, that it is in the financial interests of a university to fail marginal students so that they are obliged to repeat studies and pay additional fees. These tensions are further heightened when substantial tuition fees, forgone earnings, additional living expenses (to cover a longer stay while subjects are repeated) and applications for permanent residency status are also at stake. It is important for students to have proper recourse to grievance procedures and dispute settlement mechanisms. At the same time, it is vital for universities to maintain – and be seen to maintain – high standards of academic quality on the part of teachers and learners.

These concerns are most strongly held by critics within research-intensive universities in Australia and New Zealand, who are concerned by the growth in international student recruitment by teaching-focused universities and vocational education and training institutions. They fear that such expansion is aimed at 'lower-quality' students, and this will tarnish the national brand and deter 'high-quality' students and doctoral students from studying in Australia. The massification of these countries' international education industries is seen as detrimental to their international reputations in an era in which global league tables of universities based on research output are becoming increasingly influential (Marginson, 2007a).

All educational institutions and academic commentators, perhaps unsurprisingly, are calling for domestic students and research to be more heavily supported by government, so that institutions are not so dependent on international students for discretionary income. However, it is by no means clear that increasing universities' funding for domestic students and research would lead the institutions to recruit fewer international students, but such funding increases would likely allow institutions to provide better services to international students (Bradley, Noonan, Nugent & Scales, 2008).

Leap-frogging strategies in Asia

Until around 2000, the bulk of the growth in intra-regional student mobility in East Asia and the Pacific was accounted for by students from Asia studying in Australia and New Zealand in rapidly increasing numbers, but since that time, more East and South East Asian students are studying in nearby Asian countries. This type of mobility between neighbouring countries in the region is an excellent means of building long-lasting connections and of sharing expertise between higher education systems.

Countries with English-language higher education systems are clearly much more easily able to recruit foreign students, and in the past decade Singapore and Malaysia have taken advantage of their English-language institutions by actively marketing their education systems to foreign students. Singapore's 'Global Schoolhouse Strategy', launched in 2003, aimed to establish Singapore as a regional hub for education, with the ambitious goal of attracting 150,000 international students by the year 2015. The multi-pronged approach includes expansion of local provision, attracting prestigious foreign education providers to establish branch campuses, and enacting enhanced quality assurance and registration provisions for local private providers and consumer protection measures for students. Education is one of several sectors being promoted by the government in the context of presenting the country as a well-regulated, low-risk location where English is the official language of government, business and education – where one can undertake a Western-style education while also having the opportunity to be immersed in Asian culture and business practices.

It is clear that Singapore has become a popular destination for international students. In 2003, when the government began proactively marketing Singapore as an education hub, there were 61,000 foreign students in the city state. By 2008, international student enrolments had grown to 97,000 (Lee, 2009). Enrolments of Chinese students have grown rapidly to become the largest group of foreign students in Singapore, overtaking traditional source countries Malaysia and Indonesia (Davie, 2005). The Singapore Tourism Board, which is charged with promoting Singapore as an education destination, is now seeking to promote Singapore in more remote Chinese cities. Small numbers of students from Europe, the USA and Australia are also choosing to study in Singapore, many considering it to be a comfortable introduction to Asia, providing both the chance to get a Western education at a leading institution, and become familiar with Chinese language and business practices.

For Singapore, student recruitment is but one strand in an extensive regional hub strategy that is the contemporary continuation of the city's *entrepôt* economy. Since its foundation, Singapore has acted as a regional business hub providing a point of coordination for extensive trade and investment relationships across South East Asia. The contemporary approach to Singapore's hub strategy is to draw foreign investment by fostering concentrations of specialized services in fields that facilitate international business in the global knowledge economy: research and development, IT, finance, accounting, advertising, property development and legal services. These knowledge-intensive aspects of companies' operations require a highly trained workforce and links with a range of higher education institutions. One of the Global Schoolhouse strategy's aims is to attract top international student graduates to remain on in the country as skilled immigrants – an important consideration for a small nation with a low birth rate. Liberal immigration policies make it easy for international student graduates to stay on, and public institutions offer bonded scholarships to top foreign applicants. However, there are stresses. Just as there is some public concern about the domestic impact of large numbers of international students in Australia, there is anecdotal evidence of some local resentment of 'foreign talent' in Singapore. The presence of foreign students (and the allocation of international scholarships) adds to the pressure on locals seeking to enter the already highly selective public university system (which effectively restricts entry to the top quartile). Similarly, the presence of foreign graduates and other skilled immigrants makes the employment market more challenging.

Malaysia's higher education system includes public institutions which operate primarily in Bahasa Malaysian, the national language, and private institutions, which operate in English. The majority of international students in Malaysia are enrolled in English-medium programmes in private institutions, with a smaller number in English-language postgraduate programmes in public universities. The few international students who study in public universities in the national language are mostly from neighbouring countries who are already proficient in Malay. The Malaysian government set a target of 100,000 international students per year by 2010 and established a Marketing and International Education Division within the Ministry of Higher Education. The government's recruitment efforts focus on Islamic countries, primarily North Africa and the Middle East, while private institutions (which enrol the majority of international students) are more active in recruiting students from China and South Asia. Capitalizing on Malaysia's diversity of higher education institutions and cultural diversity, the more active recruitment strategies being employed by both government and private sectors appear to be paying off, and the country looks set to meet its targets. By 2007, international student enrolments had reached 65,000, with 48,000 (74 per cent) of these enrolled in private institutions. In 2008 the number of foreign students enrolled in private higher education institutions had grown to 71,000 (*The Star*, 2008, 2009).

The success of the recruitment strategies of Malaysia and Singapore clearly demonstrate the competitive advantage English language institutions have in recruiting foreign students, especially when supported by government policy development in areas such as student visas, overseas promotion and branding, and quality assurance of providers. As a point of comparison, it is interesting to compare the experiences of these countries with the Philippines, which has a large number of English-language institutions, but has lacked a coordinated strategy to increase international enrolments. In both Malaysia and Singapore, education export strategies were promoted by powerful central economic policy units, which have been able to coordinate whole of government responses aimed at recruiting more international students encouraging institutions to accept them, while ministries of education have remained concerned primarily with the education of the local population and the functioning of the public institutions.

Conclusion

An increasing number of governments are keen to support their institutions to recruit more students from abroad, to generate export income, enhance the ability of their educational institutions and businesses to compete internationally, and to support the broader international relations strategies. One of the key determinants of the role governments play is that small matter of who is paying the bill. The majority of internationally mobile degree students are self-funded and pay tuition fees that cover the cost of their education, and often generate a surplus to the institution. Nearly all of those fee-paying students are studying in English-taught programmes. This presents a challenge to governments of countries where the normal language of instruction is not English, where the government can either accept that it needs to heavily subsidize foreign students, or encourage institutions to develop programmes taught in English and aimed at the international market. In order to compete with the established English language destinations that dominate the global market for mobile degree students, governments must work hard at market research and promotion, visa issuance, quality assurance of providers, and either provide a low-cost alternative or access to paid work. Singapore and Malaysia have been spectacularly successful in making the transition from net importer to net exporter of education in a very short time frame. They have achieved this very deliberately, and have encouraged the development of private and transnational providers to complement their existing public institutions. As we will see in later chapters, the qualities that attract international students are often also the qualities that attract domestic students to undertake studies at home rather than study overseas.

References

Altbach, P. G. (2006). Globalization and the university: Realities in an unequal world. In J. J. F. Forest & P. G. Altbach (Eds.), *International Handbook of Higher Education* (pp. 121–139). Dordrecht, Netherlands: Springer.

Baas, M. (2006). Students of migration: Indian overseas students and the question of permanent residency. *People and Place, 14*(1), 9–24.

Bashir, S. (2007). *Trends in International Trade in Higher Education: Implications and Options for Developing Countries.* Washington DC: The World Bank.

Becker, R., & Kolster, R. (2012). *International Student Recruitment: Policies and Developments in Selected Countries.* The Hague: NUFFIC (Netherlands organisation for international cooperation in higher education).

Benson, S. J. (2006). Commodification of Asian international students in radio media discourse. *New Zealand Journal of Asian Studies, 8*(1), 96–109.

Boag, S. (2008). New Zealand 'punching above its weight' in export education (media release). Wellington: Education New Zealand.

Bradley, D., Noonan, P., Nugent, H., & Scales, B. (2008). *Review of Australian Higher Education: Final Report.* Canberra: Department of Education, Employment and Workplace Relations.

Brenn-White, M., & Faethe, E. (2013). *English-Taught Master's Programs in Europe: A 2013 Update.* New York: Institute for International Education Center for Academic Mobility Research.

Byun, K., Chu, H., Kim, M., Park, I., Kim, S., & Jung, J. (2010). English-medium teaching in Korean higher education: policy debates and reality. *Higher Education, 62*(4), 431–449. doi: 10.1007/s10734-010-9397-4.

Chaney, M. (2013). *Australia – Educating Globally: Advice from the International Education Advisory Council.* Canberra: Commonwealth of Australia.

Chen, J. (2010, 29 September). Soft power part of the curriculum. *China Daily,* p. 4.

City of Melbourne. (2013). *A Great Place to Study: International Student Strategy 2013–17.* Mebourne: City of Melbourne.

Cleverley, J., & Jones, P. (1976). *Australia and International Education: Some Critical Issues.* Hawthorn: Australian Council for Educational Research.

DAAD (2012). *2011 Annual Report.* Bonn: Deutscher Akademischer Austausch Dienst.

Davie, S. (2005, 3 December). Foreign students in Singapore a class apart. *The Straits Times.*

European Commission. (2010). The Erasmus Programme. Retrieved 26 June 2010, from http://ec.europa.eu/education/lifelong-learning-programme/doc80_en.htm

Gibbs, L. (2002). *Aesop's Fables: A New Translation.* Oxford: Oxford University Press.

Guardian (2011, 1 February). Crackdown on student visas will curb 'unpleasant' abuses, says minister.

Hudzik, J. K. (2011). *Comprehensive Internationalization: From Concept to Action.* Washington DC: NAFSA Association of International Educators.

Kapur, D. (2010). *Diaspora, Development, and Democracy The Domestic Impact of International Migration from India.* Princeton, NJ: Princeton University Press.

Knight, J. (2004). Internationalization remodeled: Definition, approaches, and rationales. *Journal of Studies in International Education,* 8(1), 5–31. doi: 10.1177/1028315303260832.

Knight, J., & de Wit, H. (1995). Strategies for internationalisation of higher education: historical and conceptual perspectives. In H. de Wit (Ed.), *Strategies for Internationalisation of Higher Education: A Comparative Study of Australia, Canada, Europe and the United States of America* (pp. 5–32). Amsterdam: European Association for International Education.

Lane, J. E., & Owens, T. L. (2012). The international dimensions of higher education's contibutions to economic development. In J. E. Lane & D. B. Johnstone (Eds.), *Universities and Colleges and Economic Drivers: Measuring Higher Education's Role in Economic Development* (pp. 205–237). New York: SUNY Press.

Lee, Y. S. (2009). Speech by the Minister of State for Trade and Industry at the Singapore Education Awards 2009, Raffles Hotel. Retrieved 4 May 2009, from http://app.stb.gov.sg/asp/new/new03a.asp?id=9964

Levi-Faur, D. (2005). The global diffusion of regulatory capitalism. *The Annals of the American Academy of Political and Social Science,* 598(1), 12–32. doi: 10.1177/0002716204272371.

Litao, Z. (2012). China as a new popular destination for international students: The role of the soft power discourse. Paper presented at the Education Mobilities in East Asia, Singapore.

Marginson, S. (2007a). Global position and position taking: The case of Australia. *Journal of Studies in International Education,* 11(1), 5–32.

Marginson, S. (2007b). The new higher education landscape: Public and private goods, in global/nationa/local settings. In S. Marginson (Ed.), *Prospects of Higher Education: Globalization, Market Competition, Public Goods and the Future of the University* (pp. 29–77). Rotterdam: Sense.

Marginson, S., Nyland, C., Sawir, E., & Forbes-Mewett, H. (2010). *International Student Security.* Cambridge: Cambridge University Press.

Martens, K., & Starke, P. (2008). Small country, big business? New Zealand as education exporter. *Comparative Education,* 44(1), 3–19.

Migration Watch. (2012). *Students: Genuine or Bogus?* Guildford, UK: Migration Watch.

MoHE. (2009). Department of Higher Education. from www.mohe.gov.my/educationmsia/index.php?article=dept

Mok, K. H. (2008). Varieties of regulatory regimes in Asia: the liberalization of the higher education market and changing governance in Hong Kong, Singapore and Malaysia. *The Pacific Review, 21*(2), 147–170. doi: 10.1080/09512740801990220.

NSF. (2013). *Doctorate Recipients from U.S. Universities: 2012.* Arlington, VA: National Science Foundation.

OECD. (2013). *Education at a Glance 2013: OECD Indicators.* Paris: OECD Publishing.

Olsen, A., Dodd, T., & Wright, R. (2009). *The Nature of International Education in Australian Universities and Its Benefits.* Canberra: Universities Australia.

Poretti, P. (2009). *The Regulation of Subsidies Within the General Agreement on Trade in Services of the WTO: Problems and Prospects.* Netherlands: Kluwer Law International.

Rodan, P. (2007). Dilemmas of dissent: International students' protest mechanisms. Paper presented at the Australian International Education Conference, Melbourne. www.aiec.idp.com/pdf/Paper_Rodan.pdf

Tan, E. (2011). Singapore: New 'cap' on foreign students. *University World News* (185).

The Star (Malaysia) (2008, 9 March). Branding Malaysia.

The Star (Malaysia) (2009, 4 April). Govt wants 80,000 foreign students for colleges, varsities this year.

Travis, A. (2011, 23 March). Visa curbs will cut overseas students by 80,000, says Theresa May. *The Guardian.*

UK Border Agency (2010 December). *The Student Immigration System: A Consultation.* Home Office.

UKCISA. (2008). *Mobility Matters: Forty Years of International Students, Forty Years of UKCISA.* London: UK Council for International Student Affairs.

UNESCO. (2009). *Global Education Digest 2009.* Paris: United Nations Educational, Scientific and Cultural Organization Institute for Statistics.

UNESCO. (2013). Data centre. Retrieved 21 October 2013 from http://www.uis.unesco.org

Universities Australia. (2010). International. From www.universitiesaustralia.edu.au/page/policy-advocacy/international

Victoria State Government. (2013). *International Education Strategy for Victoria 2013–2018.* Melbourne: Department of State Development, Business and Innovation, Victoria State Government.

Wei, I. P. (2012). Medieval universities and their aspirations. In A. R. Nelson & I. P. Wei (Eds.), *The Global University: Past, Present, and Future Prospects* (pp. 133–152). New York: Palgrave Macmillan.

Whitehead, T. (2011, 6 January). Bogus students cost country £500m a year, think-tank warns. *Telegraph.*

Ziguras, C., & Harwood, A. (2011). *Principles of Good Practice for Enhancing International Student Experience Outside the Classroom.* Hobart, Tasmania: ISANA International Education Association.

Chapter 3

Managing the outflow of self-funded and sponsored students

This chapter explores the role of governments in students' home countries in relation to outward degree mobility. In the past, governments tended to either be uninvolved in the movement of privately funded students, or to try to restrict outward mobility of their citizens. Now, many governments endeavour to manage the scale of outbound degree mobility, either to reduce or increase numbers. An increasing number of governments actively support students to study abroad by offering loan schemes or purchasing places at foreign institutions for their citizens. In addition, governments of some countries with large student populations abroad are playing a more significant consular role in support of their young citizens abroad. Most studies of students' home countries focus on government policies in relation to sponsored students but here we are also concerned with self-funded students, who comprise the majority of internationally mobile students. As early as 1980, according to the US Institute of International Education, around 85 per cent of students in the United States received no funding from the home country other than support from their families (Barber, 1985).

We have organized this chapter around two quite different types of policy objectives. In the first section we examine how states manage the extent of participation in outbound degree mobility, in some cases to reduce numbers of students going abroad, in other cases to increase mobility, and in some cases to broaden access to particular groups of students. Here governments are interested in who is studying abroad, and how to change the composition of the mobile population to meet a particular policy objective. This is not a new problem – it was pointed out long ago that 'the interests of individuals studying abroad are not necessarily congruent with national interests and that it is hard to force congruence' (Barber, Altbach & Myers,1984, p. 164). The second half of the chapter is concerned with the welfare of outbound students, both in terms of consumer protection and pastoral care. Here governments seek to ensure that their citizens are not being exploited or misled and that their welfare needs and rights are being attended to while overseas.

Managing the scale of outbound mobility

In earlier chapters we outlined international student numbers worldwide, and considered the factors that influence the individual's decision to study abroad.

Here we are concerned with the motivations and activities of governments seeking to steer the mobility of their citizens. Steps taken to reduce student outflow range from the draconian – visa restrictions and restrictions on transfer of funds (needed for fees and living expenses abroad) – to the benign: increasing the home-country availability of both domestic and international (transnational) education. Methods of facilitating mobility include the provision of scholarships or home-government funded subsidies for study abroad. In this context, we consider what implications GATS commitments have for the international mobility of student subsidies.

Restricting the ability of students to study overseas

The most draconian means of reducing the number of outbound international students who do not return is to prevent students from leaving for the purposes of overseas study, except in approved circumstances. During the twentieth century the ability of governments to regulate cross-border flows increased greatly. Many previously porous borders became tightly controlled by immigration regimes and the expansion of state intervention into daily life meant that travelling informally to another territory without 'papers' became increasingly difficult. Some countries used this new control over movement to restrict mobility for education after the Second World War. In countries where citizens required exit permits to travel abroad, as was the case in most socialist countries until the late 1980s or early 1990s, a permit was usually only available to those whose overseas study was organized and sponsored by the sending and receiving governments.

Many developing countries erected various obstacles designed to reduce outflows of students in the 1970s and 1980s, or to allow some students to travel while denying the opportunity to others. These were often part of a broader economic strategy of reducing the currency outflows associated with importation of goods and services. These restrictions on access to education often had the same effect as tariffs on imported goods, which were also considerably higher in low-income countries than in high-income countries during this period. In some cases they allowed Leftist governments to democratize access to education by ensuring merit-based access to domestic institutions and denying children of wealthy elites the opportunity to buy their way into overseas institutions. In many cases these were short-lived and were linked to broader shifts in regime and economic policy.

Measures included imposing rigorous academic requirements, limiting the field or level of studies that could be undertaken (Barber, 1985). South Korea in the late 1960s introduced restrictions on the availability of passports in order to reduce the number of students travelling abroad. This was effective in halving the number of outgoing students for a decade until the policy was abandoned in 1981 (Cummings, 1984). The Indian government also for several decades prevented self-funded students from leaving the country. Indian citizens were free to leave, but they were not free to take their money with them; currency-exchange restrictions prevented them from using funds from India to pay for study overseas. Until the 1990s, India's central bank only permitted foreign exchange for undergraduate education at three institutions (Cambridge, Oxford and Harvard) (Kapur, 2010, p. 130). As a result, most Indian students abroad before the 1990s were either supported by scholarships or relatives overseas.

Home-country measures to restrict the ability of students to study overseas fell out of favour as developing countries' economic policies shifted in the 1980s and 1990s to expand international trade rather than to contract it. Although governments were much keener to expand exports than imports, international education was often seen as an important investment in building the human capital needed to engage in a global market. With the notable exception of Cuba and North Korea, we are not aware of any states that continue to deliberately restrict the ability of students to undertake degrees abroad.

Import replacement: increasing the local supply of education

The most common means of decreasing outbound student mobility is to improve access to tertiary education locally, especially in middle-income economies where outbound mobility is in large part driven by the inability of the domestic education system to meet rapidly increasing demand. When the massification of secondary education proceeds well in advance of the massification of the tertiary education system, large numbers of young people will miss out on a place at university, heightening competition for places. Cummings (1984) argues that one of the factors that led to the former British colonies in Asia – Singapore, Malaysia and Hong Kong – having such high rates of outbound mobility in the 1970s and 80s was that school systems tended to be relatively well developed in British colonies and participation rates in schools were then significantly expanded during the 1960s. However, university systems were much less developed in those countries, leaving many high-school graduates no further education pathway at home.

Greece, China, Malaysia and Singapore have all managed to reduce their dependence on overseas education providers by expanding supply locally. In some cases, the overall number of outbound students has declined, and in others the number has continued to grow, but at a slower rate than it would have. However, in none of these countries was the desire to reduce outflows the government's primary motivation for increasing supply of places. To understand why, we need to consider the politics of access to higher education. In essence, those who are dissatisfied with the lack of educational opportunities have two options, exit or voice, to use Hirschman's (1970) classic formulation. The affluent are able to exit by purchasing a place overseas if they miss out on a place at home. The less affluent, for whom study overseas is not affordable, are more likely to exert political pressure to expand higher education provision. As a result, governments face much more immediate pressure for expansion of educational capacity from those who miss out and are unable to study overseas. In contrast, the losses caused by international student emigration are less immediate and less noticeable. We will first consider the cases of Greece and China, which have both significantly expanded access to public higher education, but for different reasons. Electoral pressure in Greece led to both major parties promising to expand access, while in China the government embarked on rapid development of the higher education system as a key feature of a much broader economic development programme.

The difficulty of admission to university had become a major political issue in Greece in the 1990s because only one in six high-school graduates was able to secure a university place (Psacharopoulos, 2003). In response the government increased intakes into Greek universities and polytechnics, which reached 45 per cent by 1998. Nonetheless, the number of Greek students abroad was equivalent to 16.6 per cent of the number of students in Greek institutions (Outbound Mobility Ratio). With further domestic growth, by 2006 the tertiary Gross Enrolment Ratio had leapt to 93 per cent and the Outbound Mobility Ratio had dropped to 5.3 per cent. The total number of students from Greece studying abroad dropped steadily during this period, from a high of 66,934 in 1999 to a low point of 28,558 in 2008. The expansion of university places primarily served to respond to political demands for greater participation, but at the same reduced overall reliance on foreign education providers. The quality of Greek universities' facilities is low, however, and students have little choice of institution or programme.

China is also well aware of the importance of producing and retaining talent if it is to sustain its economic growth over the coming decades. China's higher education sector has expanded dramatically in recent years. Since in the late 1990s, China has invested heavily in higher education with the aim of producing sufficient skilled labour to feed into the country's rapidly developing economy. While in 1995, only 5 per cent of the tertiary-aged population had access to higher education, by 2007 the ratio increased to 23 per cent. In addition, there was the hope that greater domestic options would stem the flow of Chinese students abroad. It appears that this investment is having the desired effect with Chinese students citing the improvement of Chinese higher education as an important factor in their decision to stay home for advanced study (Ryan & Dodd, 2005).

Historically the number of undergraduate places available in Singapore's domestic higher education institutions has been significantly below the level of demand from school leavers. The cohort participation rate in publicly funded degree programmes has increased considerably over the past 30 years, from 5 per cent in in 1980 to 27 per cent in 2012, but still falls far short. A similar number of students undertake degree programmes overseas or transnational programmes in Singapore. Recent workforce survey data showed that 46 per cent of 25–29-year-olds held degrees, with around half of those being graduates of public universities and half being graduates of foreign degree programmes in Singapore or overseas (Committee on University Education Pathways Beyond 2015, 2012, p. 23). This high level of reliance on foreign provision of education has been a longstanding feature of Singaporean tertiary education. Table 3.1 shows student numbers in domestic and foreign education in 2005, the most recent year for which transnational degree programmes data is available.

Table 3.1 Students in Singaporean tertiary education institutions, 2005

	Number of students	Percentage
• Polytechnics	56,048	23
• Local universities (NUS, NTU, SIM)	41,628	17
• Private institutions' own programmes	26,500	11
• Institute of technical education	19,207	8
• National institute of education	2,282	1
All domestic providers	145,665	59
Transnational programmes	80,200	33
Singaporean students enrolled overseas	19,371	8
Total	245,236	100

Data sources: Lee (2005, p. 15); MoE (2006, table 15); UNESCO (2013).

The Singapore government plans to continue to increase the cohort participation rate in public universities, to 40 per cent by 2020, through an increase in the number of places and helped by a decline in the number of students of university age. The advisory committee that recommended the expansion noted that, 'As Singaporeans become more financially able, this small proportion of students that leave Singapore to pursue a degree overseas, and who may subsequently decide to stay on in their adopted countries, is expected to grow' (Committee on University Education Pathways Beyond 2015, 2012, p. 18). The continued expansion in publicly funded places is in part a means to mitigate the risks posed by such an increased outflow of young people.

While the government was keen to expand higher educational opportunities to meet the growing demand, it was also committed to establishing Singapore as a global education hub. The rationale behind Singapore's hub ambitions is to raise foreign revenues through students as well as attract industries keen to be located alongside higher education institutions. Since 1997 the government has been actively encouraging prestigious foreign universities to offer programmes and establish centres in the country. Its Global Schoolhouse initiative set out to attract 10 world-class foreign institutions within 10 years. Singapore quickly surpassed this goal and by 2007 there were 15 such institutions, from China, United States, France, India, Germany and the Netherlands. These elite foreign institutions primarily offer niche programmes to small numbers of Singaporean and foreign students. The presence of branch campuses of elite foreign universities in Singapore was highly publicized by the government and has been the subject of much commentary in the higher education press. One fascinating feature of the Global Schoolhouse initiative, and the commentary about it, is the lack of data on the number of students enrolled in the elite foreign schools brought to Singapore by the government, and the total absence of any mention of the large number of collaborative transnational programmes that have been operating in Singapore for decades (Garrett, 2005; Koh, 2012; Ng, 2013; Sidhu, Ho & Yeoh, 2011). In a similar vein, the Ministry of Education's webpage listing the institutions that comprise the country's post secondary education system neglects to mention any private institutions, transnational programmes, or the branch campuses of Curtin and James Cook universities (Ministry of Education, 2013).

In fact, Singapore's private tertiary education institutions are large, well established and highly internationalized. In 2012 they enrolled 227,000 students, 56 per cent of whom were domestic and 44 per cent international (CPE, 2013). Since the 1980s, transnational education has been Singapore's principal means of expanding the supply of degree programmes to privately funded students, thereby stemming the outflow of Singaporean students and establishing the island nation as a major destination for foreign study. In the mid-1980s, the government allowed transnational providers to partner with local institutions to meet growing demand locally, thus stemming outward student mobility. They provide an alternative to public polytechnics for those students who miss out on a university place, and the majority of their courses are in business and hospitality, disciplines that are not well served by the polytechnics. The private institutions also partner with overseas universities to provide collaborative degree programmes, in a wide range of models (Hoare, 2012).

Students have the option of taking a whole foreign degree programme in Singapore, articulation programmes that are delivered partly in Singapore and partly at the university's home campus, and top-up degree programmes designed for local diploma graduates. The largest private institution, the Singapore Institute of Management, enrols more students than the National University of Singapore. Its partnerships with the University of London (UK) and RMIT University (Australia) have each been continuing for over 25 years and each currently enrols over 8,000 students. Each of these universities teaches more students in Singapore than there are Singaporean students studying in all institutions in either the UK or Australia. Graduates of such programmes have good employment outcomes in Singapore but tend to be paid less than graduates of public universities which have tougher entry standards (Davie, 2012b).

Despite the invisibility of private higher education in most governmental pronouncements on the education system, over the past decade the government has embarked on extensive measures to raise the standard of private institutions. A pivotal report by the Ministry of Trade and Industry (MTI, 2002), entitled *Developing Singapore's Education Industry*, was focused on the recruitment of larger numbers of foreign students but also considered ways to use the private sector to provide additional opportunities for local students. The report observed that while Singapore had a vibrant private higher education sector, it was fragmented, and quality was uneven due to an absence of a robust quality assurance framework. It noted that:

> the private sector lacks a suitable quality assurance system that will provide a minimum service level, market transparency and quality control. This results in uneven quality among the professors, teachers and instructors employed in privately funded educational institutions, which ultimately affects Singapore's branding in education.
>
> (p. 10)

Meanwhile, many other countries had successfully built the capacity and quality of private institutions over time. In Malaysia, in particular, which had a very similar history of transnational collaboration between private colleges and foreign universities, the introduction of accreditation and quality assurance systems focused on capacity building had promoted the consolidation of the sector into a smaller number of university colleges and new private universities that were increasingly attractive to both domestic and international students. The strategy proposed by MTI was for Singapore to foster large high-quality private institutions schools enrolling significant numbers of international students, complemented by smaller niche schools. The MTI report led to the establishment of the Council for Private Education, which enforces a robust quality assurance framework for the private sector and undertakes a wide range of industry development activities (CPE, 2013). Recent press reports suggest that enrolments at private institutions are increasing as the quality and reputation of the sector improves (Davie, 2012a).

Despite the lack of longitudinal data covering both public and private sector enrolments, it is clear that improvements in educational quality and capacity in Singapore have reduced outbound student numbers. As stated earlier, the number of Singaporean students studying overseas has declined since the late 1990s and has been flat, at around 20,000, since 2004. Similarly, enrolments of Singaporean students in Australia show a decline in the past decade across all levels of study apart from doctoral programmes, with the largest reduction at the bachelor level, where there has been most growth in Singapore (see Table 3.2).

Universal portability of funding

Some countries, particularly in Northern Europe, provide students with grants and loans that are portable overseas. The Netherlands, for example, provides students with a progressive scholarship that varies according to the family's income and can be used to cover tuition fees and living expenses either in the Netherlands (where all institutions charge tuition fees) or abroad. If the student completes the degree within 10 years the loan becomes a grant and does not need to be repaid.

Table 3.2 Singapore students in onshore Australian higher education and vocational education and training

	2002	2003	2004	2005	2006	2007	2008	2009	2010	2011	% change 2002–11
Sub-degree	739	723	690	662	636	635	661	714	741	684	−7
Bachelor	9,120	8,886	8,009	7,227	6,761	6,376	6,397	6,716	6,926	6,913	−24
Postgraduate	1,139	1,127	1,003	881	829	812	788	960	951	913	−20
Doctorate	146	150	172	184	215	226	244	261	285	307	110
Total	11,144	10,886	9,874	8,954	8,441	8,049	8,090	8,651	8,903	8,817	−21

Data source: AEI (2013).

Unlike competitive scholarship programmes these schemes are usually open to any student that qualifies for a university place.

One of the most interesting features of Norway's international engagement in higher education is its long-standing system of funding for overseas study, which has been in place for over five decades for students who undertake qualifications abroad and more recently has been extended to exchange students. For our purposes, Norway is an interesting case study of some of the consequences of government-funded global study options, and what policy levers are available to government to steer student flows in a global market when students' decisions don't reflect the government's strategic objectives.

Norwegian higher education students have a long history of travelling abroad for study. Before the first university was opened in 1811, scholars would normally travel to Copenhagen and due to the limited number of study options available locally the number of outbound students grew over time, peaking in the post-World War II period, at which time around 30 per cent of Norwegian university students were studying outside the country (Wiers-Jenssen, 2008a). Norwegian higher education policy has promoted a high rate of outward mobility, and has achieved this through very favourable funding mechanisms. Students receive a combination of government grants and subsidized loans through schemes operated under the Norwegian State Education Loan Fund, established in 1947. Norway now provides grants and subsidized loans that allow around 6.5–10 per cent of the student body to study overseas, which is higher than comparable nations with high GDP per capita (Wiers-Jenssen, 2008a). Students are allowed to study anywhere in the world as long as the institution is deemed by the funding body to be appropriately accredited and of suitable quality.

The most explicit policy rationales for encouraging outgoing student mobility are educational and cultural – to allow students to access a wide range of high-quality programmes and to enrich Norway's social and cultural engagement. Norway is wealthy country with a small but geographically dispersed population of five million inhabitants, and with a history of close engagement with Scandinavian and northern European countries. So study in neighbouring countries presented few linguistic, cultural or financial difficulties for students. Wiers-Jenssen (2008a) points out that there are sound economic reasons for supporting student outflows, since the provision of education in Norway is often more expensive for the government than education abroad, especially in niche programmes. One of the effects of this policy is that Norway has a higher rate of outbound mobility than most comparable countries, which is to be expected. The system of universal public support for international education broadens access considerably, but Wiers-Jenssen (2012) has found that mobile Norwegian students are still more likely to have university-educated parents, and parents who have lived abroad, than non-mobile students.

After the introduction of full fees for international students in the UK and Australia in the mid-1980s, those countries developed sophisticated marketing and student recruitment processes, as described earlier in Chapter 2. Norway proved an easy market for universities from these countries, because of the generous funding scheme, high level of English language proficiency, and quality secondary education system. By 2002, Australia had become the leading destination for Norwegian students, followed by the UK, and between them the two countries enrolled half of all outbound students (Norwegian Ministry of Education and Research, 2005, p. 49). Australia and the UK had implemented streamlined application and immigration processes for students during this period, whereas applying to a United States university remained much more difficult, for example often requiring students from across the country to travel to Oslo twice, once to sit a Scholastic Assessment Test (SAT) and again to apply for a visa. The resulting concentration of students in two export-oriented Anglophone countries is described by Wiers-Jenssen (2003) as 'an unintended result of a generous support system, and not in accordance with the government's goals. It is frequently stated as a policy objective that students should spread out in a wide range of countries' (p. 398).

Around this time a series of high-profile newspaper articles, particularly in *Aftenposten*, the country's largest-selling newspaper, suggested that many Norwegian students went to Australia for recreational purposes, at the taxpayer's expense, rather than for serious academic pursuits. In March 2005, *Dagbladet*, one of the country's leading tabloid newspapers, ran an eight-page feature article in its youth-oriented magazine, entitled 'The Australian Dream'. The article begins, 'Employers are wondering what on earth the 4000 Norwegian students in Australia are doing.' Underneath, a large photograph depicts two Norwegian students lying on a beach on Australia's Gold Coast. Terje Strømstad from Skien, holding a cigarette, asks bikini-clad Alana Ringnes from Oslo, 'can you smear my back?' (Opsahl, 2005). Through such depictions, which impugned both student motivation and academic merit, the reputation of Australia as a serious study destination was seriously damaged. The flow of Norwegian students to Australian universities plummeted from around 1,800 commencing students in 2002 to less than 700 in 2006 (AEI, 2007).

But it was not only media attention that diverted the flow of students away from Australia. The flow of students clearly was not reflecting the nation's perceived strategic interests, and it would be understandable that the government might be concerned that their young people's study choices in a global education market might not reflect broader national interests. In 2002, the number of Norwegian students studying in Australia was seven times the number studying in Germany, and ten times the number in France, both key political and economic influences on Norway. An Australian government industry briefing note from the time complains that:

> The Norwegian Government has claimed that it is not looking to promote or discourage study in specific countries, but there has been subtle encouragement for students to study in non-English speaking countries (Poland, Czech Republic, China), countries with strong trade and business ties with Norway (China, Canada and South Africa) and within Europe.
>
> (AEI, 2007)

Wiers-Jenssen (2008b) also observes that Norwegian students were encouraged, both financially and rhetorically, by the government to study in countries other than English-speaking ones. Government policy began to shift away from promoting overseas degree study to instead encourage students to study in Norway and to undertake international exchange. The government achieved this through three prongs – changes in funding to students, changes in funding to institutions, and internationalization of the curriculum.

The Norwegian State Education Loan Fund changed the funding formula for students, increasing the loan proportion and decreasing the grant proportion. This made study overseas in countries that charge tuition fees considerably more costly than studying in Norway, where most students are enrolled in public institutions that charge no tuition fees. For students who undertook degrees abroad, the change led students to consider study options that are less costly (so that less debt burden is accumulated) and that are more beneficial in the labour market (as the loan has to be repaid). Because Anglophone countries generally charge tuition fees, the greatest reductions in student numbers were felt in the two leading destinations, Australia and the UK, with less effect on non-English speaking destinations.

A second factor that reduced student outflow overall was a change to the way Norwegian universities were funded, placing greater emphasis on the number of graduating students. This provided institutions with an incentive to increase enrolments. The government encouraged Norwegian institutions to develop masters programmes in English to attract international students and to provide Norwegian students with internationalized programmes at home. The government also determined that each student in a Norwegian institution is entitled to undertake a period of study abroad, and provided generous financial support to promote both incoming and outgoing exchange (Norwegian Ministry of Education and Research, 2005). This has a strategic rationale for Norway, since institutional exchange programmes allow for much more targeted mobility, usually within Europe and facilitated by the Erasmus student exchange programme. Even though Norway is not an EU member, it participates in the Bologna Process and Erasmus and many other regional initiatives, and shifting the form of mobility from degrees to semesters allowed the government to redirect student mobility toward the EU and away from the UK and Australia.

The Norwegian State Education Loan Fund collects and analyses detailed data on the students it supports, estimated to include some 95 per cent of mobile Norwegian students. Research and analysis on various aspects of education policy and practice – including international mobility and engagement – is carried out by the Norwegian Institute for Studies in Innovation, Research and Education (NIFU STEP), funded through commissioned project work and with core funding from the Research Council of Norway. In one such project, Wiers-Jenssen (2008a) analyses data from surveys of former students between 3.5 and 5 years after graduation. The students are divided into three groups, those who did all of their studies in Norway, those who obtained Norwegian qualifications but did some study abroad, and those with foreign qualifications. Internationally mobile students found it more difficult to enter the labour market initially, but had higher wages than non-mobile students. Students who had studied abroad were, perhaps unsurprisingly, more likely to work in roles requiring international skills, English language proficiency and international travel, and more had worked outside Norway, although the vast majority returned to Norway within a few years of graduation. Therefore, unlike many other countries with large outbound student numbers, brain drain is not an issue for Norway, especially since some returnees bring partners back to Norway with them. Such detailed comparative data on outcomes for internationally mobile and non-mobile students is rare, and Wiers-Jenssen's (2008a, 2012) research shows the practical value of such research in evaluating the implications of policies supporting international mobility.

Norway's experience has shown that it can be cost-effective for governments in high-income countries to provide portable funding for students, since the cost of education abroad is often comparable or lower than in Norway. For a long period, the government of Norway has effectively outsourced higher education for a significant section of its population (between 6 and 30 per cent over the past half-century) to suitable institutions abroad. As the shapes of student flows have changed over time it has been able to adjust the funding formula to steer students towards countries in which the host government subsidizes the education of Norwegian students.

Competitive portable funding

Many governments operate significant scholarship programmes that support high-performing students to undertake a degree abroad, including Malaysia, Vietnam, China and Chile to name a few. In most of these programmes, students with exemplary undergraduate degrees are sponsored to do advanced study abroad, such as professional masters and doctoral studies in fields that are national priorities, and often with a bias toward the natural sciences (OECD & World Bank, 2010, pp. 46–52). Masters degrees are often funded by a particular government department as a way of recruiting the brightest graduates and bringing international experience into middle management. Doctoral studies are often funded by the Ministry of Education as a way of developing the country's academic labour force to support the expansion of universities.

Like the portable funding model discussed above, these schemes allow the state to purchase or subsidize foreign education on behalf of its citizens. But there are some key differences. First, scholarships are usually scarce and highly competitive. Second, recipients are nearly always required to return to the home country after completion of their studies, and usually required to work for a period of several years with a particular organization. Students who fail to meet these conditions are usually required to repay the funding they have received, along with a penalty fee in some cases. Third, scholarship funding bodies are much more selective about the institutions at which students study.

Perhaps the largest scholarship scheme in the world today is Saudi Arabia's King Abdullah Foreign Scholarship Program, which reportedly spends USD 2.4 billion per year to send 125,000 highly qualified students overseas (Bashraheel, 2013). Begun in 2005, the programme aims to meet the country's human resource development needs by helping young people to acquire the skills required to enable Saudi citizens to occupy some of the specialist jobs currently occupied by expatriates (Saudization). It also aims to provide a significant pool of bright young people with international experience, in order to develop social, cultural and economic linkages that will allow the country to move beyond its reliance on oil. The Ministry of Education has added and removed countries from the programme from time to time and screens institutions at which students are able to study, directs students interested in particular niche fields of study to targeted institutions and avoids too high a concentration of students at individual institutions. As a result of the programme, the number of Saudi students abroad grew six-fold in a period of just four years, from 14,523 in 2006 to 88,435 in 2010, with the largest destinations being USA, the UK, Canada, Australia, Egypt, South Africa and Malaysia, according to Saudi Ministry of Education figures (Denman & Hilal, 2011). Now nearly 90 per cent of Saudi students abroad are funded by the programme rather than by private sources, which has broadened access considerably, including to female students, who have increased from 31 per cent of outgoing students in 2004 to 42 per cent in 2012 (PIE, 2013; UNESCO, 2013). The scale of Saudi Arabia's scholarship programme is exceptional, and very few countries are able to publicly fund such large-scale scholarship programmes. Middle-income countries generally have much more limited scholarship programmes targeted to the most high-achieving students in fields of study identified as being of critical importance for national development.

Scholarships are expensive though, and it is notable that two of the largest schemes are supported by huge natural resource windfalls – oil in the case of Saudi Arabia and copper in the case of Chile. One way that middle-income countries without such vast foreign currency reserves can support outbound mobility for a larger number of students is through a subsidized loan scheme, and these have been introduced in quite a few countries over the past decade, particularly in Latin America. Unlike the Scandinavian schemes these are selective and operate on a smaller scale, usually for masters and doctoral studies, but like the Scandinavian schemes they steer student behaviour by varying the extent to which the funding is a grant or a loan. These are creative forms of financing that share the cost burden between students and funding bodies, which may involve a combination of government agencies, business groups and philanthropic organizations. A key feature of all of these programmes is selectivity, to ensure that scarce financial resources are directed to what the funding body considers the best students studying in the best institutions. This both ensures that the funding bodies' policy objectives are met, where grants are involved, and that the funding will be able to be repaid, where it takes the form of a loan.

For example, funding provided by Colombia's COLFUTURO programme, which we will discuss in more detail in the next chapter, must be paid back in full if the student does not return to Colombia, but if they return and stay in Colombia their loan amount will be reduced by half, and there is a further reduction for students who return to positions in the public sector or educational institutions where salaries are often lower than in the private sector. Mexico's Foundation for Education, Science and Technology (FUNED) scholarship scheme is supported by the charity Monte de Piedad (which has been providing low-interest loans to the poor since the 1770s) and the National Council of Science and Technology. It supports graduate students (numbering nearly 400 in 2012) to study in the top 200 universities or 100 programmes in a particular field according to international rankings. It has agreements in place with 50 universities that grant tuition fee discounts and provide additional services to FUNED scholars.

Implicit in all these schemes is an expectation that the international mobility of these students generates broader public benefits as well as benefiting the individuals involved. Public funding of international education is justified on the basis of these 'external' benefits, which have been well understood in relation to national systems (Weisbrod, 1962). The OECD and World Bank (2010) see schemes such as the Becas Chile Programme as highly effective use of public funds that allow 'drawing on resources of other countries to fill gaps in local capacity for human capital formation' (p. 11). In such programmes the state effectively becomes the purchaser of international education on behalf of selected students, seeking to align decisions about student characteristics, fields and levels of study and host universities with national human resource development priorities. The resulting patterns of mobility are very different from those of self-funded students, who still represent the vast bulk of mobile degree students from most countries with scholarship programmes. These organizations also see scholarship schemes as 'injecting a demand-side stimulus to reform of an insular system of higher education supply' (p. 11). By this they mean that domestic institutions must compete with foreign institutions to attract the best students, which they hope will lead to those institutions being much more responsive to student demand and interested in international standards. The return of graduates with advanced qualifications from abroad, they believe, will have the effect of 'stimulating productivity improvement by further opening up Chilean thinking to international best practices, internationalizing the Chilean workforce and connecting the next generation of Chilean leaders to international networks' (p. 11). For these reasons the OECD and World Bank have been keen to highlight the achievements of international scholarship programmes such as Chile's.

GATS and portable subsidies

For those interested in the international portability of domestic education subsidies, the interpretation of countries' GATS commitments offers intriguing possibilities.

One of the high points in the movement towards liberalization of international trade in services was the World Trade Organization's General Agreement on Trade in Services (GATS), which came into effect in 1995 (WTO, 1995). In the language of international trade agreements, student degree mobility is referred to as 'consumption abroad', a mode of delivering services in which the consumer (in our case the student) travels to the country of the service (education) provider for the transaction to take place. Perhaps the most well-known service delivered in this way is tourism, and there also is growth in consumption abroad of medical services.

Liberals advocate that governments allow their students to study overseas freely, imposing no unnecessary restrictions on their access to overseas study (the 'market access' principle) (WTO, 2001, p. 24). Such measures might include limiting students able to leave the country to study overseas, restricting the type or nationality of institutions in which they are allowed to study or blocking an overseas institution's website so that students cannot access information about its programmes. Currently, 40 WTO member states have committed to impose no market access restrictions on higher education consumed by their students abroad (Table 3.3), including many of the largest sources such as China, the European Union,

Table 3.3 GATS commitments for consumption abroad

Members	Limitation on market access for consumption abroad of higher education	Limitations on national treatment for consumption abroad of higher education	Notes
Albania	None	None	
Armenia	None	None	
Australia	None	None	Private tertiary only
Cambodia	None	Subsidies excluded	
Cape Verde	None	Subsidies excluded	
China	None	None	
Congo RP	None	None	
Croatia	None	Subsidies excluded	
Czech Republic	None	Subsidies excluded	
Estonia	None	Subsidies excluded	
European Union	None	None	
FYR Macedonia	None	None	
Georgia	None	Subsidies excluded	
Hungary	None	None	
Jamaica	None	None	
Jordan	None	Subsidies excluded	
Kyrgyz Republic	None	None	
Latvia	None	None	
Lesotho	None	None	
Liechtenstein	None	None	

(Continued)

Table 3.3 (Continued)

Members	Limitation on market access for consumption abroad of higher education	Limitations on national treatment for consumption abroad of higher education	Notes
Lithuania	None	None	
Mexico	None	None	
Moldova	None	None	
Nepal	None	None	Convertible currency limit of US$2,000 may be applied to Nepalese citizens
New Zealand	None	None	In private institutions
Norway	None	Subsidies excluded	
Oman	None	None	
Panama	None	None	
Poland	None	Subsidies excluded	
Russian Federation	None	Subsidies excluded	
Saudi Arabia	None	None	
Slovak Republic	None	None	
Slovenia	None	Subsidies excluded	
Switzerland	None	None	
Chinese Taipei	None	None	
Tonga	None	Subsidies excluded	
Turkey	None	None	
Ukraine	None	Subsidies excluded	
Vanuatu	None	None	
Vietnam	None	None	

Data source: WTO (2013).

Mexico, Russia, Taiwan and Vietnam and significant exporters such as Australia, New Zealand and Switzerland. The majority of WTO member states, however, did not make such commitments but are in practice imposing no such restrictions. The list of countries that are still not inclined to make a binding commitment to free outward mobility of their students includes some of the world's most important importers and exporters of higher education, including India, Canada, South Korea, the United States, Malaysia, Singapore or Japan (WTO, 2013).

As well as 'market access', another key aspiration of the trade liberalization movement is 'national treatment', meaning that foreign goods, services and suppliers are treated no less favourably than 'like' (same or comparable) national goods, services and suppliers. The formal treatment can be identical or different, as long as the effect is to uphold the principle of 'equality of competitive opportunity'. Any measure imposed by a government that treats overseas education providers less favourably than equivalent domestic providers would be interpreted as a breach of the national treatment principle. This might include providing funding or loans for a student to attend a local institution but not one based overseas, or applying more restrictive processes for recognition of qualifications to overseas degrees.

While restrictions on 'market access' are now quite rare – students wanting to study overseas are generally not much bothered by their governments – preferential treatment of domestic institutions is so common as to be the norm. Nearly every government has discriminatory measures in place that treat domestic providers much more favourably than overseas institutions, particularly in financing and recognition of qualifications. In the liberal world view, the purpose of the public subsidy is to fund the education of a citizen, and as long as the provider meets the required quality the government should not care whether the provider is publicly or privately owned, domestic or foreign, not-for-profit or for-profit.

In most countries, students' tuition fees are wholly or partially subsidized by government and these subsidies are rarely portable. Usually, when a student moves outside of the jurisdiction that is funded to educate them, the financing of that student's education ceases to be the home government's responsibility. In most countries funding is national, but in others such as the USA, states subsidize students from that state studying in public institutions within the state. In many countries the education of citizens, including higher education, is considered a key function of the state, and government is not simply a purchaser of education for its citizens, but also the key provider. In others, higher education is provided both in public and private institutions, with government being a significant funder of public providers but not responsible for private providers to the same extent. Government funding can flow either to the educational institution (a producers' subsidy) or to students as subsidized loans or grants (a consumers' subsidy). In either case, it is clear that when these are available only to domestic institutions in an environment where domestic and international providers are in competition then they are trade distorting (Poretti, 2009, pp. 86–87). As far as GATS is concerned, there is a huge gap between the free trade ideal of national treatment and the contemporary reality of heavy state involvement in provision of education.

The treatment of subsidies in the GATS legal framework is complicated. An OECD guide explains that

> in sectors where a WTO Member has made market access commitments under the GATS, it can maintain the ability to subsidize national service suppliers on a discriminatory basis by listing such limitations on national treatment in its schedule of commitments.
>
> (OECD, 2002, p. 71)

As Table 3.3 shows, around two-thirds of the WTO members that have made commitments on consumption abroad of higher education have not listed any limitations on national treatment while a third have explicitly excluded subsidies. However, these commitments do not reflect the reality of governments' policies. Norway, for example, does allow subsidies to be portable internationally in practice but has not bound itself to that policy in the agreement (Mathisen, 2006). And none of the WTO members that have committed to full national treatment provides the same funding to institutions abroad as they do at home.

This apparent misrepresentation of policies in the GATS stems from the ambiguity surrounding subsidies in the agreement (Poretti, 2009). For example, A 1993 explanatory note produced by the WTO secretariat, *Scheduling of Initial Commitments in Trade in Services*, which was revised in 2001, suggests that national treatment does not apply to consumption abroad:

> There is no obligation in the GATS which requires a Member to take measures outside its territorial jurisdiction. It therefore follows that the national treatment obligation in Article XVII does not require a Member to extend such treatment to a service supplier located in the territory of another Member [...] a binding under Article XVII with respect to the granting of a subsidy does not require a Member to offer such a subsidy to a services supplier located in the territory of another Member.
>
> (WTO, 2001, p. 6)

The difficulty here is that the GATS agreement in other places implies that national treatment applies to overseas providers, and in their schedules of commitments member states are required to state whether or not they extend national treatment to such providers. The meaning of these commitments remains unclear and since 1995 limited progress has been made in the WTO towards clarifying either the meaning of national treatment undertakings in relation to consumption abroad or to the treatment of subsidies provided either to producers or to consumers (Poretti, 2009).

Despite the ineffectiveness of the GATS in relation to this question, as we have noted above, more countries are experimenting with ways of expanding access to international education by creating portable funding mechanisms. Such approaches are also popular with international education professional associations, as reflected in the *International Student Mobility Charter* developed in 2012 by the European Association for International Education, with input and subsequent endorsement by the Erasmus Student Network (EU), National Union of Students (UK), Association of International Education Administrators (USA) and International Education Association of Australia. The Charter, which aims to articulate and advocate for international students' rights, includes the principle that, 'National student loans and grants should always be portable' (EAIE, 2012). The associations' focus on advocating for policies that benefit the internationally mobile student parallels liberal concern with advocating for policies that benefit the consumer.

For advocates of public education the notion that funding should be portable to non-government institutions (foreign or domestic) represents an unwelcome erosion of an already dwindling and inadequate public pie. During the WTO's Millennium round of talks, in which deepening liberalization of trade in services was supposed to be a major focus, public opposition from university associations, education unions and students groups made governments very timid about pushing for greater coverage of higher education in the GATS (e.g. AUCC, ACE, EUA & CHEA, 2001; Education International & Public Services International, 2000). The GATS provided a tangible target for groups opposed to commercialization of education on a both national and international scale (Mundy & Ika, 2003). It was widely interpreted as a key plank in a neoliberal campaign to privatize education, which involved shifting costs from the state to students and their families and shifting provision from the public sector to private institutions. Critiques of the GATS were primarily motivated by a desire to maintain public funding of students and institutions, and national public institutions in particular. Much has been written about the relative merits of public and private funding and provision in different countries, most notably by Daniel C. Levy and others involved with the Programme for Research on Private Higher Education at the University at Albany, State University of New York (Kinser et al., 2010). It is not our intention to cover that ground, but we should note that one consequence of the preoccupation with domestic public education on the part of governments, education institutions and education unions is that those students who study locally generally receive far higher levels of public support than those who travel abroad to undertake degrees. This limits access to international study for the large majority of students whose families are not affluent enough to able to fund the full cost of their education. And as we have seen above, the desire to broaden access to overseas study opportunities on equity grounds is now one of the key drivers for extending public support beyond the boundaries of the nation state.

Looking after the interests of student citizens abroad

While governments are able to exercise a significant degree of control over students they fund, the majority of international students are privately funded and therefore much less constrained. Many countries, it would seem, absolve themselves of any responsibility in relation to their citizens' foreign educational choices or outcomes, and provide only the consular support that all expatriates receive in times of trouble.

There are, however, notable exceptions. In this section we examine: the role of the Chinese government in protecting the consumer interests of its students abroad; the activities of India in relation to student safety and security; and attempts by China and Malaysia to influence students to represent home government political interests.

Scrutinizing the recruiters

In many countries, student recruitment agents – locally based private businesses – play a key role in marketing foreign universities and colleges, providing advice to students and their families and assisting with the often complex processes of applying for a place and a visa. In some cases they are paid a commission by the overseas education provider, typically around 10–15 per cent of the first year's tuition fees. This is the norm for study in the UK, Australia and New Zealand, and increasingly for institutions from a wider range of countries. Students who are applying to institutions that do not pay agents a commission, including most universities in the USA and elite universities the world over, often pay the agent directly. Like agents for other services, such as financial products or travel, education agents that are paid on commission have an incentive to steer their clients to service providers that are easily accessible and which pay a generous commission. However, the agent's preferred choice of providers may not be in the best interests of the student. Top universities are difficult to gain entry to and pay no commissions, while universities and colleges without a strong reputation are much less selective and need to pay higher commissions to interest agents. Agents can play a valuable role in assisting students and their families to make a choice of institution and programme. However, consumers have very little information about the extent of the commissions and other perks agents earn for steering the student towards a particular provider. There has been considerable interest in recent years in how governments and institutions in destination countries regulate agents, as discussed in Chapter 2, and here we consider how the government of the students' country is able to regulate this potentially fraught sector.

One of the first countries to regulate recruitment agents for outgoing students was China, which introduced in 1999 the Regulations on Agency Service for Self-Supported Overseas Students. This stipulated that agents must be registered with the Ministry of Education, that they must have a contract in place with universities they represent and must have written agreements with students outlining roles and responsibilities of each party, and that fees charged must be reasonable (Wang, 2003). This measure can allow authorities to sanction or deregister recruitment agents that have been found to be acting illegally. In some countries with well-functioning consumer protection laws, registration of agents may not be required as there are adequate avenues for authorities and consumers to take action against unscrupulous agents. In some countries, such as India, there is neither, and students are routinely lured into poor-quality or unaccredited institutions. The Australian government asked India to more closely regulate agents after a series of large-scale scams were discovered in 2009. Two years later over 1,000 Indian students were found to have enrolled in a fake university in the United States, leading the Ministry of Overseas Indian Affairs to promise to table legislation to regulate agents (Mishra, 2011). Three years later no such regulatory framework has been developed.

Like China, Vietnam also regulates recruitment agents, and in addition to registration, agents are required to deposit US$24,000 into a dedicated account that can be used to repay students in the case of an institution collapsing. The Vietnamese regulations require the head of an agency to hold a bachelor degree, be fluent in a foreign language and to have been awarded an overseas counselling certificate issued by the Ministry of Education and Training (Austrade, 2013).

Steering students in the right direction

While recruitment agents are clearly very influential in informing students' study decisions, governments are also becoming increasingly active in providing advice to outgoing students. Agencies that fund scholarships and loan schemes usually provide some level of advice and support for students, consistent with their role in steering students towards those institutions and programmes that are deemed to be in line with the priorities of the funding scheme. For independent students, it is another matter. Many countries' ministries of education provide no information on overseas study, even many countries with significant outflows such as India and Singapore.

Another major factor affecting consumption abroad is the recognition of foreign academic and professional qualifications in their home country. Globally, there has been a gradual trend towards greater cross-border recognition, led by certain regions (particularly Europe) and professions (e.g. engineering). Many governments are committed to the progressive international harmonization of national tertiary qualification frameworks, degree structures and duration of levels of education, and this is a major factor contributing to the growth of student and professional mobility. However, in some countries, pressure from professional associations dominated by graduates of domestic institutions and the domestic institutions themselves, is influential in limiting recognition of the academic qualifications of foreign-trained graduates in favour of those locally trained. Some governments selectively restrict the number of foreign institutions they recognize in particular disciplines in order to restrict the number of graduates entering the local labour market.

The Chinese government is one of very few that proactively advises self-funded overseas students, through the operations of the Ministry of Education and Foreign Regulatory Information Network (which goes by the acronym JSJ). The JSJ maintains a comprehensive website (www.jsj.edu.cn) as a resource for students and their families and publishes study warnings for students as urgent matters arise in order to prevent or assist in resolving unexpected problems abroad. Since 2003 it has published a list of reputable higher education institutions which now extends to 43 countries. It also points students to the relevant host country websites listing registered institutions (JSJ, 2013). The listings of institutions can be contentious when the JSJ's assessment does not reflect those of the host government country. The New Zealand government used bilateral free trade agreement negotiations with China to raise such concerns and managed to have the list changed. One of the achievements of the NZ–China FTA, according to the New Zealand Ministry of Foreign Affairs and Trade is that, 'China has made a binding commitment to include on the China Ministry of Education Study Abroad Website' all public universities and polytechnics as well as 'six degree conferring private training establishments duly approved and accredited by the New Zealand Qualifications Authority' (MFAT, 2010).

The JSJ's Overseas Study Warnings advise students on problems (such as college closures) and developments (including changes in regulations) in host countries, and – most importantly – advising which providers and indeed in some instances *countries* that Chinese students should avoid. The alerts are published on the MoE website and the JSJ website, and are widely reported in the Chinese media – especially in the more colourful cases of college collapses. In this context, it is notable that both delinquent recruitment agents and delinquent institutions are 'named and shamed' in the Overseas Study Warnings. For example, when in late 2006 an alert was published concerning the failure of a private Canadian institute to provide adequate services, three Chinese recruitment agencies were also cited for signing up Chinese students for the operation. The JSJ's Warnings are very often focused on private providers, warning Chinese students to be wary of colleges that are at higher risk of falling into financial difficulties or failing quality assurance audits.

Mindful that the intention of some of its citizens is to work in and migrate to the country of study, the JSJ also monitors and publicizes developments in migration regulations as they affect student visas and migration applicants. For example, when Australia reduced the list of occupations that would allow international students to apply for permanent residency, the Ministry of Education issued an Overseas Study Warning that many young hopefuls should reconsider their plans, and should not be misled by the blandishments of misguided or unscrupulous agents (JSJ, 2010):

> [A]ccording to the relevant policies to be implemented in Australia, a considerable fraction of the people who originally sought to seek jobs in or immigrate to Australia through the pathway of studying in Australia will be disappointed. To avoid disappointment, it is advised that students should not blindly seek migration by means of studying abroad, neither should they give credit to the misguided and false publicity made by several education agents and media, which proclaimed that 'there is still an opportunity to take advantage of studying abroad to immigrate to Australia'.

The passage above is a translation of the JSJ Overseas Study Warning provided by Australian Education International to the sector as part of its regular industry updates. Because such alerts can have very serious consequences for the reputation of a country's education sector, the embassies of the major exporting countries monitor them closely, along with Chinese media coverage on international education.

A vivid illustration of the power of the JSJ to influence student flows is the experience of New Zealand in the early 2000s, which saw a spectacular and destabilizing rise and fall in the number of Chinese students studying in the country. After several years of rapid growth in Chinese student numbers, in all types of providers, in 2003, a series of incidents involving Chinese students at some private English language colleges in New Zealand led the JSJ and official news agencies to advise students not to study in New Zealand (Li, 2008). Many of these students were enrolled in secondary schools or English language colleges and living with host families, with little life experience and little supervision or guidance (McFedries, 2001). Between 2001 and 2003 there was a spate of assaults, deaths and criminal activities involving such students which led first to commentary in the NZ media, with headlines such as 'Risk for Asian students revealed in study' (*New Zealand Herald*, 18 February 2002) and 'Asian students need sex ed' (*TVNZ One News*, 3 April 2002). The plight of these students was then taken up by the JSJ and the Chinese media, who according to Li (2008) represented New Zealand as a crime-ridden country that was unsafe for foreign students. The *People's Daily* reported in 2003 that, 'In the recent two years, there is an upward tendency in the immoral behaviours and the vicious cases incurred by Chinese international students in Australia and New Zealand' (p. 16). Li refers to concerns by Chinese leaders that for some international students New Zealand was a 'school for crime' with some out-of-control students becoming 'hooked on crime' (p. 7).

Drawing on Chinese and New Zealand media reports, Li found that the majority of the crimes suffered by Chinese students in New Zealand were perpetrated by other Chinese nationals, who were either fellow international students or who had gained residency. These included instances of kidnappings of wealthy students by others in the community, who then sought ransom from wealthy parents back in China, and robberies of students who were carrying a lot of cash due to the difficulties of remotely withdrawing money from China, and assaults, robberies and protection rackets. NZ police reported heavy involvement by Chinese in drug smuggling and drug trafficking: in one year, 98 per cent of captured methamphetamine ingredients had come from China, with 80 per cent of those arrested in connection with the drugs being Chinese students on short-stay visas. In a report on the sex industry the NZ Ministry of Justice estimated that up to 60 per cent of sex workers were foreigners, with most of those Chinese students (Li, 2008). Even though the incidents were concentrated on students enrolled in a small number of private colleges, which are not representative of the education system overall, the episode caused major damage to the reputation of New Zealand in China, and the flow of Chinese students to New Zealand virtually ceased. This case clearly points to regulatory failures relating to accreditation and quality assurance of institutions and the protection of student welfare, in addition to broader issues of law enforcement. These are issues for the New Zealand government that are well out of the control of the Chinese Ministry of Education, but what this case shows is that the JSJ is able to reward or punish education exporting countries very effectively through its advice to students.

Very few governments have units like China's JSJ, but there are other ways in which some governments provide information to outgoing students. The Norwegian government funds a student-run not-for-profit organization, the Association of Norwegian Students Abroad, to perform this function. Established in 1956 and staffed by former international students, it provides extensive information and advice to prospective outbound students (both exchange and full degree), provides support networks for mobile students, and liaises closely with government agencies to represent mobile students' interests. The Association is run at arm's length from government, unlike the JSJ, and is much more reliant on students' experiences being shared through formal and informal mechanisms, including a very comprehensive website, such as school visits, online forums and in-country networks. One other means of providing information to prospective students is through consular posts. Occasionally, but surprisingly rarely, some countries' foreign embassies provide information for their nationals intending to study in that country, such as the 'Studying in Australia' section of the website of the High Commission of India in Australia.

Safety and security abroad

All governments continue to take some degree of responsibility for the welfare of their citizens abroad, and provide consular assistance of various kinds to those requiring assistance, including students. In addition, large consular posts sometimes include an official responsible for education, whose title is often education consul or counsellor. In addition to managing intergovernmental and institutional relationships, these officials usually oversee the administration and well-being of their nationals studying in that country. Where there are large numbers of students from a particular country studying in one location it is common for them to establish a club or society through which to meet one another and organize social events. An education counsellor's relationship with such associations often constitutes an important point of contact between a home government and individual overseas students. Most of the time, the education counsellors and other consular staff have very little involvement in the lives of students. It is notable that in a large study of international student welfare in Australia based on interviews with 200 students (Marginson, Nyland, Sawir & Forbes-Mewett, 2010), the only time home country governments are mentioned is in relation to their advocacy role during large-scale crises. Consular posts, it would appear, are rarely called upon to assist with students' routine challenges dealing with education and accommodation providers, immigration departments and banks, but they do become involved when students are victims or perpetrators of crime, and in cases of serious injury or death.

The most extreme measure a government can take is to evacuate its students. In both 2012 and 2013 during political uprisings in Egypt the Malaysian government organized flights to assist students studying there to return home. (After the second time Prime Minister Najib suggested that it might be easier for everyone if Al-Azhar University in Cairo were to build a campus in Malaysia instead.) As Marginson et al. (2010) note, home country governments often exert pressure on host government agencies when their students are seen to be at risk. The Chinese and Indian embassies in Australia have been vociferous in demanding government action in response to assaults on students.

Like the Chinese government's role in New Zealand six years earlier, the Indian government's role was fast and furious. A key difference however, was that in China official media echoed concerns expressed by government, whereas in India the press and 24-hour news channels were swept up in unrelenting coverage of assaults on Indian students in Melbourne. The Indian and Australian governments sprang into action to be seen to be doing all they could to respond. Australia's High Commissioner to India was summoned to a meeting with Overseas Indian Affairs Minister Vayalar Ravi, who urged Australia to ensure the events were not repeated. India's High Commissioner to Australia travelled to Melbourne to convey her government's concern to Victorian police, government and educational representatives. The Prime Ministers and the Foreign Ministers of the two countries discussed the issue with their counterparts, all expressing their abhorrence at the attacks. Indian film star Amitabh Bachchan announced he would turn down an honorary doctorate from the Queensland University of Technology that he had previously agreed to accept (*The Times of India*, 2009). Bollywood's largest union, the Federation of Western India Cine Employees, called on its members to stop filming in Australia, its leader proclaiming: 'We prefer to call it a non-cooperation movement because we feel what is happening in Australia is painful and shameful. The Australian government is just not taking adequate steps to find the culprits' (Uddin, 2009). This came after a string of big-budget Bollywood films had been filmed and set in Australia in recent years.

What is perhaps most notable in this episode was the key role of non-government actors, particularly international students themselves and the media in the home country, who could connect instantly with one another. Indian students were interviewed over the phone and via Skype from Australia, and Indian media coverage was available to students online in Australia and the nature of the Indian coverage itself became a newsworthy topic for the Australian media. Both sending and host governments were criticized for being slow to react, and in both countries opposition parties were able to gain political mileage by lambasting governments for dealing poorly with the situation. In the midst of the high drama of media coverage, the Indian High Commission issued a travel advisory, which illustrates the very similar understanding of the situation held by both governments. It is worth quoting at length here, since the statement provides a very clear illustration of the role of a foreign government in relation to host government agencies and students:

> The Ministry of External Affairs cautions Indian students who are planning to study in Australia that there have been several incidents of robbery and assault on Indians in Australia, particularly in Melbourne, which has seen an increase in violence on its streets in recent years, with the offenders suspected to be mainly young people in their teens and early 20s.
>
> The most recent incident of this kind has been the fatal stabbing of a young Indian, aged 21 years old, in Melbourne on 2 January, as he was walking to his place of work late at night from a train station through a public park.
>
> These incidents are continuing to occur despite efforts by the local police to step up anti-crime measures, and are occurring all over Melbourne without any discernable pattern or rationale behind them. Increasingly also, the

acts of violence, are often accompanied by verbal abuse, fuelled by alcohol and drugs.

While, the majority of Indian students studying in Australia, especially those enrolled in Universities and reputable institutions, have a positive experience of living and studying in Australia, the number of such incidents of assault as well as of robbery has been on the rise in recent months, which has affected not only Indian students but also members of the larger Indian community in Australia.

Keeping these factors in view, the Government of India advises Indian students studying in Australia as well as those planning to study there, that they should take certain basic precautions in being alert to their own security while moving around:

- Do not travel alone late at night.
- If you are travelling alone, make sure that you have checked out your route carefully and that you keep to well-lit, populated areas as far as possible.
- Make sure that someone knows where you are going and at what time you are expected to return.
- Don't carry more cash with you than what is required.
- Do not make it obvious that you are in possession of expensive items, such as iPods or laptops.
- Always carry some identification with you as well as details of who should be contacted in an emergency.
- If in danger, dial 000 to get police help.
- In case you have a complaint, get in touch with the officer responsible for students welfare in the High Commission or the Consulate nearest to you.

(High Commission of India in Australia, 2010)

The Commonwealth and Victorian state governments remained in close contact with the Indian High Commission and responded in a range of practical ways. The measures included increasing the number of police and other security personnel on Melbourne's train lines, introducing hate crime legislation to strengthen punishment of offenders in race-based assaults, and organizing a 'Harmony Walk', which aimed to 'bring together Victorian communities to recognise and celebrate the enormous contribution of ethnic, cultural and religious communities to the state' (Victoria, 2009). Such an event runs the risk of being perceived as an empty public relations exercise, but it has was welcomed by the Federation of Indian Students of Australia as 'an important way Indian students can show the Premier and the whole Victorian community that we reaffirm Victoria's commitment to multiculturalism and racial tolerance and our total condemnation of recent racial attacks on Indian students.' In a media release announcing the event the then Premier of Victoria John Brumby makes clear not only the message but also the audience, which includes the community in Australia and government of India:

We are a community built on the understanding that while we come from different races, follow many faiths and cultures – we are all equal. That's why recent isolated incidents of racially motivated crime have been so distressing and we condemn racially motivated crimes in the strongest possible terms. Attacking a fellow Victorian – be they an international student or a father going to the aid of a stranger in the street is anathema to the values and principles that make our state one of the world's most successful multicultural communities and must not be tolerated. This was the message I relayed to the High Commissioner of India Sujathm Singh and Consul General of India Anita Nayar last week. We must not let the actions of a very small minority undermine one of the very tenets of our state. I encourage all Victorians to stand-up now to reaffirm that our tolerance and our multiculturalism are important to all Victorians.

(Victoria, 2009)

This statement marked an important rhetorical shift in the way governments describe international students, who are usually described as visitors or guests, but describing them as 'fellow Victorians' signalled a more inclusive approach.

International students as representatives of the home government

The role of consular staff is not only to support students in time of need, but sometimes also to monitor the loyalty of students and mobilize the student community to support the home government when required. In 2013 for example, a student advisor at the Malaysian Consulate in Sydney wrote to Malaysian government scholarship holders in Australia warning them not to attend a talk being presented by Malaysian opposition leader Anwar Ibrahim, whose coalition won the majority of the popular vote, but not the majority of seats, in the last national election. His email stated: 'You are smarter to think and focus on what matters rather than joining this activity that could make your hardship in maintaining good grades and earning the scholarship goes down the drain' (Lloyd, 2013). It seems the government expects loyalty from those who are the recipients of such funding.

China has been more successful in mobilizing its students in Australia when required. In 2008 when the Olympic torch relay arrived in Australia on its way to Beijing the Chinese authorities were keen to avoid a repeat of scenes in London, Paris and San Francisco, where pro-Tibet protesters had interfered with the relay. The embassy arranged buses to ferry students from Melbourne and Sydney. Thousands of Chinese students turned out to cheer the torch, dwarfing a small group of proTibet protesters. The *New York Times* reported that:

There were some ugly incidents when groups of Chinese students surrounded and intimidated isolated Tibet supporters. One frightened young man had to be pulled aboard a police boat when a rowdy group of demonstrators looked as if they might force him into the lake in the heart of Canberra, the capital. The crowd was finally calmed by an official from the Chinese Embassy.

(Johnston, 2008)

Such a political role for student citizens abroad is an interesting variation on traditional domestic student activism, and a spin on the usual exhortation offered by study-abroad advisors: 'remember that you are an ambassador for your university and your country, and act accordingly'.

Conclusion

Over time, the engagement of governments with their mobile student citizens has ranged across a spectrum from preventing travel by using visa restrictions, to encouraging study abroad by providing scholarships and subsidies. The case of China's JSJ shows that governments can play an important role in the consumer protection of students, through furnishing advice on the bona-fides and reputation of institutions, regulating the activities of home-based student recruitment agents, providing updates on developments in host countries, and negotiating with host governments keen to remain on the list of approved education providers. Where safety and security is involved, the case of India and Australia demonstrates that concerns about the welfare of students can escalate into headline news, and require concerted diplomatic action.

As the significance of other restrictions on student mobility fade away, differentials in student access to financial support for domestic and international study may become more significant in shaping patterns of trade. Most countries subsidize the tuition of their own nationals studying in domestic institutions. There is also a well-established practice of domestic funding for student-exchange arrangements of foreign study for a semester or two as part of the local degree (students of the participating universities simply swap places). Such subsidies are not normally available for those undertaking a full foreign degree. Norway is a notable exception.

There are practical and ideological reasons for the reluctance to extend domestic subsidies to international study. From a practical viewpoint it is difficult to enforce loan repayments from students who remain abroad after graduation. For those opposed to the marketization of education, the transferability of domestic subsidies could further privilege those rich enough to study abroad, and would then constitute an inequitable case of middle-class welfare. In countries where higher education is chiefly a function of the state, internationally portable subsidies would effectively mean a diminution of public funding for domestic education, a rerouting of tax revenue out of the country. For example, vouchers spent abroad would not contribute to the employment of local teachers, researchers and administrative staff, or the upkeep of libraries and lecture halls.

The arguments in favour of portable subsidies fall under two headings. First, there is the view that international experience is inherently beneficial – broadening the outlook of the individual, promoting understanding between nations, and so on – and any means of facilitating mobility is therefore a good thing. Second, there is a free-market view that governments that provide student subsidies should provide the same degree of funding for students wherever they study, as long as the provider meets requirements. In this context, the widespread practice of funding students' education in local but not equivalent overseas programmes would be interpreted as a form of protectionism. Governments will, of course, be more influenced by economic practicalities and addressing the requirements of the domestic polity, than by free-market ideologues or cosmopolitan intellectuals dreaming of free and frictionless internationalization.

References

AEI. (2007). *Market Data Snapshot: Norway.* Canberra: Australian Education International.

AEI. (2013). International student data. Retrieved 20 December 2013, from http://www.austrade.gov.au

AUCC, ACE, EUA, & CHEA. (2001, 28 September). Joint declaration on higher education and the general agreement on trade in services. Retrieved 15 May 2002, from www.unige.ch/eua/En/Activities/WTO/declaration-final1.pdf

Austrade. (2013). *Legislative Changes to the Operation of Education Agents in Vietnam.* Canberra: Australian Trade Commission.

Barber, E., Altbach, P. G., & Myers, R. G. (1984). Perspectives on foreign students. *Comparative Education Review, 28*(2), 163–167.

Barber, E. G. (1985). *Foreign Student Flows: The Significance for American Higher Education.* New York: Institute of International Education.

Bashraheel, L. (2013). Scholarship students: Big dreams, slow change. *Saudi Gazette.* Retrieved from www.saudigazette.com.sa/index.cfm?method=home.regcon&contentid=20130311156300

Committee on University Education Pathways Beyond 2015. (2012). *Report of the Committee on University Education Pathways Beyond 2015: Greater Diversity, More Opportunities.* Singapore: Higher Education Division, Ministry of Education.

CPE. (2013). *A Quality-Driven Private Higher Education Sector: Council for Private Education Annual Report 2012–2013.* Singapore: Council for Private Education.

Cummings, W. K. (1984). Going overseas for higher education: The Asian experience. *Comparative Education Review, 28*(2), 241–257.

Davie, S. (2012a, 8 June). Private institutions attracting more Singaporean students. *The Straits Times,* p. 48.

Davie, S. (2012b, 8 June). SIM grads find jobs easily, but earn less. *The Straits Times,* p. 48.

Denman, B. D., & Hilal, K. T. (2011). From barriers to bridges: An investigation on Saudi student mobility (2006–2009). *International Review of Education, 57*(3–4), 299–318. doi: 10.1007/s11159-011-9221-0.

EAIE. (2012). *International Student Mobility Charter.* Amsterdam: European Association for International Education.

Education International, & Public Services International. (2000). *The WTO and the Millennium Round: What is at Stake for Public Education.* Brussels: Education International.

Garrett, R. (2005). The rise and fall of transnational higher education in Singapore. *International Higher Education* (39), 9–10.

High Commission of India in Australia. (2010, 5 January). Important advisory for Indian students studying in Australia. from www.hcindia-au.org/travel_advisory.html

Hirschman, A. O. (1970). *Exit, Voice, and Loyalty: Responses to Decline in Firms, Organizations, and States.* Cambridge, MA: Harvard University Press.

Hoare, L. A. (2012). Transnational student voices: Reflections on a second chance. *Journal of Studies in International Education, 16*(3), 271–286. doi: 10.1177/1028315311398045.

Johnston, T. (2008, 25 April). China supporters greet Olympic torch in Australia. *New York Times.* Retrieved from www.nytimes.com/2008/04/25/world/asia/25torch.html?_r=0

JSJ. (2010). Ministry of Education Overseas Study Warning No. 2 [教育部发布今年第2号留学预警赴澳大利亚留学务必注意相关情况变化]. from www.jsj.edu.cn/index.php/default/news/index/333

JSJ. (2013). To help students studying abroad at their own expense correct choice of foreign schools in 43 countries released by the Ministry of Education list of schools. From www.jsj.edu.cn/index.php/default/index/sort/12020

Kapur, D. (2010). *Diaspora, Development, and Democracy The Domestic Impact of International Migration from India.* Princeton, NJ: Princeton University Press.

Kinser, K., Levy, D. C., Silas, J. C., Bernasconi, A., Slantcheva-Durst, S., Otieno, W., et al. (2010). *The Global Growth of Private Higher Education* (Vol. 36). San Francisco: Jossey-Bass.

Koh, A. (2012). Tactics of interventions: Student mobility and human capital building in Singapore. *Higher Education Policy, 25*(2), 191–206. doi: 10.1057/hep.2012.5.

Lee, S. J. (2005). Educational upgrading through private educational institutions. *Singapore Statistics Newsletter*(September), 15–17.

Li, M. (2008). Keeping them safe: A review of Chinese students' safety issues in New Zealand. Paper presented at the Australian and New Zealand Communication Association Conference 2008: Power and Place, Wellington.

Lloyd, T. (2013). Anwar Ibrahim visit for Adelaide Festival of Ideas prompts email threats to local Malaysian students. *The Advertiser.* Retrieved from www.theaustralian.com.au/news/anwar-ibrahim-visit-for-adelaide-festival-of-ideas-prompts-email-threats-to-local-malaysian-students/story-e6frg6n6-1226741922954

Marginson, S., Nyland, C., Sawir, E., & Forbes-Mewett, H. (2010). *International Student Security.* Cambridge: Cambridge University Press.

Mathisen, G. (2006). *Alienation of higher education? Investigating Norwegian Initiatives on the General Agreement on Trade in Services.* (Master), University of Bergen, Bergen.

McFedries, T. H. (2001). Non-English-speaking-background secondary school fee-paying Asian students living in a host family environment in Christchurch: A research report. (Master of Teaching and Learning), University of Canterbury, Christchurch. Retrieved from http://ir.canterbury.ac.nz/bitstream/10092/2868/1/thesis_fulltext.pdf

MFAT. (2010). New Zealand-China Free Trade Agreement: Most favoured nation. From www.chinafta.govt.nz/1-The-agreement/1-Key-outcomes/2-Services/2-Most-favoured-nation/index.php

Ministry of Education. (2013). Post secondary education. From www.moe.gov.sg/
education/post-secondary

Mishra, A. (2011). India: New law on overseas university agents. *University World
News*. Retrieved 5 April 2014, from http://www.universityworldnews.com/article.
php?story=20110204224357407

MoE. (2006). *2006 Education Statistics Digest*. Singapore: Ministry of Education.

MTI. (2002). *Developing Singapore's Education Industry*. Singapore: Ministry of
Trade & Industry.

Mundy, K., & Ika, M. (2003). Hegemonic exceptionalism and legitimating bet-hedging:
Paradoxes and lessons from the US and Japanese approaches to education services
under the GATS. *Globalisation, Societies and Education, 1*(3).

Ng, P. T. (2013). The global war for talent: Responses and challenges in the Singapore
higher education system. *Journal of Higher Education Policy and Management, 35*(3),
280–292. doi: 10.1080/1360080x.2013.786859.

Norwegian Ministry of Education and Research. (2005). *The Common European Objectives in Education and Training: Indicators and Benchmarks in the Lisbon Strategy – A
Norwegian Perspective*. Oslo: Norwegian Ministry of Education and Research.

OECD. (2002). *GATS: The Case for Open Services Markets* (p. 97). Paris: Organisation for Economic Co-operation and Development.

OECD & World Bank. (2010). *Reviews of National Policies for Education Chile's
International Scholarship Programme*. Paris and Washington, DC: Organisation
for Economic Cooperation and Development and the World Bank.

Opsahl, A. M. (2005, 18 March). Drømmen om Australia [The Australian Dream].
Dagbladet Fredag.

PIE. (2013). How has Saudi Arabia's KASP impacted the sector? *The PIE Review* (2),
44–47.

Poretti, P. (2009). *The Regulation of Subsidies Within the General Agreement on Trade in
Services of the WTO: Problems and Prospects*. Netherlands: Kluwer Law International.

Psacharopoulos, G. (2003). The social cost of an outdated law: Article 16 of the
Greek Constitution. *European Journal of Law and Economics, 16*, 123–137.

Ryan, C., & Dodd, T. (2005). China spends big bites. *Australian Financial Review*.
Retrieved 22 August 2007, from http://www.afr.com

Sidhu, R., Ho, K. C., & Yeoh, B. (2011). Emerging education hubs: The case of
Singapore. *Higher Education, 61*(1), 23–40. doi: 10.1007/s10734-010-9323-9

The Times of India. (2009, 30 May). Amitabh Bachchan turns down Australian doctorate as mark of protest.

Uddin, Z. (2009). Bollywood union vetoes Australian shoots. www.digitalspy.co.uk/
bollywood/news/a158572/bollywood-union-vetoes-australian-shoots.html

UNESCO. (2013). Data Centre. Retrieved 21 October 2013, from www.uis.unesco.org

Victoria. (2009, 3 June 2009). Premier to lead harmony walk to celebrate Victoria's
multiculturalism. From http://archive.premier.vic.gov.au/component/content/
article/7110.html

Wang, X. (2003). *Education in China Since 1976*. Jefferson, NC: McFarland.

Weisbrod, B. (1962). *External Benefits of Public Education: An Economic Analysis*.
Princeton, NJ: Princeton University Press.

Wiers-Jenssen, J. (2003). Norwegian students abroad: Experiences of students from
a linguistically and geographically peripheral European country. *Studies in Higher
Education, 28*(4), 391–411. doi: 10.1080/0307507032000122251.

Wiers-Jenssen, J. (2008a). Career impacts of student mobility: Stumbling block or stepping stone? In Å. Gornitzka & L. Langerfeldt (Eds.), *Borderless Knowledge: Understanding the New Internationalisation of Research and Higher Education in Norway* (pp. 79–101). Dordrecht, Netherlands: Springer.

Wiers-Jenssen, J. (2008b). Does higher education attained abroad lead to international jobs? *Journal of Studies in International Education, 12*(2), 101–130. doi: 10.1177/1028315307307656.

Wiers-Jenssen, J. (2012). Degree mobility from the Nordic countries: Background and employability. *Journal of Studies in International Education, 17*(4), 471–491. doi: 10.1177/1028315312463824.

WTO. (1995). *General Agreement on Trade in Services*. Geneva: World Trade Organization.

WTO. (2001). *Revision of the Guidelines for the Scheduling of Specific Commitments (S/CSC/W/30)*. Geneva: World Trade Organization.

WTO. (2013). Services database. from World Trade Organization http://tsdb.wto.org

Chapter 4

Even the best laid plans

Student migration policy and its unintended consequences

For countries keen to attract skilled migrants, international students would seem to be perfect candidates. They have qualifications that are recognized by employers and relevant to local conditions, they are proficient in the local language (at least where the language of instruction is the national language) and they are young. For as long as students have travelled to study, a proportion of them have remained in the place that they have studied, and often the aspects of the host country that attracted them as students also make it an attractive location to build a career. We know from OECD data that between one-quarter and one-third of international students who complete their studies in many of the largest receiving countries stay on in the country (including the United Kingdom, France, Germany, Australia and Canada) (OECD, 2011, pp. 328–330). Three-quarters of those who stayed on did so to work. It is difficult to know, however, how long these students stay for, how many return to their home country, and how many move on to third countries. In those economic and political unions where there is freedom of movement, such as within the EU and between Australia and New Zealand, the policies referred to in this chapter only apply to citizens from outside the common market. For the same reason the OECD data above excludes EU students studying in EU countries.

Until recently, governments have usually treated international students no differently from other types of migrants. Nevertheless, their qualifications, cultural familiarity and understanding of the local employment environment have provided them with a foot in the door, so to speak, which has allowed many to stay. Since around 2000, many of the major host countries for international students have been enacting policies designed to allow larger numbers of international students to remain in the host country after completion of their studies. Former international students have been given preferential treatment over other applicants for either temporary and permanent residency in the UK, Germany, Australia, Canada, New Zealand and Singapore, to name a few.

Host governments are competing both for students and skilled migrants in an increasingly globalized market for both, which Wildavsky (2010) has termed 'the great brain race' and Reiner (2010) 'brain competition policy', both drawing parallels with the much older notion of 'brain drain'. Policy settings are both internally focused, aimed at satisfying national demands for skills of various kinds, and externally focused in order to ensure that the nation remains an attractive destination for foreign nationals that others are also trying to lure. Shachar (2006) has described how competitive migration regimes allow states to use their control over residency and citizenship rights to 'advance the economic interests of certain domestic industries while at the same time competing against other nations in the global race for talent' (p. 164). A fundamental difference between the recruitment of students and skilled migrants, however, is that host countries are much more open to foreign students than they are to foreign workers, thus necessitating mechanisms to select which students should be allowed to transition from the more open category to the more restrictive category of temporary or permanent resident.

In this chapter we explore the ways in which states have sought to link their competitive student recruitment regimes and their competitive migration regimes for mutual benefit. However, this has not been smooth sailing. Policy experiments over the past decade have revealed a range of unforeseen consequences that have resulted in what the Observatory on Borderless Higher Education refers to as policy 'pendulum swings' (Lawton, 2011) in the UK and Australia, and frequent rule changes and recalibrations in many countries.

In the next section, we outline the types of regulatory measures – policy levers – that host governments employ to selectively allow some graduated international students to remain, while requiring others to leave. Then we consider the both the policy objectives that lead them to use the tools we have described, and the unexpected consequences of the measures they have enacted. In examining these issues, we review the cases of the UK, Australia and Singapore, which embraced student migration strategies wholeheartedly, only to pull back after a few years.

Regulatory measures

The first decade of this millennium saw major growth in student migration for leading education exporters UK and Australia, but by the end of the decade both countries put policies in place to drastically reduce numbers. It is instructive to look at the levers they were able to use, both to rapidly increase and rapidly decrease the influx.

The key lever is to give preferential treatment to the migration applications of international student graduates of the host country. This can be fine-tuned in terms of the type of preferential treatment, who qualifies, and under what conditions they can make application. A decade ago Australia began to grant preferential treatment to applicants for permanent residence who held Australian higher education qualifications, blazing a trail in the linking of international education and skilled migration. The successes and failures of the programme – and perhaps equally importantly responses by media and public opinion, both locally and internationally – hold lessons for the future of 'two-step' migration. The decision was based on longitudinal research on employment outcomes of earlier migrants, which showed that immigrants with Australian qualifications were more readily integrated into the labour market (Birrell & Hawthorne, 1999). Former international students had several advantages over other migrants – qualifications that were readily recognized by employers, cultural familiarity, and established social networks which were beneficial in finding employment. Previously, as in many countries, former international students were able to apply for permanent residence, but were barred from applying for three years after graduation, were required to apply from outside Australia and were assessed on the same basis as graduates of other countries. This policy was changed in 2001, allowing students to apply immediately after graduation while in Australia (Hawthorne, 2005).

A points system was introduced for skilled migration programmes, and tertiary qualifications were assigned a specific number of points according to the level of study and perceived labour market demand for graduates in each discipline. Thus Australia launched into uncharted territory in international education policy development, and was closely watched by other countries which recruit large numbers of international students and skilled migrants. Applicants for skilled migration were awarded points for various qualities that the immigration authorities judged would lead to positive labour market outcomes, such as age, proficiency in English, occupational qualifications and professional experience. Into this mix, extra points were added from 1998 for Australian educational qualifications. By 2002, international students constituted half of all applicants for skilled migration and there was early evidence that the migration pathway was stimulating demand for Australian education (Hawthorne, 2005).

Soon the UK, Canada and New Zealand introduced similar point-based schemes with extra points for national qualifications. Similarly, international graduates of German universities can obtain a work permit for employment in their field of study without being subject to needs tests (that is, the employer is not required to demonstrate that no EU national is available to fill the position). The DAAD reports that increasing numbers of students are taking advantage of this possibility. Currently around a quarter of international graduates in Germany stay on for employment, and if those who stay for family reasons (primarily as spouses) are included the rate increases to around one in three, and nearly half of the foreign academics in Germany have a German degree (DAAD, 2012, p. 72).

The flow can be reduced or increased by distributing bonus points according to the type and level of qualification. Where countries – such as the UK and Australia – have opened up vocational qualifications (such as hairdressing) to residency rights, enrolments in these fields have grown dramatically and quickly, and have subsequently been downgraded or removed from migration programmes. Typically, at present there is a sliding scale, with greatest preference given to postgraduate qualifications and least to sub-degree certificates, and more highly skilled fields such as engineering in preference to cookery.

Another measure being adopted by some host countries is to allow students to stay on in the country with work rights for a specified period after graduation. Like the points systems, post-study work rights have been adopted in a competitive fashion by Australia, the UK, Canada and New Zealand, although the UK has since reversed the policy in the face of anti-immigration sentiment. This approach retains the temporary nature of the student visa without making any guaranteed link with permanent residency but still holds out to the student the possibility of work experience and permanent residency. As a review of Australia's student visa policy put it:

> In those occupations where Australia might in the future want to recruit skilled migrants, a two year post study work visa gives employers an opportunity to "try before you buy". It would enable employers to have a good look at how someone functions within the Australian workplace before deciding whether or not to begin the fairly complicated process of sponsoring that person for migration.
>
> (Knight, 2011, p. 40)

Post-study work rights are very attractive to prospective students, and like the possibility of working part-time during studies and breaks, can allow students to both cover the cost of living and gain professional experience.

Policy objectives

What do recruiting nations hope to achieve by providing preferential treatment for former international students in their migration programmes? Here we consider four rationales and the unintended consequences that have arisen as a result of the measures that have been implemented in pursuit of these goals. First, international students are sought after because they can fill skills shortages in the labour market with nationally recognized qualifications, language skills and cultural competence in the host country. Second, international students can help to redress the ageing of the population by importing workers who are at the start of their careers. Third, providing opportunities for international students to remain in the host country can assist in recruiting students to a country's education institutions. In this context, we consider Singapore's strategy to 'achieve a net gain of talents' in the face of its own youth studying abroad in large numbers. Fourth, because international students who are resident for more than a year are counted as migrants according to international statistical standards, managing the student intake can provide governments with a means to quite rapidly change the net migration rate. Finally, we look at unintended consequences in the case of assaults on Indian students in Australia, attracted in large numbers by the prospect of migration.

Human resource development

Growth in migration is often portrayed as economically beneficial for the host economy, as it boosts GDP by expanding the number of producers and consumers. The vibrancy of high-migrant cities in turn attracts further migration as well as investment, and cultural and lifestyle benefits for the host population. Attracting skilled migrants is a rapid, cost-effective way of meeting the growing needs of the knowledge economy. More specifically, two-step migration (first step is entering the country as a student, second step is applying for migrant status at the end of the study period) is an appealing strategy. As the OECD notes:

> Virtually all OECD countries expect that there will be a need for highly skilled migrants, especially in scientific and technological occupations, in coming years. Language proficiency issues are far more significant for this type of migration, as are issues related to qualifications and work experience obtained in a developing country . . . . International student migration in particular seems a promising way of expanding highly skilled migration, all the more so because youth cohorts are declining in many OECD countries.
>
> (OECD, 2009, p. 161)

Such migration is, at least in theory, an efficient method: the student is already in the country; has sufficient academic ability and facility with the domestic language to engage in postsecondary study (presumably a good indicator for future employability); is acculturated or currently becoming acculturated to local ways (and therefore more likely to successfully integrate); will bear a host-country qualification, thereby avoiding the need to assess its provenance or equivalence; and will be well-motivated to get a job to recoup the cost of study (and therefore less likely to be a burden on the welfare system); and they will generally be in their 20s or 30s (and therefore demographically desirable).

There are, however, several counter-arguments raised by critics of this form of migration. There is always a choice to be made between developing the skills of the domestic population and importing skills. Typically, opponents of student recruitment policies will argue that the skills shortages are a product of failings in the domestic education system, and that these should be addressed for the benefit of the population rather than importing foreign talent. The quick-fix skilled labour-importation approach can be seen as a squib – giving employers and governments an opportunity not to meet their responsibility for ensuring the nation's citizens are properly educated and trained to meet society's needs. A second argument is that the economic benefits of migration are negligible – or indeed negative – for the receiving country's population. For example, a study commissioned by the UK House of Lords on the effects of migration noted whilst GDP rose 3 per cent due to migration in the period under study, the population rose 3.6 per cent. On a per-capita basis, it could therefore be concluded that the pre-migration population were in fact worse off. Third, the benefits of 'vibrancy' are offset by public concerns about overstressed infrastructure (such as congested roads, crowded public transport, overcrowded public hospital emergency rooms and so on) and the rising cost of housing, while the influx of foreign labour may be seen to disadvantage local workers by increasing competition for jobs and potentially driving wages down.

A fourth concern is that the skill gaps are not being filled despite migration. There is a risk of disjunction between nominated fields and actual employment, due to students having no intention of working in that field (but only seeking a rapid means of migrating), and students not being suitable to work in that field. Part of the problem may lie in inadequate vetting of visa applications. For example, an internal audit by Australia's Immigration Department found that in 2008–2009 there was a 37 per cent fraud rate across more than 40,000 Indian student visa applications (Ockenden, 2013). Even the genuinely well-qualified graduate may fail to gain or retain employment in the specified field. Because of the lag time between enrolling and graduating, the vacancies in the field may be filled; indeed, the field may be flooded as intended-migrants flock to qualify in the field that they think will grant the easiest path to migration. The result may then be new migrants that are unemployed or underemployed. This can alienate the domestic public, leading to criticisms of both international student recruitment and student migration.

Negative public reaction and criticisms of current skilled migration regimes has in recent years found its way into newspaper headlines in the developed world, influencing politics as well as economics, as the OECD has noted:

> [L]abour migration management has become an imperative, because of concerns about competition with native workers and the persistence of irregular migration and because the labour market outcomes of past immigrants and their children have not always been as favourable as expected. Public opinion in many OECD countries may not be willing to encourage further significant labour migration if these issues are not resolved.
>
> (OECD, 2009, p. 78)

In part this is a challenge for governments to respond to the public concerns. More importantly, such disaffection underlines the need for migration programmes to operate transparently and to be seen to successfully meet the stated policy objectives.

Improving the potential support ratio

Because most graduates will be in their 20s or 30s, migration proponents argue that there are demographic benefits for receiving nations with an ageing demographic profile. Migration (especially of the skilled young) is desirable to boost the ratio of working-age population to the retired population, ensuring that the tax base will continue to be sufficient to cover the cost of pension entitlements, health care and so on.

There are, however, numerous critics of the migration-to-replace-ageing-population argument (see for example the arguments and evidence amassed in House of Lords Select Committee on Economic Affairs 2008a, 2008b). One counter-argument is that recruiting migrants to help cover pension costs is effectively a giant, state-run Ponzi scheme, akin to a pyramid-selling scheme reliant on recruiting new 'investors' (in this case taxpaying migrants), with the broadening base (those paying in) supporting the apex (those extracting the benefits of pensions and superannuation benefits). New migrants will eventually themselves become old citizens entitled to the fruits of the welfare/superannuation state. While the massive influx of new entrants through migration postpones the inevitable collapse of the system (or at least the reduction of entitlements and the increase of the retirement age), this is only temporary, and the expansion of the population means that the day of reckoning will be all the more costly. Those Western governments placating social unrest by promising welfare state entitlements following the Second World War did not have to pay the bills, that would not be due for decades, when the baby-boomers retired. Similarly, it can be argued that current governments seeking to rapidly broaden their tax base through immigration are opting for a quick fix – again, the entitlement costs for the migrants will not be due for decades. Critics advocate reducing entitlements and raising the age at which citizens can claim pension and superannuation payments, arguing that such an approach will be more effective than any other (House of Lords Select Committee on Economic Affairs 2008a, pp. 45–46).

Increase fee-paying student numbers

It is clear that the possibility of obtaining post-study residency in a host country influences many international students' choice of country and programme of study. Some students are, from the outset, interested in emigrating. Others are unclear of their post-study plans, but even for these students the possibility of gaining work in the host country is usually quite attractive, both as a means of generating income to offset the cost of their studies and as a means of gaining work experience that will assist them to subsequently gain employment in their home country, or even in a third country. Even amongst those students who do return to their home country, some will experience such profound return culture shock that they will relocate to the country in which they studied, very often without having intended to previously (Christofi & Thompson, 2007). Robertson (2013) has documented the unclear and precarious routes that many students make through the process of international study and migration, showing that intentions are rarely clear-cut, and change over time as students experience the precariousness of temporary residence and competing allegiances and desires. Nevertheless, market research on prospective international students often reports that many students indicate that the opportunity to work in the host country is an important factor in their choice of country. For example, around three-quarters of Chinese and Indian students expressed this as in important factor in choosing the UK in 2009 (Lawton, 2011). By 2004 more than a third of international students completing Australian university degrees were obtaining permanent residency. The rate of migration varied considerably by country of origin, as Table 4.1 shows, with nearly three-quarters of graduates from South Asia obtaining permanent residency. This table includes data for 14 nationalities with the largest numbers of completions in 2004.

Table 4.1 International students in higher education in Australia: completions, permanent residency and enrolment growth

	Higher education completions 2004	PR visas issued 2004–05 as % of 2004 completions	Average annual rate of HE enrolment growth, 2000–04 (%)
Sri Lanka	583	76.8	18.7
India	3,455	73.7	41.8
Bangladesh	681	69.8	51.7
South Korea	1,058	50.2	22.7
Indonesia	3,405	45.9	3.1
China (excluding HK)	7,061	39.7	69.6
Vietnam	714	35.2	14.5
Hong Kong	2,906	34.1	12.6
Japan	935	27.4	16.4
Malaysia	4,805	27.0	12.6
Taiwan	1,313	20.7	14.0
Singapore	3,226	15.7	1.5
Thailand	2,147	11.3	20.1
Canada	820	4.5	33.2
Other countries	9,186	24.2	12.9
Total	*42,295*	*34.1*	*20.0*

Data sources: columns 2 and 3 from Birrell (2006); column 4 based on Australian Education International data.

Table 4.1 also shows the rates of enrolment growth across this period as the study-migration pathway was being established. For all nationalities, enrolments grew by 20 per cent per annum, on average. The rate of growth for students from the top seven countries with the highest rates of permanent residency combined was 33.5 per cent per annum, while the seven countries with the lowest rates of permanent residency combined grew at only 11.6 per cent per annum across this period. There are clearly many other factors driving enrolment levels for each country, and therefore much variation between countries with similar migration rates (e.g. China and Vietnam), but it is evident that enrolments grew significantly faster from those countries with higher migration rates.

At the same time, there are potential downsides for the receiving country. There is the risk of provoking a bubble of enrolments in certain fields that generate 'easy' migration points. Australia has experienced enrolment bubbles in those courses that would allow students to most rapidly accrue the desired migration points – masters programmes in computer science and accounting in the early 2000s, and vocational courses in commercial cookery and hairdressing in the late 2000s (Ziguras, 2012).

In the past decade, students seeking permanent residency, migration agents, educational institutions, and immigration officials in many countries have been engaged in an uneasy and unstable relationship with each other. By 2010 the governments of two of the world's most popular destinations for international students, which had for decades promoted education as an export industry and gone to great lengths to recruit foreign students, changed their mind. The UK and Australia both lost their appetite for growth, and for almost exactly the same reasons.

It was not surprising that governments would eventually act to stem the rapid growth in enrolments in sub-degree for-profit institutions. While there are some very good private colleges operating in both countries, the last few years have seen the emergence of many 'visa mills', offering young people with a thirst for travel an easy opportunity to live and work in the UK and Australia. There was a lot of money to be made by investors willing to work through the relatively simple processes for establishment of a private college and then tapping into the immense network of overseas agents advising students. It turned out to be easier for entrepreneurs to establish colleges than for authorities to scrutinize and close them. The number of foreign students in Australian private colleges hit 100,000 in 2002, doubled to 200,000 in 2007, and peaked at over 330,000 in 2009 (AEI, 2013). Accreditation and quality assurance agencies were found wanting and immigration authorities took up the regulatory slack, revoking some colleges' visa-sponsoring licenses with the stroke of a pen, or more likely the clicking of a delete button.

In Australia, the immigration department finally severed the pathway from vocational diploma to permanent residency, which had been clearly driving a huge bubble in enrolments in any area that provided extra points to prospective migrants. Melbourne and Sydney were awash with hairdressing and cooking schools catering for foreign students, which all closed in 2010, leaving little trace apart from tens of thousands of graduates who are now in residency limbo on temporary visas waiting for their migration applications to be lifted from the bottom of the pile. A high proportion of students in Australian private colleges were from South Asia, particularly Punjab, and they were particularly vulnerable. Compared to students from East and South East Asia who tend to study in universities, students from South Asia tend to be male, living on low incomes in poor neighbourhoods, working in precarious employment in fast-food outlets and convenience stores or driving taxis, and reliant on public transport. As a result, these students were unwittingly exposed to the most dangerous pockets of urban violence, especially around train stations late at night.

The private college enrolment bubble grew over several years in both countries; the only surprise was how long it would take governments to respond to the obvious quality shortcomings at the bottom end of the market. A clampdown was always going to result in a reduction in student numbers in private colleges and we saw this transpire in 2010 in both countries.

Achieving a 'net gain of talents': the case of Singapore

One option for a country facing a loss of students abroad is to adopt the same approach as the destination countries and import those skills by recruiting students from other countries to stay on after graduation. This would appear logical – if it is a loss of skills that is the problem, then find the skills elsewhere. This approach is actually quite rare, mainly because most countries experiencing an outflow of students also have a large pool of graduates from domestic institutions (Ziguras & Law, 2006). In India, China, Greece and Malaysia, governments are focused on reducing rates of graduate unemployment and incoming international students are normally not allowed to stay on in the country. Singapore is rare in having sought to balance the brain drain of outgoing students with an immigration programme that targets incoming international students.

Singapore has been successful in using immigration, or 'attracting foreign talent', as a means of human resource development. The ex-Prime Minister Lee Kuan Yew observed that, despite the outflow, Singapore 'will make a net gain of talents' by recruiting from the region, even if most of those recruited do not settle permanently (quoted in J. Ng, 2008). As a result, Singapore's population has grown by 2.88 per cent per year over the past decade, increasing from 4.1 million in 2003 to 5.3 million in 2012 according to World Bank data.

Like most high-income countries, Singapore has an ageing population and low birth rate, and its population policy is primarily concerned with maintaining the size of the working-age population (Singapore Government, 2013). This involves a combination of strategies to boost the birth rate and reduce emigration as well as immigration, which is framed as, 'complementing the Singaporean core with a foreign workforce' (Singapore Government, 2013, p. 40). This involves recruiting low-skilled migrants to work in jobs that are not attractive to Singaporeans, particularly in construction and social services, and in highly skilled migrants to support the global competitiveness and flexibility of the workforce. The recruitment of former incoming international students into the Singapore workforce is a key means of attracting those in the latter category, an approach that has also been adopted in Australia, New Zealand, Canada and the United Kingdom over the past decade (Robertson & Runganaikaloo, 2013).

Singapore's education hub ambitions have resulted in growing numbers of foreign students choosing to study in Singapore, many of whom accept attractive employment opportunities post graduation (Daquila, 2013). A generously funded research sector equipped with state-of-the-art facilities and staffed with top talent from around the globe has created a highly desirable environment for local and foreign graduates. In addition, Singapore has been keen to brand itself as a 'global city', epitomizing the 'New Asia'. While the Economic Development Board is largely responsible for steering Singapore Global Schoolhouse strategy, the Singapore Tourism Board, with its extensive network of international offices and educational specialists, markets Singaporean higher education to foreign students.

Reliable data on the number of international students in Singapore is not available, and it is one of the only countries (and the only major exporter of education) not to provide such data to UNESCO. The Council for Private Education states that in 2012, private institutions enrolled 99,880 international students, accounting for 44 per cent of total private sector enrolments (CPE, 2013). No such data is available for public universities or polytechnics; however, the government has revealed that international students account for 18 per cent of students in public universities (Tan, 2011).

Foreign students with high grades, particularly those from elite schools in China, India and South East Asia are offered scholarships and stipends to study at one of Singapore's public universities. These do not involve any obligation to stay on in Singapore after graduation but the government expresses expectations that these top students will go on to make a contribution to the country (Koh, 2012). Other international students at public universities pay tuition fees subsidized by the government. They may apply for government grants to cover their tuition fees and in return they are required to work for at least three years for a Singapore-based company after graduation (P. T. Ng, 2013). However, for the bulk of international students in Singapore, who study in private and foreign institutions, there is very little available in the way of government subsidies, and these students do not enjoy streamlined access to permanent residency. There is no data available to indicate how many of the more than 100,000 international students in Singapore stay on after graduation and enter the workforce, but it is clear that this group of students represents a ready pool of labour and that many of these students would welcome the opportunity to stay on in the country.

Koh (2003, 2012) has pointed to limitations facing an immigration response to brain drain in Singapore. Koh (2003) describes the 'subterranean tensions that underlie state arguments and discourse on foreign talent', arguing that while Singaporeans are convinced of the need to attract foreign talent to Singapore, they remain ambivalent about their presence. According to Koh their ambivalence stems from the asymmetrical treatment given to foreign talent who enjoy superior employment opportunities and benefits without enduring civic obligations such as national service. It appears that while 'foreign talent' offers an economic solution to Singapore's limited pool of skilled labour, this strategy could pose significant social challenges. In 2008, reports of a surge in applications by foreign students to public universities provoked debate as to whether Singapore should reserve its limited public education resources for its own population (Davie, 2008). The apparent rise of local-versus-foreign tensions in education and the workplace have since received significant attention from the government, and in 2011 authorities undertook not to increase the number of international students in public institutions (Koh, 2012; Tan, 2011). Similarly, the country's new population policy promises to slow the rate of immigration and focus immigration policy on complementing rather than competing with the domestic workforce (Singapore Government, 2013).

Singapore's policy of attracting top scientists came under fire after the departure of several high-profile scientists (Overland, 2007). Like other leading Asian cities, Singapore aims to encourage foreign talent to stay permanently. However, the majority of foreign residents do not become citizens despite considerable government efforts to entice expatriates to remain. In fact, remaining permanently in one place is at odds with the very nature of the so called 'global nomads' who are likely to view somewhere like Singapore as a temporary location in their career trajectory (Ong, 2007). This is especially the case if taking up Singaporean citizenship requires a permanent resident to renounce their existing citizenship status of another country. Singapore might be better served by accumulating global expertise via successive waves of foreign experts and returnees rather than aspiring to permanence (Ong, 2007).

In summary, the government has been successful in recruiting a large number of international students into the country, which far exceeds the number of Singaporean students studying overseas. Given the numbers, it would seem to be much simpler for the government to recruit incoming students to stay than it is to entice ambivalent outgoing Singaporean students to return. However, in Singapore, as in the United Kingdom and Australia, immigration of international students is politically sensitive, and governments often respond to populist fears of competition by limiting the flow of students into both education institutions and into permanent residency.

Massaging net migration rates in the UK and Australia

Since the financial crisis began it was obvious that many countries would temporarily scale back their migration intake in response to lack of employment opportunities. Clearly, this would reduce the appeal of the UK and Australia, to which many students were attracted by the opportunity to stay on after graduation. What happened next, though, was astounding. Political parties promised to reduce immigration rates dramatically for short-term electoral gains. When politicians looked at recent statistics on net immigration (the number of migrants arriving minus the number leaving) they saw that international students made up a significant proportion of the total – not former international students who had stayed on after their studies, but people on temporary student visas who had been counted as 'migrants' because they had resided in the country for more than 12 months.

Migration was a central issue in national elections in both countries. In the UK the Tories were elected on a platform of reducing net migration down from hundreds of thousands to tens of thousands. This target cannot be met by reducing the number of working migrants alone, and will require a reduction in the number of students from outside Europe studying in the UK. The Australian conservative party also vowed to dramatically reduce net migration, with the party's leader arguing that students were 'by far the largest contributor to net overseas migration'. The Australian Labor Party, which went on to retain government narrowly, countered that it had already been actively reducing net migration rates (partly by making student visas more difficult to obtain) and were on track to better the cuts proposed by the conservatives. It is clear to everyone involved in migration policy that reducing student numbers will have no effect on long-term population growth rates, but it is the easiest way to be able to quickly sell an anti-migration policy to the electorate.

The UK and Australia both saw a strong rise in immigrant numbers during the 1990s and 2000s. Following the Global Financial Crisis, the desirability of continued rapid expansion was revisited. The Cameron government declared its aim to reduce net immigration to below 100,000 by the year 2015, down from the 242,000 reported for the year 2010. One of the key targets is the reduction of international student numbers. Following a report that student visa numbers to the UK went up 35 per cent to more than 360,000 in 2009, the immigration minister concluded that student immigration numbers were 'unsustainable' (BBC, 2010). Noting that international students and their dependents accounted for two out of three visas of non-EU migrants, the Home Secretary stated that the 'most significant migrant route to Britain is the student route. And so we must take action . . .' (Travis, 2011). Further, the government cited figures showing that some 20 per cent of students remained in the country five years after they had completed studies – a clear but unsurprising indicator of a link between study and migration (BBC, 2010). Whatever the merits of either case, it is clear that non-EU international students pose a relatively soft target for numbers reduction, as they are more easily within the government's ability to regulate, unlike mobile fellow EU members. The desire of international students to settle permanently was portrayed as illegitimate in both countries. The UK immigration minister promised to 'drive abuse out of the system . . . . The primary objective of studying in the UK must be to study, not to work or to acquire long-term residency status' (quoted in *Guardian*, 2011). The Australian government introduced a requirement that each student visa applicant must be able to demonstrate that they are a 'Genuine Temporary Entrant', meaning that they have no desire to stay on in Australia after graduation.

Predictably enough, responses from the education sector were scathing, arguing that while changes to permanent residency application procedures may be warranted, those on temporary student visas should not be included in migration statistics. The chief executive of Universities UK explained that students 'are not here for economic reasons, their time in the UK does not count towards any later application for settlement, unlike workers, and they have no recourse to public funds' (Travis, 2010). The general secretary of the University and College Union warned that 'Populist policies on immigration might play well domestically, but on the global stage we risk looking foolish' (BBC, 2010). The National Union of Students held that to 'suggest that the levels of those coming to the UK to study is too high is a politically motivated misinterpretation of the huge contribution which international students make to our colleges' (BBC, 2010).

Despite protestation from education providers, both governments took steps to reduce the number of international students, focusing on private college enrolments but also affecting university enrolments. While the UK Conservative government was bound by a numerical election pledge to continue to reduce numbers, the Australian government has since loosened its restrictions. As the UK cancelled post-study work rights, Australia, with a much more buoyant economy, extended them, resulting in renewed growth in enrolments. The irony in both countries is that a statistical convention that includes students on temporary visas of 12 months or more in a country's net migration figures, has in two of the world's largest destination countries led governments to deliberately reduce international student numbers. This served the ruling parties well in the short term by catering to anti-immigration populism, but will only harm to the nation's economy but do nothing to reduce permanent migration rates.

Unintended consequences: Assaults on Indian students

A series of serious assaults against Indian students in a one-month period in 2009 in Melbourne and Sydney resulted in street protests in both cities and a media storm in India, with serious political repercussions in both countries. The episode reveals much about the social cost of migration-linked international student recruitment, particularly for the most vulnerable students who often have the most to gain from the prospect of achieving permanent residency in a high-income country.

On 9 May, Sourabh Sharma, 21, a hospitality management student was beaten up on a train by a group of teenagers. He was returning home in the evening after a shift at KFC (Johnston, 2009). Four teenagers were charged over the assault. Security video footage of the attack, made public later in May, was broadcast extensively in Australia and India, showing a group of teenage boys, who appeared to be of diverse racial backgrounds, repeatedly punching and kicking Sourabh, who sustained a broken jaw and extensive bruising from the attack. On 25 May, Baljinder Singh, 25, an Indian cookery student, was stabbed in the stomach in an attempted robbery while leaving a suburban railway station. The following day, four Indian students were attacked when a birthday party at their home was gatecrashed by two teenage boys.

The political response in India was fast and furious. On 29 May, Australia's High Commissioner to India was summoned to a meeting with Overseas Indian Affairs Minister Vayalar Ravi, who urged Australia to ensure the events were not repeated (Hodge & Clayfield, 2009). India's High Commissioner to Australia travelled to Melbourne to convey her government's concern to Victorian police, government and educational representatives. The Prime Ministers and the Foreign Ministers of the two countries discussed the issue with their counterparts, all expressing their abhorrence at the attacks. On 30 May, Indian film star Amitabh Bachchan announced he would turn down an honorary doctorate from the Queensland University of Technology that he had previously agreed to accept. On 6 June, Bollywood's largest union, the Federation of Western India Cine Employees called on its members to stop filming in Australia. This came after a string of big-budget Bollywood films had been filmed and set in Australia in recent years.

A major incident in early June 2009 in Sydney highlighted the complexity of the racial issues. Indian students staged large protests in a low-income neighbourhood where, in recent years, Indians have surpassed Lebanese as the largest ethnic group. The protests were sparked by an attack on an Indian student by a group of young men of Middle Eastern background. Indian students claimed that the police were not doing enough to protect them from Lebanese gangs. Indian protesters attacked three uninvolved Lebanese men and police brought in the reinforcements to control the crowd.

But why Indian students? Over 600,000 international students studied in Australia in the 2009 academic year, but Indian students who make up around one sixth of the total seemed to be over-represented as targets of violent assaults, and particularly Indian students studying in vocational programmes in private colleges. The students who were attracted to such programmes were usually from less affluent backgrounds, and with lower levels of English language proficiency, compared with those who studied in more expensive and selective university programmes (Baas, 2006; Singh & Cabraal, 2010). In India, students were able to obtain loans with which they could meet the financial means test to obtain a student visa to Australia, but then were understandably reluctant to draw down on those loans, and instead sought to earn enough in Australia to pay their tuition fees and living expenses. Compared with other international students in Australia, students from India were to be more dependent upon income from shift work, such as driving taxis, stacking supermarket shelves, and working in convenience stores and as security guards. Being less affluent, they were more likely to be living in outer suburbs with cheaper housing, and therefore travelling late on trains more often, and in areas where street violence is more common. Gender is an issue too, as assaults against strangers on and around public transport are generally perpetrated by young men on other young men; the vast majority of Indian students are male, whereas East and South East Asian students are evenly split by gender.

The Australian government responded by stepping up policing in dangerous areas of capital cities such as around suburban train stations. But the government also changed the permanent residency application process, making it much more difficult for students in vocational programmes to remain permanently, and as a result new applications for such programmes ceased very quickly. The financial means tests for low-income countries were made much more stringent, as were checks for fraudulent documentation during the visa application process, particularly in South Asia.

Indian media attention also deterred many Indian students from studying in Australia. Throughout 2009 the Indian media remained hyper-sensitive to any news from Australia involving harm to Indian nationals, but in 2010 a series of murders of Indian nationals committed by their compatriots in Australia changed the tone of media reporting dramatically. Matters came to a head with the high-profile case of the tragic death in early 2010 of an Indian toddler living in Melbourne. Before the culprit was found, some Indian media outlets decried this as a yet more brutal racist atrocity, providing airtime to Right-wing nationalist politicians, and predicting anti-Australian riots and the downgrading of diplomatic relations between the two countries. When an Indian national was apprehended by police and confessed to the crime, much of the heat went out of the anti-Australian hysteria.

Conclusion

Approaches to student migration are characterized by unstable policies, vulnerable to swings in political mood, swayed by the competing influences of employer demands for skilled labour and anti-immigration arguments. They have had mixed success in meeting their stated goals. Looking back over the past decade, a pattern is evident in which enrolments surge in those programmes that provide the cheapest and shortest pathway to permanent residency. Educational institutions then expand those programmes to meet booming demand. This leads within a few years to an oversupply of skilled migrants with particular qualifications, and immigration authorities respond by closing down those pathways. Student demand shifts quickly into the next best migration pathway and the cycle repeats.

However, despite the frequent changes, some features appear to be rather consistent. A significant proportion of students continues to attracted to the possibility of remaining in the host country after graduation and, one way or another, many manage to stay on. It is now well understood that those countries that are able to provide such opportunities have an advantage in recruiting students, and so we expect to see more experimentation in such policies in those countries that are most determined to increase numbers of incoming degree students.

References

AEI. (2013). International student data. Retrieved 14 January 2012, from www. austrade.gov.au/Export/Export-Markets/Industries/Education/International-Student-Data

Baas, M. (2006). Students of migration: Indian overseas students and the question of permanent residency. *People and Place, 14*(1), 9–24.

BBC. (2010). Student immigration levels unsustainable, says minister. www.bbc. co.uk/news/uk-politics-11191341

Birrell, B. (2006). Implications of low English standards among overseas students at Australian universities. *People and Place, 14*(4), 53–64.

Birrell, B., & Hawthorne, L. (1999). Skilled migration outcomes as of 1996. In *Review of the Independent and Skilled-Australian Linked Categories.* Canberra: Australian Government Department of Immigration, Multicultural and Aboriginal Affairs.

Christofi, V., & Thompson, C. L. (2007). You cannot go home again: A phenomenological investigation of returning to the sojourn country after studying abroad. *Journal of Counseling and Development, 85,* 53–63.

CPE. (2013). *A Quality-Driven Private Higher Education Sector: Council for Private Education Annual Report 2012–2013.* Singapore: Council for Private Education.

DAAD. (2012). 2011 *Annual Report.* Bonn: Deutscher Akademischer Austausch Dienst.

Daquila, T. C. (2013). Internationalising higher education in Singapore: Government policies and the NUS experience. *Journal of Studies in International Education.* doi: 10.1177/1028315313499232

Davie, S. (2008, 14 December). There are many paths to the top. *The Straits Times.* Retrieved from http://news.asiaone.com/News/Education/Story/A1Story20081211-107115.html

Guardian (2011, 1 February). Crackdown on student visas will curb 'unpleasant' abuses, says minister.

Hawthorne, L. (2005). "Picking winners": The recent transformation of Australia's skill migration policy. *International Migration Review, 39*(3), 663–696.

Hodge, A., & Clayfield, M. (2009, 30 May). Delhi carpets our man over attacks. *The Australian.* Retrieved from www.theaustralian.news.com.au/story/0,25197,25558985-25837,00.html

House of Lords Select Committee on Economic Affairs. (2008a). *1st Report of Session 2007–08. The Economic Impact of Immigration. Volume I: Report.* London: The Stationery Office Limited.

House of Lords Select Committee on Economic Affairs. (2008b). *1st Report of Session 2007–08. The Economic Impact of Immigration. Volume II: Evidence.* London: The Stationery Office Limited.

Johnston, C. (2009, 16 May). Scarred, scared and wanting to go home. *The Age.* Retrieved from www.theage.com.au/national/scarred-scared-and-wanting-to-go-home-20090515-b64p.html

Knight, M. (2011). *Strategic Review of the Student Visa Program 2011 Report.* Canberra: Government of Australia.

Koh, A. (2003). Global flows of foreign talent: Identity anxieties in Singapore's ethnoscape. *Sojourn, 18*(2), 230–256.

Koh, A. (2012). Tactics of interventions: Student mobility and human capital building in Singapore. *Higher Education Policy, 25*(2), 191–206. doi: 10.1057/hep.2012.5.

Lawton, W. (2011, 20 April). Political pendulum: Shifting attitudes on international students and immigration. *Borderless Report,* pp. 2–4.

Ng, J. (2008). MM Lee says Singapore facing brain drain problem. Retrieved July 24, 2009, from www.channelnewsasia.com

Ng, P. T. (2013). The global war for talent: responses and challenges in the Singapore higher education system. *Journal of Higher Education Policy and Management, 35*(3), 280–292. doi: 10.1080/1360080x.2013.786859

Ockenden, W. (2013). Immigration Department audits reveal large-scale fraud of visa system by Indian students and workers. Australian Broadcasting Corporation. Retrieved from http://www.abc.net.au/news/2013-07-22/immigration-audits-reveal-large-scale-visa-fraud/4833710

OECD. (2009). *International Migration Outlook.* Paris: OECD Publishing.

OECD. (2011). *Education at a Glance 2011: OECD Indicators.* Paris: OECD Publishing.

Ong, A. (2007). Please stay: Pied-a-terre subjects in the megacity. *Citizenship Studies, 11*(1), 83–93.

Overland, M. (2007, 13 December). British stem-cell scientist is latest prominent researcher to leave Singapore. *The Chronicle of Higher Education.* Retrieved from http://chronicle.com/article/British-Stem-Cell-Scientist-Is/40141/

Reiner, C. (2010). Brain competition policy as a new paradigm of regional policy: A European perspective. *Papers in Regional Science, 89*(2), 449–461. doi: 10.1111/j.1435-5957.2010.00298.x.

Robertson, S. (2013). *Transnational Student-Migrants and the State: The Education-Migration Nexus.* Basingstoke, UK: Palgrave MacMillan.

Robertson, S., & Runganaikaloo, A. (2013). Lives in limbo: Migration experiences in Australia's education-migration nexus. *Ethnicities, 14*(2), 208–226.

Shachar, A. (2006). Competition for skilled migrants. *New York University Law Review, 81*, 148–206.

Singapore Government. (2013). *A Sustainable Population for a Dynamic Singapore: Population White Paper*. Singapore: Singapore Government National Population and Talent Division.

Singh, S., & Cabraal, A. (2010). Indian student migrants in Australia: Issues of community sustainability. *People and Place, 18*(1), 19–30.

Tan, E. (2011). Singapore: New 'cap' on foreign students. *University World News* (185).

Travis, A. (2010, 7 December). Government confirms plans to curb international student numbers. *The Guardian*.

Travis, A. (2011, 23 March). Visa curbs will cut overseas students by 80,000, says Theresa May. *The Guardian*.

Wildavsky, B. (2010). *The Great Brain Race: How Global Universities Are Reshaping the World*. Princeton, NJ: Princeton University Press.

Ziguras, C. (2012). Learning the hard way: Lessons from Australia's decade of innovation in student migration policy. In D. Neubauer & K. Kuroda (Eds.), *Mobility and Migration in Asian Pacific Higher Education* (pp. 39–52). New York: Palgrave Macmillan.

Ziguras, C., & Law, S. F. (2006). Recruiting international students as skilled migrants: the global 'skills race' as viewed from Australia and Malaysia. *Globalisation, Societies and Education, 4*(1), 59–76.

Chapter 5

Outgoing student migration
Steering the circulation of brains

For as long as students have travelled abroad to study, some have chosen not to return home. In this chapter we consider three questions concerning the approach of governments in countries which face an outflow of international students, a proportion of whom will not return home. First, what factors influence the proportion of international students who do not return to their home countries? Second, when and why does the non-return of international students come to constitute a policy problem warranting the attention of government? Third, if governments are concerned, what policy options are available to them and what are the factors that influence the particular approach they adopt?

While we have some data, discussed in the previous chapter, on the stay rates of international students in host countries, very few sending countries collect data on the departure and return of students. Another challenge is the extended time-frame involved. While students may eventually return to their home country, before that they may spend years or decades abroad, either in the country in which they have studied or in another location altogether.

The problem of student migration has for decades been framed within broader conceptualizations of 'brain drain' and 'brain circulation' (Gaillard & Gaillard, 1997). While in recent years these concepts have been applied mainly to mobility from the global south to the global north, the British Royal Society is credited with coining the term 'brain drain' to refer to the outflow of scientists from Europe to the USA and Canada in the 1950s and 1960s (Cervantes & Guellec, 2002). Later, the term was taken up much more broadly to describe the widespread flow of skilled migrants from low-income to high-income countries. Many developing countries that were experiencing a serious outflow of skilled people launched scathing critiques of the continuing exploitation of poor countries by rich countries through the poaching of human resources, just as in the colonial era they had poached natural resources.

It is often suggested that high levels of international student mobility can have negative consequences because sending countries inevitably lose the highly educated who play a vital role in ensuring innovation, building institutions and implementing programmes (Egron-Polak, 2004; Kapur & McHale, 2005). The International Association of Universities has recently stated that brain drain arising from the internationalization of education risks 'undermining the capacity of developing countries and their institutions to retain the talent needed for their prosperity, cultural advancement, and social well-being' (IAU, 2012, p. 3). At a recent Boston College symposium to honour his influential career, Philip Altbach told *Times Higher Education* that the growth of student mobility had fuelled a brain drain in which 'the developing and emerging economies are subsidizing the rich countries by educating many through the bachelor's degree and then losing them' (quoted in Matthews, 2013). Such remarks are often heard in forums in which international educators gather, particularly those held in the North East of the United States and the North West of Europe. Echoing decades of anti-imperialist critiques informed by dependency theory, the global trade in education is denounced for exacerbating inequalities by exploiting students' desire for a better life. Education-exporting countries are seen to be extracting both wealth and brains from the 'global south'. This view was once widely held in developing countries but as we show in this chapter, much has changed.

This is a well-meaning expression of solidarity from the political Left, but it implies that sending countries would be better off if their students were studying at home or, if they do undertake degrees abroad, returned home upon graduating. We are sceptical of such abstracted claims that student migration is inherently detrimental, and converse claims (though rarer) that student emigration is necessarily beneficial. There are several problems with such claims. First is the question of who we should be concerned about – the home country (which is the unit of analysis favoured by brain drain critics), the student's family (which is often the locus for decision-making), the individual student (who liberals are concerned with), the host country (which immigration policy cares about), or a transnational value such as scientific progress or European integration (which are strengthened by mobility). Clearly there are many different interests involved, and the costs and benefits for each are difficult to disentangle. In Chapter 4 we considered the views and policies of governments in education exporting countries, while in this chapter we examine the views and policies of governments in importing countries. We are interested in how they perceive the costs and benefits, and in how they endeavour to steer their students' migratory pathways.

The second problem with abstract claims about brain drain is the question of what constitutes a cost or a benefit. There have been many econometric attempts to quantify national gains and losses to sending countries from skilled emigration, but such efforts invariably smooth over the complexity, diversity and temporality of mobility to the point that such numbers become meaningless.

We examine in this chapter the particular priorities of seven quite different sending countries – China, Greece, India, Malaysia, Singapore, Timor-Leste and Vietnam. Each of these faces a unique set of challenges and has interpreted the actual and potential positive and negative effects of outmigration of mobile students in its own way. There are a range of questions about benefits that governments in education importing countries commonly ask. Is there labour market demand for the skills that returning graduates possess? Is the non-return of particular types of graduates hampering progress towards specific development objectives? Will students who stay abroad contribute to the flow of remittances, or to growth in trade and investment? Is it better for graduates to work abroad before returning to gain professional experience and repay the cost of their studies? How can we capitalize on the presence of highly qualified expatriates to further diplomatic goals or to deepen important social and cultural relationships? The consequences of student emigration are by no means straightforward, and rather than attempt to judge from afar, we are interested in the ways in which governments arrive at evaluations that influence policy, and this is the focus of the first half of the chapter.

The second half of the chapter examines a range of policies that governments have put in place to shape outflows of students. On the other side of the political spectrum from critics of brain drain are liberals who argue that home country governments should support the choices made by students rather than trying to control where and how they should live and work. After all, they would argue, the principle of freedom of movement is enshrined in the United Nations Universal Declaration of Human Rights, which states that 'Everyone has the right to leave any country, including his own, and to return to his country.' What business does a government have to force its citizens to study at home rather than abroad, or to return home upon completion of studies? Sceptical of initiatives that seek to restrict freedom of movement of students in the belief that it is in the public interest for that student to study, reside or work in a particular place, liberal proponents of student mobility advocate for the right of individual students to make decisions that suit their own interests without interference by government. An article in NAFSA's *International Educator* magazine expresses this view well:

> There is nothing wrong – and indeed much that is positive – with international students voluntarily choosing to return to their home country after earning a degree in the United States. But there is also nothing wrong with such individuals deciding to stay in America if they can make a positive contribution and achieve gainful employment. The reality is that those international students who desire to leave their home – the most ambitious – will go to other countries if they are not allowed to stay in the United States. Rather than attempting to choose for an individual whether or not they would be 'better off' in their home country, the United States should err on the side of freedom.
>
> (Anderson, 2010, p. 7)

We are sympathetic to the notion of maximizing the freedom of mobility, but it is fanciful to pretend that states are not involved in regulating mobility. While NAFSA may want the United States to 'err on the side of freedom', any foreigner who has ever visited that country will know that its border controls and immigration practices are intended to tightly regulate who may enter, and how, rather than promoting 'freedom' of movement. While the governments that we consider in this chapter have over time become more liberal in the way they deal with outgoing students and migrants, they think strategically about how to influence mobility in ways that generate benefits for the home country.

When does student emigration become a policy problem?

Aggregate global trends of the proportion of students who stay on in the host country after graduation mask considerable variability within the student population, with students from some countries much more likely to stay on than students from others. We would expect that the greater the income differential between home and host country, the higher the level of migration, so students from less developed countries would have a lower return rate. In neoclassical economic terms, the return on a privately funded student's investment in their education is much higher if they gain employment in affluent countries. This 'wage-pull' is a major factor in explaining migration rates in OECD counties (Lowell, 2009). Applied to education, it suggests that the bigger the income difference the greater the incentive to stay on rather than returning home. Data on rates of migration of former international students from different countries that could be used to test this hypothesis is difficult to come by. In one of the few studies to explore this relationship, Birrell (2006) estimated the proportion of the 42,295 graduating international students who had been granted permanent residency in Australia in one year. When one considers the percentage from each country who obtain permanent residency (see Table 4.1), it appears (from this limited data set) that students from low-income countries tend to have higher rates of stay than students from high-income countries. However, even among low-income countries there are significant variances. One stark pattern here is the difference between low-income countries in South Asia, with student migration rates between 70 and 80 per cent, compared with low-income countries in East Asia with migration rates between 35 and 45 per cent.

This can be explained by income disparities. While low-income countries might tend to have a higher proportion of outbound students that do not return, there are several factors that cause student emigration to be less likely to pose a serious policy concern for governments. The notion of the 'migration hump' has long been used to describe the tendency of low-income and high-income economies to have lower rates of outward skilled migration than middle-income economies. This is because people in middle-income countries have access to the levels of education, skills and experience that enable migration to high-income countries. In a nutshell, people in lower-income countries lack the resources to migrate and those in high-income countries lack the motivation (Martin & Taylor, 1996). The same is true of student migration, for several reasons.

Students in high-income countries usually have access to quality education options at home and therefore low rates of degree mobility. Some graduates may live and work abroad but not in significant number to be of any concern, and the skills that they possess are rarely in short supply in the home country. In most low-income and lower-middle-income countries, overseas study is limited to a small proportion of the population, comprising scholarship students and a wealthy elite able to privately fund a foreign education. Most low-income countries have less than one in every 200 students of tertiary age studying overseas, that is a Gross Outbound Enrolment Ratio below 0.5 per cent, including countries as diverse as India, Indonesia, Papua New Guinea, El Salvador and most of Africa (UNESCO, 2012a). These countries understandably tend to be much more concerned about the plight of the more than 99.5 per cent of the tertiary age population that stays at home than those few who study abroad.

Of the mobile degree students from low-income and lower-middle-income countries, we need to distinguish between some very different patterns. Concerns about student brain drain usually focus on self-funded students travelling to high-income countries in which students seek to work after graduation. As the data in Table 5.1 shows, students from low-income countries are more motivated to stay. However, there is a large proportion of students from low-income countries that do not fit this profile. First, some of the students who go to high-income countries are on scholarships that require them to return after graduation. Second, South–South mobility is surprisingly common, allowing students in low-income and lower-middle-income economies to access educational opportunities in affordable countries (often neighbours) that have more developed educational systems. For example, Malaysia, South Africa and Jordan are upper-middle-income economies that are significant destinations for students from lower-income countries. These destinations tend not to have active programmes to recruit international students as permanent migrants, and those who do stay on after graduation are unlikely to settle permanently. Where there is a concern about brain drain in low-income countries, this often concerns students who have been educated at home and then use their qualifications to leave rather than self-funded international students. To illustrate the context in which student emigration occurs in low-income countries, consider the cases of Timor-Leste and Vietnam.

Table 5.1 Outbound student mobility and emigration rates

	Outbound mobility ratio (% of tertiary students abroad)	Gross outbound enrolment ratio (% of age cohort studying abroad)	Stock of emigrants as % of population	Emigration rate of tertiary-educated population (%)
India	1.0	0.2	0.9	4.3
China	1.8	0.5	0.6	3.8
Vietnam	2.4	0.5	2.5	27.1
Greece	5.0	5.0	10.8	12.0
Malaysia	5.5	2.2	5.5	11.1
Singapore	9.4	na	6.1	15.2
Timor-Leste	20.2	3.4	1.4	15.5

Sources: Ratha, Mohapatra, & Silwal (2011); UNESCO (2012a, 2013).

Scholarships and South–South mobility: the case of Timor-Leste

The situation in Timor-Leste, one of the world's newest countries, starkly illustrates the challenges faced by many low-income and lower-middle-income economies. Until 1986 there were no tertiary education institutions in Timor-Leste, so students wishing to study at a tertiary level were required to travel. Under the period of Portuguese colonial administration to 1975, a few students studied in Portugal, but during the period of Indonesian occupation between 1975 and 1999 a growing number of Timor-Leste students travelled to key Indonesian educational centres, particularly Jogjakarta, to attend universities. Jones (2003) notes that a high proportion of students did not return to Timor-Leste because the employment prospects for indigenous Timorese graduates was poor. Instead, many remained on in Indonesia if they could find work. During the period of Indonesian occupation, there was a very different flow to other countries, with 20,000 people relocated to Australia, 10,000 to Portugal and smaller numbers to other countries, many of whom were opposed to Indonesian rule (Wise, 2004).

Since Independence in 2002 the prevalence of mobility has continued. Although Indonesian is no longer the language of instruction in schools, and students now require a visa to study in Indonesia, still around three-quarters of outbound international students are studying in Indonesia (UNESCO, 2013). The vast majority of these students are privately funded. While there is no available data on return rates of overseas students, it is likely that more of the students who study in Indonesia now return to Timor-Leste, as employment prospects improve due to the withdrawal of the largely Indonesian bureaucratic class after independence and recent economic growth. Those who travel to other destinations are almost exclusively funded by scholarships, including Cuba, which receives 19 per cent of students, and much smaller numbers of students to Saudi Arabia, Australia, Portugal, the United States and others. These scholarship-funded students are usually bound to return to Timor-Leste. It is striking that over 90 per cent of outbound students are studying in other middle-income economies.

After independence in 2002, Portugal provided scholarships to Timor-Leste students, but it soon became apparent that students were having difficulty learning the language, following course content and adjusting to the culture. After some Timorese students absconded from their courses and sought work elsewhere in Europe, the Timor-Leste government asked Portugal to redirect its funding support into the local higher education sector in Timor-Leste, predominantly through the Universidade Nacional Timor Lorosa'e (National University of East Timor). Meanwhile, the primary focus of the Timor-Leste Government has been to ensure access to basic education since at that time over half the adult population had little or no schooling (SEAMEO, 2006). The biggest aid donors, Portugal and Australia, provide significantly more aid to building basic education and training capacity in country than they do in scholarships for university students.

With economic growth and increased rates of secondary school completion, demand for higher education often increases faster than the capacity of the domestic higher education system, resulting in growth in outbound mobility. But even in periods of rapid growth in outbound mobility in middle-income countries, international student emigration rarely appears to be characterized as a policy problem. The case of Vietnam illustrates the circumstances in which student migration arising from increased outbound mobility can be elevated onto the political agenda.

Growing concern in Vietnam

Through the twentieth century a small but steady stream of Vietnamese students have studied abroad, their destinations determined by the politics of the time. The father of national liberation Ho Chi Minh, after attending a French-style secondary school travelled to France and applied unsuccessfully to study at the French Colonial Administrative School. After travelling and working for several years in Europe and the United States, he received his formative political education through the French Communist Party in Paris.

During the Cold War the destinations of students from the South and the North of Vietnam diverged markedly. Between 1950 and 1975 South Vietnam was the third-largest source country for Australian government-sponsored students, after Indonesia and Malaysia, reflecting Cold War alignment of the South with the West (Cleverley & Jones, 1976, pp. 26–29). From the North, students instead headed to the Soviet Union and Eastern Europe in large numbers, supported by similar government-to-government programmes designed to build solidarity across the socialist bloc. Between 1951 and 1989, former socialist countries reportedly helped train over 30,000 Vietnamese undergraduates, 13,500 postgraduates, 25,000 technicians and thousands of other scientists (Kelly, 2000).

While in the past, Vietnamese overseas students were government funded, since the 1990s the vast majority of Vietnamese students studying abroad have been privately funded, but overseas undergraduate study is an option only for the wealthiest students. According to UNESCO, in 2011, there were 47,639 students from Vietnam studying abroad in programmes of one year or longer, up markedly from 9,843 a decade earlier (UNESCO, 2012b). The Ministry of Education and Training publishes occasional reports on the number of Vietnamese students abroad based on data sourced from receiving countries, and most recently has estimated that around 100,000 Vietnamese students are studying overseas (Dân Trí Việt Nam, 2012). This higher number includes students studying in China and Singapore, who are not reported in UNESCO data, and students in postsecondary sub-degree programmes (certificates, diplomas, etc.) which are not included in the UNESCO data.

Until recently, the Vietnamese government appeared unconcerned about outbound student migration. Recipients of government scholarships almost always return to Vietnam since those who fail to return, or their families, are forced to repay the funding they have received (Welch, 2010). In the mid-2000s, we heard a common understanding of student migration expounded by Ministry of Education and Training officials, education officials working with foreign governments, student recruitment agents, employer groups and alumni associations. All were aware that many, and perhaps most, privately funded students remain abroad after graduation both to gain professional experience and to earn a financial return on their investment in an overseas qualification. Their common view was that with such a young population and a growing number of graduates of local universities, there was no shortage of skills and so this outflow of skilled young people did not constitute a problem. The Gross Outbound Mobility Ratio at the time was less than 0.5 per cent. When the opportunity arose for those young people to find jobs back in Vietnam they would return. Remittances sent by overseas Vietnamese constituted a significant source of foreign income. In 2008, remittances were estimated at US$8 billion and growing rapidly (World Bank, 2014). Vietnam's looming accession to the WTO in January 2007 was expected to increase foreign direct investment and trade growth, resulting in significant employment growth in key industries such as banking (John, 2007). Such jobs might lure back overseas-educated Vietnamese, but they now face stiff competition from the growing pool of unemployed graduates of local universities (H. Pham, 2013b).

In 2008, the deficiencies of the higher education system were elevated into the public spotlight by an examination held by Intel to recruit staff for its new plant outside Ho Chi Minh City, which was at the time the largest ever foreign investment in Vietnam. There were more than 2,000 Vietnamese applicants. Only 8.5 per cent passed the exam, forcing Intel to recruit staff from overseas. The skills shortage is not limited to the information technology sector, with professions such as law, engineering and architecture also reporting a shortage of qualified staff (Szabo, 2008). One effect of the widely reported story was to focus the government's attention on the need to internationalize and modernize the higher education system. A second consequence was to focus attention on the skills shortages that threatened to slow the rate of economic development. It suggested that Vietnam may well be able to absorb returning overseas trained students more quickly than had earlier been anticipated. There has since been much more discussion of brain drain in Vietnam, and the government appears to be concerned about the perceived low rate of return of self-funded students (Gribble, 2011). In late 2009 the Ministry of Education and Training issued a draft regulation that appeared to propose to extend government control over self-funded outbound students (VietNamNet, 2009a, 2009b). As of January 2013 all Vietnamese students studying overseas are expected to register in an online system operated by the Ministry of Education and Training which promises to facilitate data collection and communication with overseas students (Socialist Republic of Vietnam, 2013).

The rise and fall of concern about brain drain in Greece, Malaysia, China and Singapore

Greece has long had a high rate of outward student mobility compared with other countries at its level of economic development and a high proportion of tertiary educated population living abroad. Most Greek students abroad study in the EU, with around 40 per cent in the UK alone and smaller numbers in Italy, Germany and France. With the current debt crisis brain drain has become a high-profile issue in Greece, as many highly qualified Greeks seek better opportunities in countries less affected by austerity and those who have foreign qualifications and connections will find it easier to leave. Before the crisis, the non-return of international students was an issue for students and their families but not high on the agenda of government. Students who study abroad tend to return quite often to Greece and keep in close contact with their friends and family and most would like to return to Greece. However, the process for having foreign qualifications recognized in Greece has long been bureaucratic, cumbersome and slow. Finding graduate positions back in Greece, even before the current crisis, often takes time and is reliant on cultivating personal and professional relationships that eventually lead to ongoing employment. For both these reasons, it has been common for many graduates to work abroad for several years while waiting until they can arrange work back in Greece. Despite occasional public statements of officials lamenting the loss of skills, government has not put in place any measures in response. Glytsos (2006) has noted that, 'Unfortunately, no practical effective policies accompany this wishful thinking for motivating the return of the educated Greeks from abroad' (p. 13).

Malaysia, too, has a long history of international student mobility but little government interest in the emigration of international students. From the 1950s when many Malaysian students went abroad under schemes such as the Colombo Plan, the majority of Malaysian students studying abroad were sponsored by either Malaysian or foreign governments, but strong economic growth led to greater numbers of privately funded students. While in 1962 there were 5,524 Malaysian students abroad (Guruz, 2008), this had grown steadily to 54,112 by 1998. Then, due to the effects of the Asian Financial Crisis the number of outgoing students declined sharply, dropping by over one-quarter to 39,420 within three years. Numbers have grown slowly since then to return in recent years to the same level as the pre-crisis peak (UNESCO, 2013). During the mid-1990s, Malaysia was concerned about the number of students studying abroad, not because they might not return but because of the currency outflow this was causing. In 1995, the 20 per cent of Malaysian students who were studying abroad reportedly cost the country around US$800 million in currency outflow, constituting nearly 12 per cent of Malaysia's current account deficit (Silverman, 1996). In response, during the 1990s the government fostered the growth the fledgling private higher education sector, through better regulation, quality assurance and allowing branch campuses of foreign universities. When the financial crisis hit, these institutions were able to significantly increase enrolments of students who would otherwise have gone abroad.

So why was Malaysia concerned about currency leaving the country but not young people? Malaysia's policy of affirmative action for the majority Malay population, introduced in 1971, limited the number of places for non-Malays at public universities, and resulted in many Chinese and Indian students studying abroad. In 1980, according to Silverman (1996), 19,515 Malaysian students were studying abroad, only slightly less than the 20,045 studying in local universities. Three-quarters of the outbound students were non-Bumiputera (60.5 per cent ethnic Chinese, 15.9 per cent ethnic Indian).

As well as allowing for easier entry to public universities for Bumiputera (Malay and indigenous) students, affirmative action policies reserve most government jobs for Bumiputera graduates. While some Chinese and Indian students return to Malaysia, mostly to work in the private sector, many choose to remain abroad because of limited opportunities at home. The World Bank estimates that 11.1 per cent of Malaysian graduates reside outside the country, which is a significant proportion, but very few of these are ethnic Malays, who nearly always return to Malaysia where they have excellent career prospects. Until recently the government, which is committed to maintain race-based economic and employment policies, has not appeared too concerned about this outflow, apart from an unsuccessful attempt to lure back highly skilled individuals to the biotechnology sector in the 1990s. Since the mid-2000s, however, as we will discuss below, the government has begun to actively encourage graduating students to return.

The Chinese government has been more concerned about the non-return of students, but the outflow does not appear to have hampered China's development. While in 1960 there were just 119 Chinese students abroad, by 1978 the number had risen to more than 20,000 as the country began to relax its border controls. Today China is the world's largest source country for international students, with over half a million students undertaking degree studies overseas. While continuing to recognize the benefits associated with overseas study, the non-return of overseas Chinese students has been of concern to the Chinese government since it became apparent that many students were choosing to remain in the host country. Between 1978 and 1992 the government's emphasis was on sending students abroad and inviting foreign scholars to China, but in 1993 there was a shift in Chinese government policy, placing greater emphasis on encouraging overseas Chinese students and scholars to return home as well as a push to attract foreign students and internationalize curricula (Guruz, 2008). According to the Chinese Ministry of Education, a total of 1.07 million state-funded and self-funded students have studied between 1978 and 2006, however, only 275,000 had returned (Watts, 2007). While these appear to be large and worrying numbers, they represent a tiny percentage of the Chinese population. Of all the countries discussed in this chapter, China has the smallest percentage of both citizens and graduates abroad, and of this group only India has a smaller proportion of students abroad. As we will see later in the chapter, the Chinese government has not sought to restrict outbound mobility but has implemented programmes to support the return of specific types of graduates, particularly academics and researchers, motivated by the need to build domestic capacity in higher education and research and development. Over time, China's booming economy and public investment in universities has lured back many former international students, and in recent years the economic downturn in most destinations countries has provided additional incentive for Chinese graduates to return home.

Of all the countries we consider in this chapter, it is in Singapore that student migration has been of most significance as a policy issue. Despite a strong economy, quality educational institutions, state-of-the-art research and development facilities and a high standard of living, Singapore has grappled with the problem of how to retain students and encourage those who do go abroad to return. Concern about an international student brain drain emerged in the late 1990s when it became apparent that some top Singaporean students on government scholarships at prestigious foreign institutions were not returning home upon graduation. The decision by the then Chairman of the Economic Development Board (a central and strategic government agency) to publicly name, and thereby shame, holders of government scholarships who broke their bonds led to much public debate. The ensuing discussion centred around whether those who received government scholarships are morally obligated to return home and contribute to nation building or whether the scholarship is merely a contractual agreement which could be broken in return for the stated penalties (Hussain, 2008). The issue emerged again in 2002 after Prime Minister Goh Chok Tong in his National Day rally speech referred to two categories of Singaporeans, 'stayers' and 'quitters'. 'Stayers' were described as those Singaporean who were 'rooted to Singapore' whereas 'quitters' were 'fair-weather Singaporeans' (Tan, 2008). It is not unusual for speeches by senior Singapore government officials to call for loyalty to the nation in the face of external challenges to island state, but the emotive and pejorative language used to denigrate overseas Singaporeans was clearly shocking to many. As Koh (2012) notes, official concern about Singapore's demographic vulnerabilities have aired prominently for some time, and has been centred on the challenge of meeting the human resource needs of the country's economic development strategy, particularly in the face of a consistently low birthrate.

While there is no official data on the return rates of Singaporean students, there are various estimates. Senior Minister Goh Chok Tong in 2009 presented figures stating that more than 20 per cent of the top students who graduated with A levels between 1996 and 1999 were working in Singapore a decade later. Of those who had studied at universities overseas without a scholarship bond, more than 33 per cent were living abroad. According to one report about half of recent Singaporean graduates from US Ivy League colleges, and the majority of those attending the world's best business schools choose to work overseas (Singapore Overseas Network, 2002a). Another survey revealed that 79 per cent of 153 Singaporean undergraduates at 15 top US universities would prefer to work in the United States after they graduate (AsiaOne, 2009).

According to the most recently available data, presented in Table 5.1, there are 297,234 Singaporeans living abroad, equal to 6.1 per cent of the country's population. However, a much higher proportion, 15.2 per cent, of Singapore's tertiary educated population is living abroad (Ratha, Mohapatra & Silwal, 2011). In other words, Singaporeans with a degree are 2.5 times more likely to be living abroad than Singaporeans without a degree. This group includes both former international students, and those who have studied in Singapore and then migrated. The ex-Prime Minister Lee Kuan Yew in 1998 worried publicly that the country is 'losing about four to five percent of the top 30 percent' of its population every year, resulting in a 'pretty serious brain drain problem' (J. Ng, 2008).

The government stresses the importance of skilled young people for several reasons. The Deputy Prime Minister in a 2010 speech on population argued that a continuing downward demographic trend would have dire economic and social consequences: 'With fewer young people, our workforce and society will lose our vitality and vibrancy. This will mean that Singapore will become less attractive to foreign investors' (Wong, 2010, p. 7). The knock-on effect of a devitalized economy would be further loss of bright young people to greener pastures: 'Our own young talented Singaporeans may leave our shores for better opportunities in more dynamic economies' (p. 7). Furthermore, he noted, the survival of the nation is at stake since, 'With fewer young Singaporeans, we will face grave challenges to maintain the strength and efficacy of our citizen armed forces, security and law enforcement agencies' (p. 7). As we will see in the second half of this chapter, Singapore has implemented a wide range of strategies to address these concerns.

Policy responses to student emigration

There is a range of measures that sending countries can adopt to address concerns about student emigration. Some of these are responses to skilled emigration generally, which have been well documented (Lowell, 2001; Meyer, 2003; Wickramasekara, 2003). There are three broad approaches (Gribble, 2008). First, 'retention' polices are designed to create conditions and opportunities in the home county that will deter the highly skilled emigrating in the first place. Second, 'return' policies aim to encourage those that have gone abroad to return and contribute to their home country. The third approach is variously described as 'diaspora', 'network' or 'engagement', the intention of which is to ensure that overseas skilled professionals contribute to the home country from afar. While the measures adopted by countries wishing to regulate the flow of students differ from those used to manage the movement of skilled labour, the broad categories are useful when organizing the range of measures used to manage international student migration.

Here, we adopt Lowell's (2001) classificatory framework, adapting it slightly for the purposes of analysing student emigration policies rather than skilled emigration generally:

- *Restriction of international mobility of students.* In the past, some countries used restrictive emigration policies to prevent students from travelling freely, either by restricting access to passports, exit visas or foreign currency. This strategy has been discussed in Chapter 4. In the past, prevention of emigration, particularly from socialist states, was a primary rationale for restriction of student mobility, but such policies are very rarely used today.

- *Retention though educational development.* The outflow of students may be reduced by strengthening and expanding domestic educational institutions. Students who study in the home country are much less likely to emigrate than those who have studied overseas. This strategy has been discussed in Chapter 4. In the countries we have considered in detail, the expansion of domestic supply has had an appreciable impact on outbound student numbers, and therefore on the outmigration of students.

- *Return of students to their source country.* The return of students soon after completion of their studies abroad, or after several years of professional experience abroad, is a means of harnessing overseas graduates' human capital for the domestic economy. We discuss this strategy in detail below.

- *Reparation for loss of human capital.* The destination country compensates the source country, or former students are required to pay taxes to their home country. We are not aware of such policies being adopted in relation to student emigration.

- *Engagement with the diaspora.* Former international students living abroad can be harnessed as a resource for the home country, by encouraging ongoing engagement through communication, travel, knowledge transfer, remittances and investment. We discuss this strategy in detail below.

- *Recruitment of international migrants.* Domestic shortages of skilled workers could be filled by nationals of another country rather than by emigrating students. Skilled workers can be recruited directly by firms, or incoming international students could be offered post-study residency and work rights. This strategy is discussed in detail below.

Return of students to their home country

While the expansion of access to degree programmes described in Chapter 5 clearly has an impact on the number of outgoing students, nevertheless many students will continue to choose to study overseas. Some young people are keen to emigrate, and pursue overseas study for that reason. For example, a recent survey of over 2,000 Singaporeans between the ages of 19 and 30 found that over a quarter agreed that they would 'actively examine the possibility of emigrating to another country within the next 5 years', with those who were more highly educated and who spoke English at home more likely to aspire to living abroad (Leong & Soon, 2011). Others seek professional experience abroad after graduation, which may improve their career prospects back home as well as providing an opportunity to stay in the host country for some time. However, we should not assume that students' life choices are so clear-cut. As Robertson, Hoare and Harwood (2011) have shown, the transition from study to work is a complex one for students in international education, involving the negotiation of family relationships, residency requirements, employment options and a wide range of personal aspirations. Students often have very little knowledge of what life may have in store for them after graduation, and even after the completion of studies, graduates are often tentatively exploring a range of opportunities for some time before committing to a particular place or career.

High-performing students who receive government or company scholarships from their home country to study in elite universities will continue to gratefully grasp those opportunities as long as the funds keep flowing. One popular scholarship magazine in Singapore lists 187 types of scholarships for degree studies from a wide range of government agencies, philanthropies and corporations, most of which are portable to overseas universities (Scholarship Guide, 2012). These scholarships usually require the recipient to work for the funding body for several years upon graduation, so they nearly always return after graduation, but once their bonded period is completed they may leave. Students who do not return are usually required to repay the funds they have received, plus interest or a penalty payment, and may be subject to other penalties. For example, in the late 1990s some senior officials in Singapore took to publicly naming and shaming recipients of government scholarships who chose to repay the scholarship rather than return in order to dissuade other recipients from doing the same (Hussain, 2008).

The majority of outbound students, however, are funded by their families (sometimes in combination with subsidies or scholarships provided by host governments or institutions), and are not required by funding agencies to return after graduation. For these students, sometimes financial inducements may prove effective.

One option is conditional grants, which provide support to students on the condition that they then return after graduation. An example of one such measure is the 'Pre-Employment Grant' scholarship provided by Singapore's public health system to some medical and dental students in recognized overseas programmes. Students apply mid-way through their degree and are funded for one or two years, covering up to 60 per cent of the remaining years of tuition fees, with a maximum grant of S$150,000. Recipients of this funding are then required to work in the public health system for a number of years upon their return to Singapore. This appears to be a cleverly targeted strategy to address a specific student group, and is possible for a high-income country like Singapore.

In Colombia, the COLFUTURO loan programme has supported more than 7,000 students to undertake postgraduate studies abroad, providing students with up to US$50,000. If a student stays overseas after graduating they must repay the full amount of the loan plus interest, but if they return to Colombia, most students receive a 50 per cent discount (less for MBA studies) and an additional 10 per cent if they are employed in a public, academic or research organization. COLFUTURO is a non-government organization funded partly by government and partly by corporate donations. Such schemes allow agencies to support overseas study without imposing onerous conditions on students, and ensures that subsidies are directed to those that meet the funding bodies' objectives, which in this case is to develop human resources in Colombia while not preventing students from working abroad.

Governments can promote return of graduates by supporting recruitment channels that students use to find employment back home at the completion of their studies such as careers events, guides and online recruitment services. Malaysia has been doing this very actively, with the involvement of student groups, the private sector and government agencies. Since 2006, the UK and Eire Council for Malaysian Students (UKEC) has organized career fairs in London as a way of providing Malaysians studying in the UK with information about employment opportunities both in the UK and Malaysia. They now partner with Graduan, a firm that recruits graduates for positions in Malaysia by publishing an annual guidebook and holding careers fairs in Malaysia, USA, Canada, Australia, Singapore, New Zealand and the UK. The UKEC website says of the event:

> Working hand in hand with the same aim of overcoming Brain Drain and contributing to our nation's economic development, we and our corporate partners invite over 40 Malaysian firms and businesses to recruit the finest young Malaysian assets in the country.

Such initiatives are likely to be more effective when run by non-governmental and private organizations, but governments have a key role to play in supporting and promoting them.

A combination of growing prosperity and targeted government programmes has persuaded many Chinese students to return home. Under the slogan 'improving services for returned students' the government offers a range of incentives, including employment introduction centres for returned students, generous salary and housing packages, increased support for scientific research and greater contractual flexibility for students to move between jobs or research centres. The flow of delegations of company and government representatives recruiting in Silicon Valley is more evidence of the government's efforts to encourage overseas Chinese to engage in business development in China (Saxenian, 2007). Over the years there have been numerous schemes to promote the return of talented Chinese. The latest scheme is the 'One Thousand Talents scheme' which targets academics with full professorships or the equivalent in developed countries offering them generous relocation packages. This latest scheme follows other similar approaches such as the One Hundred Talents scheme and the Yangtze River Scholar scheme, which have lured back more than 4,000 researchers in the past 15 years (Qui, 2009). The return of these scholars has played a pivotal role in the development of science and technology in China in recent decades, with former overseas scholars comprising 81 per cent of members of the Chinese Academy of Sciences and 54 per cent of the Chinese Academy of Engineering (Zhou & Leydesdorff, 2006). However, programmes and facilities aimed at luring back students and academics appear to have created some hostility between those who went abroad and those studied in China (Zweig, Fung & Han, 2008). The announcement of the One Thousand Talents scheme has also created discontent among researchers already in China with the news about the salary of a researcher recruited from Princeton University causing an outcry (Qui, 2009).

These programmes are targeted at luring back the highly qualified overseas Chinese experts by, in the words of the vice-president of the Chinese Academy of Sciences, 'making their research and living conditions as good as they are abroad' through salary support and research funding (quoted in Xinying, 2013). However, such policies are not concerned with the bulk of international students, who are more likely to be self-financed students in undergraduate commerce-related degree programmes. For those students, broader employment conditions in China are much more significant, and as incomes and opportunities have developed, so has the rate of return climbed, from 14–23 per cent in the early 2000s to 40–47 per cent by the end of the decade (Tharenou & Seet, 2014).

The Malaysian government has also taken more direct measures, especially in relation to emerging industries. Despite having invested millions of dollars into science parks and research facilities, Malaysia's biotechnology sector struggled in the 1990s due to a shortage of qualified scientists. In the last two decades the government has implemented a number of programmes in an attempt to encourage the return of highly skilled Malaysians residing abroad. In 1995 the government introduced a Brain-Gain scheme to encourage the return of Malaysian scientists and recruit foreign talent. However, the scheme attracted only 23 Malaysians and its failure was attributed to low wages and poor working conditions in Malaysia. The scheme was suspended in 1997 following the Asian Financial Crisis (Kanapathy, 2008). In 2001 the government relaunched the Brain-Gain scheme, offering greater incentives for returning professionals, including tax exemption for income repatriated. All personal belongings, including two cars, would be exempted from import duty, and non-Malaysian spouses and children would be given permanent resident status within six months. By 2008 the programme had attracted 400 returnees, which is an improvement but a relatively small figure considering the programme had been running for seven years (MOHR, 2008).

The taxation system can be used in various ways to support return, including tax deductibility as a post-hoc subsidy for students who return. In Singapore, a Member of Parliament has suggested that, considering the shortage of local university places, the government should allow parents of students who study overseas in approved courses and then return to Singapore to claim tax rebates equivalent to the subsidy that their children would have received had they studied at a local public university (G. Ng, 2008). This is a rather elegant proposal which would make public subsidy for overseas study conditional upon return, similar to the COLFUTURO model. A key difference between these approaches, however, is that only children of relatively affluent families are able to benefit from tax deductibility, because the family must fund the overseas study themselves, whereas the COLFUTRO model is available also to students who lack the resources to fund their own studies.

The taxation system could also be used in a more punitive measure. The idea of states taxing their citizens abroad, as the United States does, has a long history but has proved difficult to implement, and so far no developing countries have successfully implemented such a 'Bhagwati tax', as they are known after their original proponent (Gaillard & Gaillard, 1997). The Vietnam Ministry of Education, in a 2009 draft regulation, proposed such a tax on outgoing Vietnamese international students, who would be allowed to work abroad for several years after graduation on the condition that they pay tax in Vietnam on income earned abroad after the completion of studies. After Vietnamese students abroad voiced their outrage online and prominent figures in Vietnam openly criticized the proposal, the Ministry clarified that the proposals were only intended to apply to state-sponsored students (VietNamNet, 2009a, 2009b). The proposal appears not to have been implemented even for scholarship holders, who are still required to return immediately after graduation.

There are sometimes regulatory barriers in place that hinder the return of students, and removing these can help. For example, until 2008, India did allow doctors with Indian undergraduate degrees but foreign medical qualifications to practice in India. Facing a serious shortage of doctors, it permitted the recognition of medical graduates from Britain, the United States, Canada, Australia and New Zealand as long as they were recognized in their respective countries (Neelakantan, 2008). In Singapore, in response to a perceived shortage of lawyers that was slowing the country's aspiration to become a regional commercial hub, the government streamlined recognition of foreign law degrees, removing the requirement for overseas qualified Singaporeans to complete a one-year Diploma in Singapore Law course before being allowed to practice (Hong, 2009).

At the other extreme, some countries' systems appear designed to dissuade students from returning. Although Greece had for many years a high proportion of students studying overseas, the government and professional associations have never exactly welcomed them back with open arms. Returning students faced convoluted and time-consuming bureaucratic obstacles to recognition of their qualifications for the purposes of employment in the public sector, for academic credit in Greek universities, or for professional practice. In the early 2000s, the qualifications recognition agency, DIKATSA, was receiving 20,000 applications from returning students each year, with an average processing time of over one year (Psacharopoulos, 2003). Faced with such delays many students would in the meantime remain overseas and seek employment in the host country, where their qualifications were readily accepted. Others would remain unemployed in Greece while waiting. One study of Greek students who returned to the country with foreign qualifications found that they have a higher rate of unemployment than graduates of Greek universities, and a quarter considered themselves overqualified for the jobs they were employed in (Lianos, Asteriou & Agiomirgianakis, 2004). In such circumstances, many of those students who were able to secure employment abroad did so, with the hope of one day working in Greece when they were able to secure a relevant position.

Professional bodies in Greece have long been resistant to recognizing foreign qualifications, and students complain that the further studies and exams they must do in Greece are simply means of privileging local graduates (who dominate the professional associations) over those who have instead studied overseas. Supporters of the professional associations see it as a matter of national sovereignty to be able to uphold what they see as Greece's higher standards. There is an interesting political context at play in Greece. While domestic university entry is competitive and meritocratic and there are no tuition fees, the entry requirements at overseas institutions are often lower, and access is dependent on a student's family's capacity to fund the cost of overseas study. In addition, the duration of studies is sometimes not as long in foreign programmes as in Greek programmes, prompting questions about quality. Liberals may focus on the benefits of mobility and the rights of the individual, but in Greece there have long been many who argue that unquestioning recognition of foreign graduates' qualifications is inequitable given these access issues.

Finally, the easiest strategy for a government to implement, but which may be effective in some cases, is to promote a sense of moral obligation to return. Senior officials in Singapore have from time to time issued warnings to young people that if they do not return to serve their nation, the country will, in the words of then Prime Minister Goh in 2001, 'descend into mediocrity and will no longer be able to provide a safe and prosperous home for people' (quoted in Koh, 2012, p. 196). A quick scan of the comments posted on online discussion boards in relation to emigration from Singapore quickly shows that many young people do not share the government's sentiments. Leong and Soon (2011), after considering the views of young people regarding emigration, concluded that:

> The results suggest that there is a need for policymakers to increase engagement with the young, mobile and highly educated Singaporeans. In this endeavor to retain Singaporeans, it is important for policymakers to complement the current emphasis on national obligations with policies that would encourage stronger family and friendship ties, which emerged as a critical factor of rootedness.
>
> (p. 12)

In the following section we consider the ways in which the governments can maintain and build such ties with the nation's diaspora.

Engagement with the diaspora

Over time most governments have realized that despite their best efforts to encourage students to return after their studies many will remain abroad, and some have even come to the conclusion that students can make a more positive contribution to the nation from abroad rather than by returning. In part this is in recognition that contemporary migration, and especially skilled mobility, is no longer necessarily one-directional and permanent as the brain drain concept implies, and is better described as brain circulation (Saxenian, 2005). This approach came to prominence in light of the growth of return migration to India and China in the late 1990s, and has been increasingly used to emphasize the ways in which contemporary mobility of students is not simply from south to north, but also increasingly intra-regional and involving mobility between several countries (e.g. de Wit, 2008). While the brain drain concept implies that people and skills are lost forever, those who focus on circulation contend that benefits to both the migrant and the home country are maximized by allowing emigrants to move freely, engage with the home country from abroad and return home at the point at which the conditions are right for them to do so. While there has been considerable research on diaspora engagement policies over the last decade, little of this has focused on engagement with students and recent graduates, so in this section we examine the ways in which three countries that have been previously concerned about brain drain have sought instead to maximize the benefits that might flow from their international students who have not returned.

China

The evolution of the Chinese government's attitude towards international student mobility is emblematic of this shift. China's stance shifted radically in recent decades from viewing Chinese expatriates as unpatriotic, to seeing them as a valuable resource to be harnessed. The economic reforms and policy of opening up China to the outside world that began in 1978 also resulted in large numbers of Chinese students and scholars studying abroad. In 1978 the Chinese government began to actively encourage study abroad as a way of building capacity in science and technology, industry, agriculture and defence. However, in the late 1980s the government began to realize that many students were not returning. In response, some Chinese leaders advocated restraining the outflow of students and scholars (as had been the practice previously) while others, recognizing advantages in having Chinese students and scholars abroad and worried that the Chinese labour market might not cope with large numbers of returnees, portrayed the potential brain drain as 'storing brain power overseas' (Zweig et al., 2008). The Tiananmen Square crackdown resulted in many foreign students and scholars who did not return being considered class enemies, but by 1992 the emphasis was on encouraging return but offering people the freedom to come and go. By 2001 there was another policy shift with the government recognizing the benefits of brain circulation and promoting the idea that Chinese citizens could serve their country without returning (Zweig et al., 2008). The Chinese diaspora, estimated to be around 35 million worldwide, is now considered a potential resource and drawing on the diaspora is now a priority (Welch & Zhen, 2008).

The government established numerous organizations throughout China to liaise with overseas Chinese and encourage them to contribute to their homeland. By 2000, in Europe alone there were more than 100 organizations in over 20 countries (Barabantseva, 2005). As early as 1992 the Chinese government began to encourage citizens who remained overseas to come back for short to medium periods of time. The Ministry of Foreign Affairs began issuing long-term multiple entry visas to facilitate the free flow of overseas students and scholars, and the creation of industrial parks to foster high-technology industries successfully attracted many members of the Chinese diaspora. Expatriate Chinese are responsible for the vast majority of foreign direct investment and have played a critical role in accelerating technology exchange. While many have returned permanently to China, a significant portion of overseas-educated mainlanders who set up enterprises do not reside permanently in China (Kuznetsov & Sabel, 2006; Zweig et al., 2008).

India's 'strategic brain drain'

The Indian government's attitude toward student emigration has followed a similar path. In the post-war period currency controls prevented self-funded students from taking their money out of the country. The situation is very different today. Indian students have a reputation for being strongly driven by the desire to emigrate, and enrolment patterns of Indian students abroad are very responsive to immigration policy changes (Ziguras, 2012). The Indian government does not consider this outflow a problem, as might be expected, and has not embarked on any serious efforts to lure students back to India. Nevertheless there has been a slow but steady increase in skilled immigration to India, both return migration from the Indian diaspora and immigrants from other countries. Giordano and Terranova (2012) have commented on this lack of interest on the part of the Indian state in skilled migration:

> A particularly striking facet of Indian migration, more striking than the metamorphosis itself, is that Indian politics has played a rather marginal role in shaping the phenomenon. While countries such as Australia, Canada and the US invest historically vast sums of public resources in attracting overseas talent and facilitating the return of their own talent – more recently this is also true of China – the Indian government has done, substantially, little or nothing. It has, in effect, delegated this role to the market.
>
> (p. 25)

As the case of Greece shows, India is not unique in this regard, although perhaps for different reasons. Giordano and Terranova point out that with a huge and young population, India seeks the return of remittances and investment from the diaspora rather than the return of people or their skills. Rather than worrying about the negative effects of the emigration of its skilled citizens, the Indian government now sets strategies in place to benefit from its mobile population. Al Barwani, Chapman and Ameen (2009) label this policy 'strategic brain drain', in which governments promote the acquisition of internationally recognized educational qualifications, both at home and abroad, that will enable graduates to work abroad, either temporarily or permanently.

Rather than being concerned about brain drain, India is seeking to emulate the 'labour export' strategy that the Philippines has adopted over several decades across various levels of unskilled and skilled labour. There the private higher education sector, and private higher education financing, support large numbers of nursing students who obtain internationally recognized qualifications enabling them to earn much higher incomes abroad than they can at home (Martin, 2004). Oman has adopted a similar strategy, using finite oil revenues to fund a dramatic expansion in higher education, well beyond the needs of the local labour market, in the expectation that many graduates will need to work outside the country (Al-Barwani et al., 2009).

The Strategic Plan of the Ministry of Overseas Indian Affairs, established in 2004, outlines this approach starkly. It conceives of its citizenry as a strategically mobile global workforce, and seeks to 'leverage the demographic dividend' of its large, relatively young and mobile population by positioning Indians as the nationality of choice to meet labour shortages, including in the knowledge economy, in foreign countries (MOIA, no date, p. 8). The Ministry argues that the ageing demographic profile of the North offers opportunities for the burgeoning young populations of the South. It posits that such international labour mobility is indeed the next key phase of globalization:

> In a world where barriers to the movement of goods, capital and technology are diminishing, the next frontier of globalization will be mobility of workers and professional[s] across international borders. The pace and direction of international migration in the future will be shaped substantially by global demography – of ageing populations in the northern hemisphere and young populations in parts of Asia. In most countries of Europe and the West, large labour supply gaps are expected to emerge. This asymmetry in the demand for and supply of workers will be a structural problem not a cyclical one. Most ageing econom[ies] will therefore have to source foreign workers . . . . India needs to seize this opportunity.
>
> (p. 12)

In this light, the Ministry argues that the country should implement a 'skills for employment abroad' programme that would involve developing India's fields of comparative advantage in terms of internationally in-demand skills and then 'identify the select destination countries where on a demand-driven basis, we can then match the skill-set required over the medium to long term' (p. 13).

This will be a huge challenge for India, considering that its education system struggles to provide education and training of sufficient quantity and quality to meet domestic needs, let alone fill labour shortages abroad. What is significant for our purposes is that the Indian government does not see the migration of outbound students as a problem but as a significant resource to support its development strategy.

While the Indian's government's ambitions are lofty, its resources are very limited and its diaspora is enormous. At the other extreme, with a relatively small diaspora and well-resourced state, is Singapore, and an examination of that country's diaspora engagement strategy may provide some examples of the types of practical initiatives that may be effective.

Singapore

Since the 1990s, as the Singapore government grew concerned about the increasing numbers of educated Singaporeans living overseas, it has experimented with ways to better integrate the diaspora into the 'imagined community' of the nation. Importantly, many of the diaspora engagement strategies discussed below also serve the purpose of encouraging the return of overseas Singaporeans and attracting foreign talent.

The government has taken practical steps to implement this approach. The Singapore International Foundation supported the establishment of Singapore social clubs and business associations around the world (which numbered 92 in 2003) and between 1996 and 2009 it ran Camp Singapore, a summer camp in Singapore for children of the diaspora (Remaking Singapore Committee, 2003). In 2002 the influential Ministry of Trade and Industry established Singapore Overseas Networks in the United States and Hong Kong, which sponsored a series of forums, weekly meetings and email discussions. These culminated in reports providing policy recommendations to the Singapore government concerning its engagement with the diaspora and engagement with global business more generally (Singapore Overseas Network, 2002a, 2002b).

In 2006, the Overseas Singaporean Unit was established to strengthen the diaspora's connection to home and fellow Singaporeans, providing coordination, support and funding for overseas Singaporean communities, including business networks and student societies (Gomes, 2009). 'Singapore Day' events have since been held in several key expatriate centres, including New York (2007), Melbourne (2008), London (2009), Shanghai (2011) and Brooklyn (2012). Their purpose was clearly articulated by the Deputy Prime Minister in his speech at the inaugural event in New York:

> The message we want to send to Overseas Singaporeans is this – even though you are away from home, we remember you and count you among us. Home may not be where you are; it is where your heart resides. Stay connected!
>
> (Seng, 2007)

These events cleverly use food, nostalgia for Singaporean popular culture, and patriotic messaging to bring together overseas Singaporeans, thus providing an opportunity to encourage return migration by promoting the latest developments in housing, education, infrastructure and employment along with practical advice for potential returnees (Gomes, 2009).

However, the government's extensive efforts to engage with citizens abroad is hampered by the inability of Singaporeans to hold dual citizenship. Around 1,000 Singaporeans abroad renounce their Singaporean citizenship each year (AsiaOne, 2012). Once an expatriate has given up citizenship, returning temporarily or permanently to the home country becomes significantly more difficult (Lowell, 2001). All of the major destinations of Singaporean students abroad allow dual citizenship – including Australia, UK, USA, Canada and New Zealand. In effect, the Singapore government is asking a mobile and highly educated expatriate population to choose between mutually exclusive competing national loyalties, in a manner which would appear at odds with the desire to retain ongoing connections with those who reside abroad. This policy has particular impact on children born to Singaporean citizens abroad, who are eligible for Singapore citizenship on condition that they do not have citizenship in the country of their birth. Around 2,000 new citizens are born overseas each year (Singapore Government, 2013, p. 26).

We should not assume that governments are necessarily keen to engage the diaspora in the social and economic life of the country. For many countries, and particularly those with a history of conflict or political instability, the expatriate community may be antagonistic to the government or politically divided. Such schisms can make relations between institutions in the home country and those abroad difficult or impossible. Government policy towards Vietnamese abroad, for example, is complicated by the history of frosty relationships between the government and those who fled the country at the end of the war in the mid-1970s, who constitute the bulk of Vietnamese abroad. Most of the large pool of tertiary-educated Vietnamese abroad shown in Table 5.1 are part of this group, or their children. They were viewed with suspicion, and government policies were not accommodating of their reintegration into Vietnam or close relationships with their homeland, but Resolution 36/NQ-TU in 2004 represented an explicit shift to a much more positive relationship. Subsequent regulations have simplified remittances and visas and fostered more formal and informal linkages with the diaspora (A. T. Pham, 2010). In recent years, the significance of this educated diaspora to the country's development has become more and more apparent, and there is much discussion about policy options aimed at luring overseas educated Vietnamese back home or creating favourable conditions for their continued engagement with Vietnam (H. Pham, 2013a).

Recruiting international students to fill the void

One option for a country facing a loss of students abroad is to adopt the same approach as the destination countries and import those skills by recruiting students from other countries to stay on after graduation. This would appear logical – if it is a loss of skills that is the problem, then find the skills elsewhere. This approach is actually quite rare, mainly because most countries experiencing an outflow of students also have a large pool of graduates from domestic institutions (Ziguras &

Law, 2005). In India, China, Greece and Malaysia, governments are focused on reducing rates of graduate unemployment, and incoming international students are normally not allowed to stay on in the country.

Of the countries in our study, only Singapore has sought to balance the brain drain of outgoing students with an immigration programme that targets incoming international students. Singapore's strategy to achieve a 'net gain of talents' through immigration was discussed in detail in Chapter 4. For Singapore, incoming international students in Singapore now offer a plentiful source of graduates that far exceeds the number of outgoing students who fail to return. Singapore's geographical position, diverse population, cosmopolitan atmosphere, excellent amenities and strong government promotion make it attractive to international students. The presence of a large number of English language educational institutions, both Singaporean and transnational is also of critical importance in its success as a regional hub. For most countries, attracting international students is not so easy. A second issue is competition between local and international graduates, and many countries make it difficult for international students to remain through fear of them taking jobs that could otherwise be filled by locals. For example, while Malaysia shares many features with Singapore, and Kuala Lumpur has a similarly vibrant international student population, because of high rates of graduate unemployment among domestic graduates Malaysia has never promoted itself as a migration destination to international students (Ziguras & Law, 2006).

Conclusion

The massification of higher education in education importing countries is clearly having a significant influence on cross-border higher education in a number of ways. Education-importing counties as diverse as China and Greece have over the past decade seen the proportion of their students who study overseas decline as a result of significantly expanded supply of domestic higher education. In relation to the emigration of students this has two effects. First, growth in capacity and quality of domestic education options reduces demand for overseas education, and students who study locally are much less likely to migrate than students who study overseas. The second impact is to reduce the significance of those outbound students who don't return. If local institutions are producing the quantity and quality of graduates required to meet the country's developmental needs, then it matters less whether students return or not.

Students who do go abroad and are not bound by scholarships to return will make up their own minds, and efforts of governments to create a moral climate in which they feel compelled to return have tended to provoke anger in students rather than national pride. In some circumstances, students may be swayed by favourable taxation incentives. Singapore's approach of partial payment of tuition fees of overseas medical students on condition that they work in public institutions on their return is an interesting approach that may have much wider application, since it is able to be applied in fields of particular need at short notice. In an era in which overseas students continue to be closely connected with friends and family in many locations through social media and cheap telecommunications, and employers advertise online, it is much easier for overseas students to monitor the situation back home.

It is expensive to return home for an interview with no guarantee of a position at the end of the process, but transnational careers fairs like those held by Malaysian recruiters and student organizations can help by providing opportunities for students and employers to meet in a range of locations. Given the involvement of key stakeholders, a little government support for such initiatives can achieve much.

Many countries are establishing agencies for this purpose, and their missions usually reflect the specific character and needs of the diaspora population. Ensuring that these agencies provide the types of services and support needed by recent graduates, even if they form a small part of the diaspora population, is one way to maximize ongoing engagement and possible return, as is allowing dual citizenship.

References

Al-Barwani, T., Chapman, D. W., & Ameen, H. (2009). Strategic brain drain: Implications for higher education in Oman. *Higher Education Policy, 22*(4), 415–432. doi: 10.1057/hep.2009.1

Anderson, S. (2010). Debunking myths about international students and highly skilled immigrants. *International Educator*, 4–7.

AsiaOne. (2009). Overseas students don't want to work in Singapore. Retrieved 28 July 2009 from Singapore Press Holdings: http://news.asiaone.com/News/Education/Story/A1Story20090728-157641.html

AsiaOne. (2012). 1,000 Singaporeans renounce their citizenship annually. Retrieved 9 January 2012 from Singapore Press Holdings: http://news.asiaone.com/News/Latest+News/Singapore/Story/A1Story20120109-320813.html

Barabantseva, E. (2005). Trans-nationalising Chineseness: Overseas Chinese policies of the PRC's Central Government. *ASIEN – German Journal for Politics, Economy and Culture, 96*, 7–28.

Birrell, B. (2006). Implications of low English standards among overseas students at Australian universities. *People and Place, 14*(4), 53–64.

Cervantes, M., & Guellec, D. (2002). The brain drain: Old myths, new realities. *OECD Observer* (230).

Cleverley, J., & Jones, P. (1976). *Australia and International Education: Some Critical Issues.* Hawthorn: Australian Council for Educational Research.

Dân Trí Việt Nam. (2012). Việt Nam 'xuất siêu' du học. Retrieved 24 April 2013 from http://dantri.com.vn/giao-duc-khuyen-hoc/viet-nam-xuat-sieu-du-hoc-556901.htm

de Wit, H. (2008). Changing dynamics in international student circulation: Meanings, push and pull factors, trends and data. In H. de Wit, P. Agaral, M. E. Said, M. T. Sehoole & M. Sirozi (Eds.), *The Dynamics of International Student Circulation in a Global Context* (pp. 15–46). Rotterdam and Taipei: Sense.

Egron-Polak, E. (2004). Comments in response to Karine Tremblay on links between academic mobility and immigration. Paper presented at the Symposium on International Labor and Academic Mobility: Emerging Trends and Implications for Public Policy, Toronto, Canada. www.wes.org/ewenr/symp/EvaEgron-PolakResponseNote.pdf

Gaillard, J., & Gaillard, A. M. (1997). The international mobility of brains: EXODUS or circulation? *Science Technology & Society, 2*(2), 195–228. doi: 10.1177/097172189700200202

Giordano, A., & Terranova, G. (2012). The Indian policy of skilled migration: Brain return versus diaspora benefits. *Journal of Global Policy and Governance, 1*(1), 17–28. doi: 10.1007/s40320-012-0002-3

Glytsos, N. P. (2006). *Is Brain Drain from Albania, Bulgaria and Greece Large Enough to Threaten Their Development?* Warszawa: Centrum Stosunków Międzynarodowych (Center for International Relations).

Gomes, C. (2009). Keeping memories alive: Maintaining Singapore nationalism abroad. *Asia Journal of Global Studies, 3*(1), 37–50.

Gribble, C. (2008). Policy options for managing international student migration: the sending country's perspective. *Journal of Higher Education Policy & Management, 30*(1), 25–39.

Gribble, C. (2011). National policies on skilled labour and the cross-border student market, with a focus on Vietnam. In S. Marginson, S. Kaur & E. Sawir (Eds.), *Higher Education in the Asia-Pacific* (Vol. 36, pp. 291–307) Dordrecht, Netherlands: Springer.

Guruz, K. (2008). *Higher Education and International Student Mobility in the Global Knowledge Economy.* New York: State University of New York Press.

Hong, J. (2009, 18 September). 2009 Amendments to the Legal Profession Act. *Singapore Law Review.*

Hussain, Z. (2008, 24 July). Still adamant that scholarship holders serve their bonds. *The Straits Times.* Retrieved from http://next-stop-wonderland.blogspot.it/2008/07/st-still-adamant-that-scholarship.html

IAU. (2012). *Affirming Academic Values in Internationalization of Higher Education: A Call for Action.* Paris: International Association of Universities.

John, K. (2007, 12 January). Vietnam's WTO hopes and dreams. *Asia Times.*

Jones, G. (2003). East Timor: Education and human resource development. In J. J. Fox & D. B. Soares (Eds.), *Out of the Ashes: The Destruction and Reconstruction of East Timor.* Canberra: Australian National University Press.

Kanapathy, V. (2008). Malaysia. *Asian and Pacific Migration Journal, 17*(3–4), 335–348.

Kapur, D., & McHale, J. (2005). *Give Us Your Best and Brightest: The Global Hunt for Talent and Its Impact on the Developing World.* Washington, DC: Center for Global Development.

Kelly, K. (2000). The higher education system in Vietnam. *World Education News & Reviews 13*(3). Retrieved 5 April 2014 from https://www.wes.org/ewenr/00may/feature.htm

Koh, A. (2012). Tactics of interventions: Student mobility and human capital building in Singapore. *Higher Education Policy, 25*(2), 191–206. doi: 10.1057/hep.2012.5

Kuznetsov, Y., & Sabel, C. (2006). *Global Mobility of Talent from a Perspective of New Industrial Policy: Open Migration Chains and Diaspora Networks* (Vol. 144). Helsinki: World Institute for Development Economics Research, United Nations University.

Leong, C.-H., & Soon, D. (2011). A Study on emigration attitudes of young Singaporeans. *IPS Working Papers* (Vol. 19). Singapore: Institute of Policy Studies, National University of Singapore.

Lianos, T. P., Asteriou, D., & Agiomirgianakis, G. M. (2004). Foreign university graduates in the Greek labour market: Employment, salaries and overeducation. *International Journal of Finance and Economics, 9*(2), 151–164.

Lowell, B. L. (2001). Policy responses to the international mobility of skilled labour. *International Migration Papers.* Geneva: International Labour Organisation

Lowell, B. L. (2009). Immigration 'pull' factors in OECD countries over the long term. In *The Future of International Migration to OECD Countries* (pp. 51–138). Paris: OECD.

Martin, P. L. (2004). *Migration and Development: Toward Sustainable Solutions.* Geneva: International Institute for Labour Studies.

Martin, P. L., & Taylor, J. E. (1996). The anatomy of a migration hump. In J. E. Taylor (Ed.), *Development Strategy, Employment and Migration: Insights from Models* (pp. 42–63). Paris: Organisation for Economic Cooperation and Development.

Matthews, D. (2013, 12 April). Expansion causing 'chaos' across the world. *Times Higher Education.*

Meyer, J.-B. (2003). Policy implications of the brain drain's changing face. Retrieved 20 August 2009 from www.scidev.net

MOHR. (2008). More incentives to attract experts to return. Retrieved 12 June 2009 from http://search.pmo.gov.my/i/search

MOIA. (no date). *Strategic Plan.* New Delhi: Ministry of Overseas Indian Affairs.

Neelakantan, S. (2008, 28 March). Facing a doctor shortage, India will recognize foreign medical degrees. *Chronicle of Higher Education, 54.*

Ng, G. (2008, 29 February). Cut scholarship bond to stem brain drain. *The Straits Times.*

Ng, J. (2008). MM Lee says Singapore facing brain drain problem. Retrieved 24 July 2009 from www.channelnewsasia.com

Pham, A. T. (2010). The returning diaspora: Analyzing overseas Vietnamese (Viet Kieu) contributions toward Vietnam's economic growth. *DEPOCEN Working Paper Series No. 2011/20.* Hanoi: DEPOCEN.

Pham, H. (2013a, 6 April). Diaspora talent is lured back, but fails to stay. *University World News* (266).

Pham, H. (2013b, 13 July). Graduate unemployment and 'over-education' rising. *University World News* (280).

Psacharopoulos, G. (2003). The social cost of an outdated law: Article 16 of the Greek Constitution. *European Journal of Law and Economics, 16,* 123–137.

Qui, J. (2009). China targets top talent from overseas. *Nature, 457*(522).

Ratha, D., Mohapatra, S., & Silwal, A. (2011). *Migration and Remittances Factbook 2011.* Washington, DC: Migration and Remittances Unit, World Bank.

Remaking Singapore Committee. (2003). *Changing Mindsets, Deepening Relationships.* Singapore: Singapore Government.

Robertson, S., Hoare, L., & Harwood, A. (2011). Returnees, student-migrants and second chance learners: Case studies of positional and transformative outcomes of Australian international education. *Compare: A Journal of Comparative and International Education, 41*(5), 685–698.

Saxenian, A. (2005). From brain drain to brain circulation: Transnational communities and regional upgrading in India and China. *Studies in Comparative International Development, 40*(2), 35–61.

Saxenian, A. (2007). Brain circulation and regional innovation: the Silicon Valley-Hsinchu-Shanghai Triangle. In K. R. Polenske (Ed.), *The Economic Geography of Innovation*. Boston: Cambridge University Press.

Scholarship Guide. (2012). *The Scholarship Guide: The Definitive Guide to Scholarships in Singapore*. Singapore.

SEAMEO. (2006). Education in Timor-Leste. From www.seameo.org/index.php?option=com_content&task=view&id=93&Itemid=99

Seng, W. K. (2007). Inaugural Singapore Day draws thousands: Largest-ever turnout by overseas Singaporeans for an event. Retrieved 17 October 2013 from www.singaporeupdate.com/previous2007/230407_inauguralsingaporedayatcentralparkinnewyork.htm

Silverman, G. (1996, 14 November). Silence of the lambs. *Far Eastern Economic Review*, 24–26.

Singapore Government. (2013). *A Sustainable Population for a Dynamic Singapore: Population White Paper*. Singapore: Singapore Government National Population and Talent Division.

Singapore Overseas Network. (2002a). *Report of the Singapore Overseas Network (US) Working Group*. Singapore: Ministry of Trade and Industry.

Singapore Overseas Network. (2002b). *Report to the Economic Review Committee by the Singapore Overseas Network (SON) in Hong Kong*. Singapore: Ministry of Trade and Industry.

Socialist Republic of Vietnam (2013). *Quy định việc công dân Việt Nam ra nước ngoài học tập* [Rules for Vietnam citizens studying abroad].

Szabo, R. (2008, 23 July). Vietnam: Skill shortage leaves firms short. *Asian Legal Business News*.

Tan, J. (2008). Singapore: Country report. Paper presented at Facing Global and Local Challenges: The New Dynamics for Higher Education, Macao SAR, People's Republic of China.

Tharenou, P., & Seet, P.-S. (2014). China's reverse brain drain: Regaining and retaining talent. *International Studies of Management & Organization, 44*(2).

UNESCO. (2012a). *Global Education Digest 2012: Opportunities Lost: The Impact of Grade Repetition and Early School Leaving*. Paris: United Nations Educational, Scientific and Cultural Organization Institute for Statistics.

UNESCO. (2012b). Global flow of tertiary-level students. Retrieved 4 November 2012 from www.uis.unesco.org/Education/Pages/international-student-flow-viz.aspx

UNESCO. (2013). Data centre. Retrieved 21 October 2013 from www.uis.unesco.org

VietNamNet. (2009a, December 2009). MOET regulations target only state students. Retrieved 24 April 2013 from http://myspecialenglish.blogspot.com.au/2009/12/moet-regulations-target-only-state.html

VietNamNet. (2009b, 20 December 2009). Opponents call overseas students regulations 'unsuitable'. Retrieved 24 April 2013 from www.lookatvietnam.com/2009/12/opponents-call-overseas-students-regulations-unsuitable.html

Watts, J. (2007, Saturday June 2, 2007). China fears brain drain as its overseas students stay put. *The Guardian*. Retrieved from www.guardian.co.uk/world/2007/jun/02/internationaleducationnews.highereducation

Welch, A. R. (2010). Internationalisation of Vietnamese higher education: Retrospect and prospect. In G. Harman, M. Hayden & T. N. Pham (Eds.), *Reforming Higher Education in Vietnam: Challenges and Priorities*. Dordrecht, Netherlands: Springer.

Welch, A. R., & Zhen, Z. (2008). Higher education and global talent flows: Brain drain, overseas Chinese intellectuals, and diasporic knowledge networks. *Higher Education Policy, 21*, 519–537.

Wickramasekara, P. (2003). Policy responses to skilled migration: Retention, return and circulation. *Perspectives on Labour Migration*. Geneva: International Labour Office.

Wise, A. (2004). Nation, transnation, diaspora: Locating East Timorese long-distance nationalism. *Sojourn, 19*(2), 151–180.

Wong, K. S. (2010). *DPM's Speech on Population at the Committee of Supply, 4 Mar 2010* (pp. 1–8). Singapore: Government of Singapore National Policy and Talent Division.

World Bank (2014). Personal remittances, received (current US$). Retrieved 5 April 2014 from http://data.worldbank.org/indicator/BX.TRF.PWKR.CD.DT?page=1

Xinying, Z. (2013, 11 July). Grants to lure native talent back to China. *People's Daily*. Retrieved from http://english.peopledaily.com.cn/90882/8321069.html

Zhou, P., & Leydesdorff, L. (2006). The emergence of China as a leading nation in science. *Research Policy, 31*(1), 83–104.

Ziguras, C. (2012). Learning the hard way: Lessons from Australia's decade of innovation in student migration policy. In D. Neubauer & K. Kuroda (Eds.), *Mobility and Migration in Asian Pacific Higher Education* (pp. 39–52). New York: Palgrave Macmillan.

Ziguras, C., & Law, S. F. (2005). Recruiting international students as skilled migrants: The global 'skills race' as viewed from Australia and Malaysia. Paper presented at Global Pedagogies: Equity, Access and Democracy in Education. Proceedings of the 32nd Annual Conference of the Australian and New Zealand Comparative and International Education Society, Australian Catholic University.

Ziguras, C., & Law, S. F. (2006). Recruiting international students as skilled migrants: the global 'skills race' as viewed from Australia and Malaysia. *Globalisation, Societies and Education, 4*(1), 59–76.

Zweig, D., Fung, C. S., & Han, D. (2008). Redefining the brain drain: China's 'Diaspora option'. *Science Technology & Society, 13*(1), 1–33.

Chapter 6

Offshoring higher education

Regulating and promoting overseas provision

We use the term 'transnational' education (TNE) here to refer to forms of education in which students are located in a different country from the one in which the provider is based. The OECD refers to this as programme and institutional mobility (PIM). It is sometimes called offshore education. Compared with the mobility of students, this is a relatively novel phenomenon, and involves a smaller number of students and education providers. The regulatory challenges for governments, though, are complex and have evolved considerably over the past decade with the expansion of transnational provision and the involvement of a larger number of providers. In this chapter we consider the regulation of transnational higher education by governments in the education-exporting countries in which the transnational institutions, and the qualifications they issue, are based. In the following chapter we consider the ways in which governments of importing countries regulate such programmes.

Over the past decade many countries have established regulatory frameworks to support the provision of education through cross-border supply. Previously, transnational programmes were often overlooked by accreditation and quality assurance systems in both the exporting and importing country, effectively slipping between the cracks of national systems. Quality assurance and accreditation processes in the major education-exporting countries (the UK, Australia and the USA) now routinely scrutinize programmes that operate abroad, whether these are offered in conjunction with local partners, or through distance education without a local presence. In this chapter we argue that governments of exporting countries have three major concerns: they enact quality assurance regimes in order to ensure that overseas operations do not damage the nation's reputation abroad; they monitor the financial arrangements of institutions operating abroad to ensure that public funds are not being used for purposes for which they were not intended; and they promote the growth of overseas provision by encouraging governments to adopt regulatory frameworks conducive to the expansion of transnational education. As in other chapters, we endeavour to differentiate national behaviour from that of institutions and students.

Governmental reports are usually state-centric, in that they describe the shape of TNE as being the result of decisions made by governments. For example, a recent and very detailed British Council report notes:

At the country level, the drivers and rationales for TNE are often different for sending and host countries. For example, sending countries are often interested in generating revenue or developing international research linkages, while host countries are often interested in expanding domestic capacity or developing new academic programmes and administrative processes. The interesting point is that both sets of objectives can be achieved when sending and host countries work together.

(McNamara, 2013, p. 9)

In discussing national approaches, it is easy to forget that the programmes and campuses are usually initiated by institutions based on what they perceive to reflect student demand. We shall return later to this point.

Understanding the scale of this form of cross-border education is difficult. Unlike degree mobility, there is no intergovernmental agency that collects data on transnational enrolments. A growing number of countries publish information about national programmes that are delivered outside their borders, but such programme statistics do not reveal much about the overall scale of transnational education, and only two 'exporting' countries, the UK and Australia, regularly publish enrolment data (McNamara, 2013). The United States is the other large-scale provider of transnational education, especially in the form of branch campuses, and a growing number of other countries' institutions are offering programmes overseas, albeit on a smaller scale, including India, New Zealand, Malaysia, Germany, China and Singapore, to name a few.

Table 6.1 shows the most recent offshore student numbers for the UK and Australia, both in universities, and in further/vocational education institutions. Validation here refers to programmes of study which are not taught by UK universities but whose students are eligible to take out the validating university's qualification upon completion. These will be discussed in more detail below when we briefly consider the main forms of transnational education, but are separated out from the registered UK students here because there is some contention as to whether they should be included in aggregate data.

For these two nations, transnational education is clearly a very significant activity. It accounts for around one-third of the international students registered in UK

Table 6.1 Foreign students enrolled in British and Australian transnational programmes

	UK	Australia
University registered / enrolled	227,480	82,468
University validation	343,190	–
Further education / vocational education and training	345	58,561
Total	571,010	141,029

Data sources: Department of Industry (2013); DIISRTE (2012); HESA (2012).

Notes: UK data is for 2011–12, Aust FE is for 2012, Aust VET is for 2011 and includes only public providers.

universities and a quarter of those enrolled in Australian universities (DEEWR, 2011; HESA, 2012). It should come as no surprise then that these two countries have been leading the way in developing regulatory frameworks governing their overseas programmes, and they will feature heavily in this chapter. It is likely that offshore students constitute a much smaller proportion of international students in US universities, and the US government has been less active both because of the smaller relative scale, and because of the federal government's limited role in regulation of higher education.

For the UK and Australia there are huge differences in offshore enrolment patterns by students' nationality, however, with students from some countries much more likely to be studying transnationally than onshore in the host country, and vice versa. Table 6.2 shows the proportions of students from each country who are studying offshore. Australian universities have large-scale transnational operations in some of the countries with high proportions enrolled offshore, including Singapore, Kuwait, South Africa, Malaysia, Vietnam and Hong Kong. Note that the table shows students by country of birth rather than study location, and we expect that most of the offshore students from Botswana and Zimbabwe are actually studying in South Africa, while those from Myanmar are enrolled in Australian programmes and campuses in Singapore and Malaysia. At the other end of the spectrum, what is notable is the small proportion of transnational students in China and India, two of Australia's major source countries, mainly due to regulatory environment in those countries, which we will consider in the next chapter.

Table 6.2 Proportion of international students in Australian universities enrolled offshore, by country of birth, 2010

Country of birth	Total enrolled in Australian universities	Proportion studying offshore (%)
Botswana	1,595	80
Singapore	27,013	67
Kuwait	1,017	61
South Africa	1,856	48
Burma (Myanmar)	1,194	46
Malaysia	33,153	42
Vietnam	15,746	41
Mauritius	2,455	40
Zimbabwe	1,968	38
Hong Kong (SAR)	18,261	36
United Arab Emirates	1,796	25
Sri Lanka	5,200	22
France	2,076	20
Indonesia	12,250	19
Japan	2,896	18
Kenya	1,607	17

Canada	4,452	12
Pakistan	3,282	12
China (excludes SARs)	91,918	11
Philippines	1,890	9
Iran	2,220	9
India	21,705	9
United Kingdom	1,442	7
Bangladesh	2,664	7
Russian Federation	1,015	6
Thailand	4,062	5
Germany	3,453	3
Korea, Republic of (South)	8,170	3
Taiwan	3,433	3
Saudi Arabia	5,374	2
United States of America	7,599	2
Norway	1,804	1
Colombia	1,091	1
Nepal	3,547	1
All countries	335,273	23

Note: Only those countries which have more than 1,000 students enrolled are listed, but the total in the last row includes all countries.

Data source: DEEWR (2011).

There is now a growing body of literature on the regulation of transnational education, consisting of both scholarly case studies and institutional reports. Early on, Chambers and Cummings (1990) produced an excellent analysis of the difficulties faced by US universities in their efforts to establish campuses in Japan during the 1980s, highlighting the role that government and accreditation agencies in each country played in the failure of many initiatives. With the growth of branch campuses over the past decade, there have also been quite a few studies of individual initiatives that touch on regulatory issues, including case studies of RMIT University in Vietnam (Wilmoth, 2006), University of Nottingham and Xi'an Jiaotong-Liverpool University in China (Feng, 2012), Curtin University in Singapore (Forde, 2011), Cornell University in Qatar (Hajjar & Gotto, 2013), New York University in the United Arab Emirates (Sexton, 2012) and Carnegie Mellon University's degree programmes in various locations (Kamlet, 2010). Two bodies stand out in the contribution to research on transnational education, both based in the UK, the largest exporting country. The Observatory on Borderless Higher Education has for a decade published numerous reports on transnational education regulation and campuses (Banks, Kevat, Ziguras, Ciccarelli & Clayton, 2010; Lawton & Katsomitros, 2011; OBHE, 2002; Verbik & Jokivirta, 2005a, 2005b; Verbik & Merkley, 2006), and more recently the British Council has published several comprehensive reports on transnational provision (British Council, 2012a, 2012b; McNamara, 2013).

Modes of delivery

We consider four modes of delivery of cross-border programmes, characterized by different in-country provision: online/distance education programmes without local partners; international branch campuses of institutions (usually universities); partner-supported programmes; and validation.

As the rush of interest in Massive Open Online Courses has demonstrated, the growth of flexible delivery and fully-online programmes has the potential to significantly expand access to education, particularly for working professionals. However single courses and whole programmes pose very different regulatory challenges for governments. Single units of study, such as MOOCs, that do not result in a nationally recognized qualification are generally not regulated by any government, except perhaps through consumer protection laws where fees are paid, but even these are difficult to enforce in relation to cross-border transactions. Whole programmes studied online are another matter, and online degrees of all kinds are usually subject to similar regulation and quality assurance as on-campus programmes. The enrolment of overseas students in fully online degrees does not usually trouble regulators greatly, since the programme offering is the same for local and overseas students. But when an overseas partner is involved, regulators tend to show more interest, as we will see below.

Compared with fully online degrees, the regulatory burden involved with establishing and operating an international branch campus is at the other extreme. One of the first issues is that there is no agreed definition of what constitutes a branch campus, and it is not uncommon for a university and a host government to use different definitions. The most commonly accepted definition of an international branch campus was developed by the UK-based Observatory on Borderless Higher Education:

> A higher education institution that is located in another country from the institution which either originated it or operates it, with some physical presence in the host country, and which awards at least one degree in the host country that is accredited in the country of the originating institution.
>
> (Lawton & Katsomitros, 2011, p. 2)

Globally, in 2011 there were 200 institutions in existence that met the OBHE definition and 38 more in development. Various definitions, however, are employed by higher education institutions themselves and by governments, which can complicate regulating such activities. For example, according to its definition the OBHE identified 17 branch campuses in India, while the Indian Association of Indian Universities believes there are five foreign university campuses, and the All India Council for Technical Education's list of Unapproved Institutions mentions only one foreign campus (Lawton & Katsomitros, 2011). Governments usually regulate the establishment and operation of branch campuses very extensively, and in practice these initiatives only succeed where they have the support of both home and host governments.

There is a long history of universities being established with foreign support, often by colonial authorities but also by non-government religious and secular groups. US-based religious groups established American universities in Beirut, Rome, Cairo and other cities, Boğaziçi University in Istanbul, and many institutions in China including Tianjin and Soochow universities, amongst others. Many Catholic universities were similarly established within a global network. However, these institutions, while often initially using imported curriculum, pedagogical models and staff, award their own degrees and are not branches of a parent university. They are typically regulated in the same way as other universities by authorities, even though in some cases they use a different language of instruction from the national system and may have foreign accreditation.

We use the term partner-supported programmes to describe foreign programmes that are delivered on the campus of a partner. The university that awards the qualification is ultimately responsible for curriculum design and assessment, but the teaching and provision of student services are shared between the partners. In most cases students do not receive a degree from the local partner. These programmes are often referred to as 'franchising' in the UK (although that term is considered distasteful elsewhere, reminiscent of a hot-dog vendor's stand) when the student completes the whole programme on the partner's campus, and 'twinning' when students are required to spend some time on the university's home campus to complete the programme. Increasingly, collaboration between universities in different countries allows students to take out degrees from both institutions, usually referred to as 'double' or 'dual' degree programmes, or a 'joint degree' which is one qualification awarded and badged by both institutions (McNamara, 2013, p. 15). British and Australian universities have been the major providers of these programmes. Perhaps the first such provider, and still the largest, is the University of London, whose extra-mural studies programme was established late in the nineteenth century with many local study centres supporting correspondence studies, especially in Africa. Partner-supported programmes pose less financial and reputational risk to the awarding university but nonetheless have come under increasing scrutiny of authorities in the university's home country, who have a brief to ensure that recognized national qualifications offered offshore meet the expectations that would be placed on the programme were it to be delivered in the institution's home country.

The fourth mode of delivery of transnational programmes we consider here is validation. It is common practice in many countries for universities to grant credit (sometimes called 'advanced standing') to students for studies they have completed at a recognized institution. Sometimes in international education these can be formalized in articulation agreements in which students complete a programme of study at an institution (often a diploma-level programme) in their home country and this is in turn recognized as equivalent to the first year or two of an undergraduate degree by a foreign university. Such arrangements tend to cause few problems for regulatory agencies. While universities in most countries are limited in the amount of credit they are able to award (typically two years of an undergraduate degree in the USA and Australia for example), British universities can provide credit for the entirety of their programme.

This allows British universities to confer a degree on students who have not actually enrolled with or completed any units of study with the awarding university, but who have completed a course of study that the university judges to be equivalent to its own degrees. What is more, the British university is able to confer degrees to students of partner institutions that it does not actually offer itself. For example, students in SAE College in many countries can study with SAE to obtain a Bachelor of Arts (Hons) Audio Production awarded by Middlesex University, even though Middlesex University does not actually teach such a programme itself.

The UK Quality Assurance Agency (QAA) appears not to have been overly concerned with validation until recently, but now these practices are the subject of much discussion, for two quite different reasons. First, the scale of validation practices has only come to light since the Higher Education Statistics Agency began publishing data on offshore students (HESA, 2009). Each year the number of students in validation programmes has grown, and now more than half of all offshore students who will earn a UK degree are in validation programmes, as Table 6.1 shows. Most of the validation students, the data reveals, are studying in just one university, Oxford Brookes. Students who enrol in the final examinations for the Association of Chartered Certified Accountants are automatically registered with the university for ten years, and upon passing the exams can submit a thesis and £135 and be awarded a BSc (Hons) in Applied Accounting (Healey, 2013a). The second factor drawing attention towards validation was the collapse of the University of Wales in 2011, which at its height had around 20,000 students studying with 130 foreign partner colleges (Healey, 2013b). A critical report by the QAA was picked up by an investigative journalist at the BBC resulting in a damaging exposé of poor oversight of the quality of validated qualifications and the low standard of some partner institutions (BBC, 2011).

Healey (2013a, 2013b) argues that validation arrangements pose significant reputational risk both to the awarding universities, and to UK higher education overall, while generating very little benefit for the university. The amounts paid to the university by partner institutions and individual students are small and they do not contribute to the broader internationalization of the university. The reputational effects are generally negative, since those partner institutions with the least established reputations relied most on the cachet of their franchising university to market their programmes. So while low-status partners would display prominently the university's name and logo, high-status partners tended not to since they could recruit students on their own merits, even if they require a university partner to be able to confer a degree. Healey argues that the real beneficiaries of validation are the academic and professional staff in the UK universities who manage the relationships, who are often treated lavishly by their partner institutions during visits and who earn discretionary income for their department. Healey found that staff involved in managing the relationships with partner institutions did not have incentives to increase income from them or to expand the range of staff involved to enhance staff development and broader internationalization. He concludes that:

> the operational management of the franchise partnerships fell into the hands of less senior academics and administrators, who appear to have maintained and controlled the development of the franchises in their own interests. The flow of modest but 'easy money' discouraged senior managers from looking more critically at the real benefits of continuing these partnerships, while the significant financial returns to the private entrepreneurs of the franchise arrangement gave them a very strong incentive to nurture their relationships with their key academic and administrative contacts. The result was that the scale of the franchises grew organically, as the private colleges expanded, without ever being a strategic objective of the universities at a corporate level.
>
> (Healey, 2013b, p. 198)

In the wake of QAA and media scrutiny of validation, some institutions are closing such programmes as university leaders become more aware of the risks involved (Healey, 2013a). It is likely that regulatory reform will ensue also, to bring the UK's credit transfer rules into line with other major education exporters. As we will see in the next chapter, key education importing countries are also regulating to prevent institutions in their country from issuing validated awards.

Business regulation

The development of early offshore programmes often went unnoticed by the institutions' home governments. Many of the earliest offshore programmes were started as distance education, or 'correspondence', courses which involved sending a package of materials abroad for students who studied either individually or enrolled through a local study centre. The University of London's external programmes have been offered for over a century and the university remains the world's largest provider of transnational education. Similarly, most of the Australian universities that pioneered the country's partner-supported provision in Asia in the 1990s were those that had over the past decade established nationally funded distance education centres, which provided them with the capacity to package curriculum materials for students both in Australia and abroad (Clayton & Ziguras, 2011).

Some public institutions, particularly in the USA and Australia, were constrained from acting outside of the jurisdiction in which they are established. The story of the rise and fall of Australia's first transnational programme is very revealing, demonstrating that institutions were being held back from providing transnational education by Australian regulatory agencies before the policy changes of the mid-1980s. The Darling Downs Institute of Advanced Education's External Studies Department between 1981 and 1984 partnered with the

University of the South Pacific in Suva in Fiji to provide an engineering diploma programme (Brimblecombe, 1996). However, the Queensland Government's Board of Advanced Education ordered the programme be terminated in 1984 on advice from the state's Solicitor-General. Despite this setback, DDIAE remained committed to delivering fee-paying overseas distance education programmes. In 1985 Queensland Cabinet gave approval for DDIAE to proceed with a pilot programme in Hong Kong, which had 170 enrolments by the end of the year. New ventures quickly developed, leading *The Australian* newspaper to observe in 1986 that DDIAE 'has enrolled more than two-thirds of all foreign paying students undertaking Australian-based tertiary courses' (Clarke & McDonald, 2007). The DDIAE went on to become the University of Southern Queensland, and these early initiatives laid the foundations for substantial transnational operations and by 2010 the university enrolled over 5,000 offshore students studying in partnerships in 11 countries.

Australia's early offshore programmes were initiated by enthusiastic individuals with entrepreneurial zeal, who pioneered new ways of delivering programmes across borders. One of these was Tony Adams, who in 1989 established one of RMIT's first offshore programmes, a Master of Business (Information Technology), in partnership with the Singapore Institute of Management (SIM). He later recounted the creative approaches such endeavours required:

> In those early programs we didn't have a rule book or the best practice case studies we have today. We wrote contracts from a blank sheet of paper and invented faculty and institutional procedures for approval. It was messy, non strategic and would have failed as a business planning process in an MBA.
>
> (Adams, 2010)

Indeed, the first programme Adams took offshore was one that RMIT did not previously offer but was instead developed in response to a request from the partner and offered in Singapore first before being subsequently adapted for delivery in Melbourne. The new programme was advertised to prospective students in Singapore before it had been formally approved by RMIT. Offshore programme development processes were usually outside the scope of existing programme approval process and oversight was much less formal than it is today:

> Apart from signing the agreement and asking the legal and finance offices to have a cursory look over the project there were really no other procedures. It wasn't until the Director and the Chair of Council, who we would now call the Chancellor, attended our first graduation overseas and entered the ballroom of the Westin Hotel in Singapore to 800 parents and loved ones applauding and ceremonial pipers playing the theme from Star Wars that they knew something important was up.
>
> (Adams, 2010, p. 6)

While the origins of the RMIT–SIM partnership established in 1987 were rough and ready, it has endured to become one of Australia's longest-standing and largest-scale offshore higher education relationships. Now RMIT, through SIM, enrols more students studying in Singapore than there are Singaporean students in Australia with all education providers.

Where governments have been most involved in regulating institutions overseas operations has been in relation to the use of public funds, especially in public institutions. Chambers and Cummins (1990) have described the efforts of state governments in the USA to ensure that universities and community colleges operating in Japan in the 1980s were not diverting funds or other resources that were provided to the institution to support its primary mandate of providing education to the state's residents. The same view holds in Australia, where in 2005 during a financial audit of universities' overseas campuses a senior state government official explained that from the government's point of view the 'primary purpose of offshore delivery is to generate net revenue to support the domestic activities of Victorian universities' (Auditor General Victoria, 2005). In such contexts, institutions sometimes must engage in extensive consultation with regulatory agencies in their home country, which can be complicated by the fact that those governments in many countries provide a diminishing share of institutional income. Government and quasi-government entities operating in a marketized manner are sometimes referred to as 'hybrid organisations' (Koelman & Vries, 1999). Ideally, the well-functioning hybrid organization has the benefits *inter alia* of reducing demands on the public purse, responding more swiftly to opportunities and threats, and having the ability to address market demand more effectively. Thus the pursuit of overseas initiatives is very much in line with many governments' efforts to encourage institutions to diversify their sources of income.

Governments nevertheless want to be assured that international entrepreneurial activities do not compromise commitment to the institution's community service responsibilities and do not place at risk public funds and the reputation of the institution or of the government. Koelman and De Vries (1999) articulated a set of principles that should be adopted in regulating universities acting as hybrid organizations, in such activities as transnational education:

> the public duty (teaching and research) may not be endangered; students should not become victims of entrepreneurial activities; the prestige of the university as a public institution should not be harmed; and entrepreneurial risks should not be shifted onto the taxpayer.

(p. 175)

These principles appear to have been widely adopted by the major exporters.

Some governments, by contrast have provided considerable public funds for the establishment of loss-making offshore programmes and campuses that are intended to foster educational, cultural or political connections. The German government, through DAAD, supports many such initiatives (Becker & Kolster, 2012). National and provincial governments in China have been supportive of its universities investing in new campuses in Laos, the UK and Malaysia in line with China's broader 'going out' strategy of promoting Chinese investment abroad. These include proposed branches of Soochow University in Vientiane, Laos, a joint initiative between Zhejiang University and Imperial College in London and a campus of Xiamen University in Malaysia.

Quality assurance

As we have discussed at length elsewhere (McBurnie & Ziguras, 2007), transnational education is inherently more prone than domestic provision to disconnection and negligence due to geographical and operational distance from the 'centre' of the awarding institution. In cases where fees are charged, there is always the possibility of friction between academic and commercial priorities, and the potential for academic standards to be compromised. These risks underline the need for sound and effective quality assurance on the part of governments in exporting countries to ensure that the reputation of both the provider institution and by extension the provider country are not endangered.

In the absence of external quality assurance, governments can rely to some extent on the self-interest of institutions to maintain their own reputations by putting in place internal quality assurance measures. And in many institutions, such controls work effectively most of the time. However, as Chambers and Cummings (1990) noted, 'Reputation operates best as a control on overseas quality where institutions already have a national or international reputation worth protecting' (p. 120). The reputational considerations within a large and established university are likely to be very different from those shaping decisions in a newly established for-profit institution, for example. A second limitation on the capacity for reputational concerns to drive internal quality assurance is the fact that the senior leaders held responsible for guarding the reputation of their institution may actually be far removed from the reality of their institution's overseas operations, which are often a small part of the institution's operations and managed by individuals who may benefit from practices that might undermine the reputation of the institution as a whole, as we saw in the case of validation described above.

National standards were put in place in the three largest provider countries around the same time: 1997 in the USA, 1999 in the UK and in 2000 in Australia. In 1997, US regional accreditation bodies agreed on a common set of expectations for offshore campuses and programmes, articulated in the *Principles of Good Practice in Overseas International Education Programs for Non-U.S. Nationals* (Council of Postsecondary Accreditation, 1997). Chambers and Cummings (1990) observed that US accreditation bodies had previously had different expectations of offshore operations, and because these were such a small part of the institution they were rarely closely scrutinized. They concluded that 'U.S. overseas programs essentially operate at a level three times removed from federal oversight, and an accredited institution can run substandard programs overseas with little effect on its formal status at home' (p. 118). They argued that the small scale of US universities' transnational operations in relation to the overall size of the university meant that even the most poorly executed overseas operations were unlikely to jeopardize an institution's accreditation. Given the lack of transparency in the accreditation process in the USA, as compared with the UK and Australia, which we will discuss in further detail below, it is difficult to know how seriously an institution's offshore operations are scrutinized. Now that the expectations of US overseas operations have been clearly articulated and are enforced by all the regional accreditation bodies, it may be the case, as Kinser (2011) argues, that a poor-quality overseas operation could put an entire university's accreditation at risk.

In Australia the universities association had adopted in 1995 a *Code of Ethical Practice in the Provision Offshore of Education and Educational Services by Australian Higher Education Institutions* (AVCC, 1995), but like most voluntary industry codes this was not able to be enforced. The same year that the US principles were adopted, the UK Quality Assurance Agency was established, and two years later produced its *Code of practice for the assurance of academic quality and standards in higher education* (QAA, 1999). The Council of Europe (2001), then developed its own *Code of Good Practice in the Provision of Transnational Education*, which made reference to the three countries' recent national frameworks. The Australian University Quality Agency, which was established in 2000, set out its expectations for transnational provision in its audit manual (AUQA, 2002).

In these four jurisdictions, accounting for the vast majority of the world's transnational provision, a similar set of principles was adopted over a five-year period between 1997 and 2002 that clearly articulated expectations of institutions awarding a qualification taught overseas. These held that, even though a local partner may be involved, the awarding institution must:

- ensure that the standard and quality of any programme conducted in its name is consistent (or 'comparable') wherever and however the programme is offered;
- comply with regulations in place in both the sending and receiving countries;
- where a partnership between institutions is involved, ensure that the partner is suitable and that the relationship is formalized in a written agreement specifying the responsibilities of each institution;
- ensure that curriculum and pedagogy are localized to meet the needs of learners in each location while maintaining equivalent standards;
- ensure that information provided to prospective students about the programme, including by partner institutions and agents, is accurate;
- ensure that staff engaged in teaching are suitably qualified and proficient;
- ensure that students have access to appropriate support services and complaints procedures.

These principles appear to be widely accepted by governments, and more recent regulatory frameworks that have been developed in China (Zhu & Zhu, 2011) and India (Mukul, 2009) have incorporated most of these principles. However, some of the newer exporters have yet to put in place quality assurance regimes for their providers operating abroad, despite sometimes having well-developed approaches to managing the quality of incoming programmes. For example, Malaysian universities' six overseas campuses (Lawton & Katsomitros, 2011) are not subject to scrutiny by the Malaysian Qualifications Agency, which currently appears concerned only with the quality of education in Malaysia. If it follows the trajectory of other exporters, however, it will develop a closer concern.

In the USA, UK and Australia, the key features of the quality assurance process for transnational operations is similar, involving an institutional self-review, visits by a panel of external auditors, and the production of a report on the institution. None of these agencies has the ability to force the closure of programmes or institutions, but in the US case they can cease the institution's accreditation, or threaten to do so if changes are not made (Kinser, 2011). The major difference between them is the degree of transparency. Reports of the UK QAA and AUQA in Australia are published on the organizations' websites and are easily accessible. When issues are identified in these reports they are covered by national and international media, so reputational damage is a real possibility. Reports of US accreditation agencies, however, are not made public. Publication of audit reports has had a very significant impact in Australia and the UK over the past decade.

In Australia, the first round of AUQA audits between 2002 and 2007 led to a dramatic transformation in institutional governance. The audit reports identified some common failings: strategic plans for transnational education rarely extended beyond commercial imperatives; offshore operations were often not well understood across the university; and the university's usual quality assurance arrangements often were not fully implemented offshore (Banks et al., 2010). In response to AUQA's public scrutiny, universities centralized the management and quality assurance of offshore programme delivery and greatly increased internal scrutiny of what were previously locally managed entrepreneurial initiatives. As a result, between 2003 and 2008 nearly half of the country's offshore programmes were closed, but student numbers remained stable. This shake-up was welcomed by AUQA as a sign of the organization's success. A 2006 review of transnational audits by the agency's executive director and an audit director argued that the large-scale closure of programmes 'ought to be viewed in a constructive light' (Carroll & Woodhouse, 2006, p. 86). They explained that:

> Most early growth in the 1990s was ad hoc rather than managed through carefully coordinated university processes. This is changing quickly, although the change process is rendered complicated as universities establish systems for new transnational operations while still managing legacy operations. Many universities now find themselves in a position where some of those

legacy operations are not able to be transformed to align with the new, more robust quality assurance arrangements. It is entirely reasonable that such activities should be closed down.

(Carroll & Woodhouse, 2006, p. 86)

In the UK, public scrutiny of transnational operations is also transforming offshore provision. The University of Wales case, mentioned above, is a good example. In June 2011, QAA published an institutional audit report which concluded that 'Confidence can reasonably be placed in the soundness of the institution's present and likely future management of the academic standards of its awards' (QAA, 2011a). But on the same day it published a report on one of the University's partnerships in Singapore that found serious systematic failings in its oversight of collaborative programmes (QAA, 2011b). Anyone reading the report on the Singapore programmes would have difficulty understanding the QAA's stated confidence in the university's academic standards, and this was enough to alert journalists to underlying problems that they then exposed with devastating consequences for the University of Wales. Within six months of the publication of the QAA reports, the university's partnerships were closed down and the structure of the university was dramatically overhauled (BBC, 2011).

Positive assessments do also have an impact on institutional behaviour. For senior managers, affirmations of support for good institutional practice in quality assurance agencies can represent a very public endorsement, and these often have implications for one's career progression, especially in relatively open higher education systems where senior academic administrators commonly move between universities.

These quality assurance processes do not cover all institutions, however. In the USA the accreditation process is voluntary, and there are a range of non-recognized accreditation organizations willing to rubber-stamp providers. These 'accreditation mills' are exploited by low-quality transnational providers. There are many dubious institutions outside the USA that claim to be US accredited but without providing details of which agency they are accredited by.

Promoting intergovernmental cooperation and trade liberalization

Exporting governments often play a role in facilitating the expansion of their institutions' overseas operations. At the micro level they support specific initiatives through various government-to-government contacts, reassuring host governments of the bona fides of their institutions and assisting in negotiations with regulatory agencies. Education counsellors and trade advisors from the major exporting countries sometimes work closely together when issues of mutual concern arise in countries where their institutions are active. In the case of major initiatives like branch campuses, senior government officials such as ambassadors and even ministers may be involved during negotiations and ribbon-cutting ceremonies, providing a significant reputational boost in the eyes of both the host government and of prospective students. At the macro level, which we focus on here, governments of education-exporting countries enter into bilateral and multilateral trade agreements, as discussed in Chapter 1, in an effort to foster conducive regulatory environments in host countries. They also provide 'market intelligence' to their institutions, through agencies such as the British Council, the US Institute for International Education, and Australian Education International.

The UK and Australian governments have been most active in global efforts to enhance the legitimacy of transnational education since the 1990s. An Australian government-funded research project on developments in transnational education, leading to the report *New Media and Borderless Education* (Cunningham et al., 1998) had significant impact in both Australia and the UK. It led to follow-up parallel research projects in both countries that delved deeper into the business of borderless education, with each team publishing influential reports in 2000 that examined emergent technological and commercial opportunities and the ways in which these were eroding the significance of national borders (Bjarnason *et al.*, 2000; Cunningham *et al.*, 2000). This work laid the groundwork for the establishment in 2001 of the Observatory on Borderless Higher Education, a collaborative initiative between the Association of Commonwealth Universities and Universities UK. The Observatory became part of the International Graduate Insight Group in 2010 and is still one of the world's leading think-tanks on TNE. The OBHE continues to have strong links to Australian universities, in terms of both contributors and subscribers, and its staff has been consistently multinational, but its advisory board membership remains exclusively British. Looking back now on the legacy of that early collaboration, we can see now that an inspired strategic partnership in the late 1990s between key UK and Australian institutions and researchers influenced subsequent research, policy development and institutional strategy in both countries. OBHE conferences, which have been held in London, Kuala Lumpur and Vancouver in recent years, are among the most influential forums at which thought leaders in TNE gather together.

More recently, in 2011 the British Council, Australian Education International and the Malaysian Ministry of Higher Education jointly sponsored a conference in Kuala Lumpur, *Excellence in Transnational Education: Partnerships for the Future*. It brought together speakers from institutions from the three countries very effectively, showcasing best practice in transnational education as well as candidly sharing concerns and challenges faced by institutions and governments. Significantly, the forum was also attended by senior ministry of education officials from Indonesia, Nepal, the Philippines, Thailand, India and Vietnam, many of whom were invited and sponsored by the host governments. For these officials, the forum illustrated vividly the success of the Malaysian model, in which liberalization of market restrictions coupled with robust quality assurance have supported the growth of a high-quality internationally oriented private higher education sector and positioned Malaysia as a net education exporter and a key regional provider.

The British Council has held similar forums focused on transnational education over recent years in key host cities including Hong Kong and Athens in 2013 as well as holding their large Going Global conferences every second year outside the UK, with the first two also held in key transnational education hubs, Hong Kong and Dubai. Australia has continued to be active in Asia-Pacific Economic Cooperation (APEC), which because of its focus on regional economic integration provides an opportunity to engage with officials responsible for trade policy, economic development strategy and education policy. In 2013 the Australian Department of Foreign Affairs sponsored a two-day forum in Kuala Lumpur to consider the ways the APEC leaders' stated desire to enhance educational collaboration could be supported by trade liberalization. Events like these, where like-minded institutions and governments showcase the long-term benefits of open regulatory environments and high-quality transnational provision, have been influential in encouraging governments to promote similar conditions elsewhere.

In addition to such activities aimed at international audiences, the British Council, Australian Education International and similar agencies in other exporting countries have also been actively encouraging their institutions to expand abroad. While decisions are taken within institutions, the presence of a clear government policy directed towards offshore growth can go a long way in steering institutional decision makers in that direction. In New Zealand the Export Education Innovation Program in the mid-2000s provided grants to institutions seeking to establish new offshore programmes and funded a series of reports for the sector. More recently the British Council has been sponsoring research on the regulatory and commercial environments in a range of countries of interest to UK universities (British Council, 2012b; McNamara, 2013).

Governments support offshore expansion for a range of reasons besides revenue generation, as we have discussed above, but revenue is clearly a major motivation and has become more so as these countries have faced constraints on their ability to recruit international students onshore, namely visa regulations in the UK and an overvalued currency in Australia. Healey (2013a) argues that government effort to foster transnational growth is based on an overestimation of the income from transnational students, since:

- Half of all those counted are in a single university's validation programme which generated income of just £135 per graduate.
- Tuition fees for offshore students paid to the UK university are much lower than for onshore students.
- Many offshore students are enrolled part-time.
- The costs involved in running quality offshore programmes are much higher than is often acknowledged.
- Given academic staff incentive structures, many are loathe to dedicate time to such activities when they could be focusing on research.

We can note, therefore that some of the concerns raised internally by proponents of TNE reflect points raised by its opponents, discussed further in the next chapter.

Conclusion

Transnational education has evolved in recent decades from a peripheral activity to a major aspect of cross-border higher education. It has moved from falling between the regulatory cracks – paid little or no heed by exporting or importing governments – to the current situation where a programme may come under the scrutiny of, variously: the exporter government; the importer government; local and international professional associations; and the quality assurance approaches of the provider institution and the local partner. Even where governments are relatively hands-off, as in the case of some recent entrants to the export of transnational education, we can anticipate a continuation of the trend for closer scrutiny due to the potential for reputational damage and, where the entrepreneurial institution receives public subsidies, the question of whether and how taxpayer money may be used for educational activities outside the home country.

The rewards and risks of transnational education are the obverse of each other: if financial gain is one of the rewards sought for by successful entrepreneurial activities of universities, financial loss is the flipside. By extension, exporter governments and their domestic publics gain if successful enterprise helps to fund the educational mission; conversely, they lose if such activities eat into taxpayer-funded resources and reduce the ability of institutions to carry out their domestic responsibilities. Similarly, there is the perceived effect of enhanced international reputation for the successful exporter, and reputational damage if a country's offerings are seen to be substandard or prone to collapse or sudden withdrawal. We have emphasized at the outset that the governance of cross-border higher education at the state level should not be conflated with the issues that must be considered at the level of the higher education institution.

References

Adams, T. (2010, 15 April). Inaugural Martand Joshi Memorial Address, CQU International Campus Melbourne. Retrieved 29 October 2011 from http://uninews.cqu.edu.au/UniNews/viewStory.do?story=6813

Auditor General Victoria. (2005). *Results of Financial Statement Audits for Agencies with Other than 30 June 2004 Balance Dates, and Other Audits, May 2005*. Melbourne: Auditor General Victoria.

AUQA. (2002). *Audit Manual: Version 1*. Melbourne: Australian Universities Quality Agency.

AVCC. (1995). *Code of Ethical Practice in the Offshore Provision of Education and Educational Services by Australian Higher Education Institutions*. Canberra: Australian Vice-Chancellors' Committee.

Banks, M., Kevat, P., Ziguras, C., Ciccarelli, A., & Clayton, D. (2010). *The Changing Fortunes of Australian Transnational Higher Education*. London: Observatory on Borderless Higher Education.

BBC. (2011, 3 October). University of Wales to stop validating other degrees. Retrieved 14 November 2011 from www.bbc.co.uk/news/uk-wales-15157119

Becker, R., & Kolster, R. (2012). *International Student Recruitment: Policies and Developments in Selected Countries*. The Hague: NUFFIC (Netherlands organisation for international cooperation in higher education).

Bjarnason, S., Davies, J., Farrington, D., Fielden, J., Garrett, R., Lund, H., et al. (2000). *The Business of Borderless Education: UK Perspectives*. London: Committee of Vice-Chancellors and Principals and Higher Education Funding Council for England.

Brimblecombe, E. (1996). *Pheonix Rising: The First Twenty One Years of Darling Downs College of Advanced Education*. Toowoomba: University of Southern Queensland.

British Council. (2012a). *Student Insight Hot Topics,* September: *Portrait of the Transnational Education Student*. London: British Council.

British Council. (2012b). *The Shape of Things to Come: Higher Education Global Trends and Emerging Opportunities to 2020*. London: British Council.

Carroll, M., & Woodhouse, D. (2006). Quality assurance issues in transnational higher education – developing theory by reflecting on thematic findings from AUQA audits. In J. Baird (Ed.), *Quality Audit and Assurance for Transnational Higher Education* (pp. 65–89). Melbourne: Australian Universities Quality Agency.

Chambers, G. S., & Cummings, W. K. (1990). *Profiting from Education: Japan-United States International Educational Ventures in the 1980s*. New York: Institute on International Education.

Clarke, J., & McDonald, A. (2007). *USQ: The First 40 Years*. Toowoomba: University of Southern Queensland.

Clayton, D., & Ziguras, C. (2011). Transnational education: Delivering quality Australian programs offshore. In D. Davis & B. Mackintosh (Eds.), *Making a Difference: Australian International Education* (pp. 302–330). Sydney: UNSW Press.

Council of Europe. (2001). Code of good practice in the provision of transnational education. From www.coe.int/t/dg4/highereducation/recognition/code of good practice_EN.asp

Council of Postsecondary Accreditation. (1997). *Principles of Good Practice in Overseas International Education Programs for Non-U.S. Nationals*. Council of Postsecondary Accreditation.

Cunningham, S., Ryan, Y., Stedman, L., Tapsall, S., Bagdon, K., Flew, T., et al. (2000). *The Business of Borderless Education*. Canberra: Department of Education, Training and Youth Affairs.

Cunningham, S., Tapsall, S., Ryan, Y., Stedman, L., Bagdon, K., & Flew, T. (1998). *New Media and Borderless Education: A Review of the Convergence between Global Media Networks and Higher Education Provision*. Canberra: Department of Employment, Education, Training and Youth Affairs.

DEEWR. (2011). Student 2010 full year: Selected higher education statistics. Retrieved 28 October, 2011 from www.deewr.gov.au/HigherEducation/Publications/HEStatistics/Publications/Pages/2010StudentFullYear.aspx

Department of Industry. (2013). *2012 Student Full Year: Selected Higher Education Statistics* (Vol. 2013). Canberra: Australian Government Department of Industry.

DIISRTE. (2012). *Delivery of VET Offshore by Public Providers, 2011.* Canberra: Department of Industry, Innovation, Science, Research and Tertiary Education and the National Centre for Vocational Education Research.

Feng, Y. (2012). University of Nottingham Ningbo China and Xi'an Jiaotong-Liverpool University: globalization of higher education in China. *Higher Education.* doi: 10.1007/s10734-012-9558-8

Forde, P. (2011). Curtin University's development of a campus in Singapore. In A. Stella & S. Bhushan (Eds.), *Quality Assurance of Transnational Higher Education: The Experiences of Australia and India* (pp. 127–136). Australian Universites Quality Agency and the National University of Educational Planning and Administration.

Hajjar, D. P., & Gotto, A. M. (2013). Launching of an American medical college in the Middle East: Educational challenges in a multicultural environment. *International Journal of Higher Education, 2*(2). doi: 10.5430/ijhe.v2n2p67

Healey, N. (2013a). Is UK transnational education one of Britain's great growth industries of the future? *Higher Education Review, 45*(3), 6–35.

Healey, N. (2013b). Why do English universities really franchise degrees to overseas providers? *Higher Education Quarterly, 67*(2), 180–200. doi: 10.1111/hequ.12012

HESA. (2009). HESA students in higher education institutions 2007/08 reveals 197,000 students studying overseas for UK HE qualifications. Press Release 133. Retrieved 26 June 2010 from www.hesa.ac.uk/index.php/content/view/1398/161/

HESA. (2012). *Aggregate Overseas Student Record.* UK: Higher Education Statistics Agency.

Kamlet, M. (2010). Offering domestic degrees outside the United States: One university's experience over the past decade. In M. B. d'Ambrosio, P. J. Yakoboski & D. B. Johnstone (Eds.), *Higher Education in a Global Society.* Cheltenham, UK: Edward Elgar.

Kinser, K. (2011). Multinational quality assurance. In J. E. Lane & K. Kinser (Eds.), *Multinational Colleges and Universities: Leading, Governing and Managing International Branch Campuses* (pp. 53–64). San Francisco: Jossey Bass.

Koelman, J. B. J., & Vries, P. d. (1999). Marketisation, hybrid organisations and accounting in higher education. In G. Neave, P. Maassen & B. Jongbloed (Eds.), *From the Eye of the Storm: Higher education's changing institution.* Dordrecht: Kluwer.

Lawton, W., & Katsomitros, A. (2011). *International Branch Campuses: Data and Developments.* London: Observatory on Borderless Higher Education.

McBurnie, G., & Ziguras, C. (2007). *Transnational Education: Current Issues and Future Trends in Offshore Higher Education.* London: RoutledgeFalmer.

McNamara, J. (2013). *The Shape of Things to Come: The Evolution of Transnational Education: Data, Definitions, Opportunities and Impacts Analysis.* London: British Council.

Mukul, A. (2009, 10 January). Govt lays down stricter norms for setting up offshore campus. *The Times of India.* Retrieved from http://articles.timesofindia.indiatimes.com/2009-01-10/india/28027388_1_offshore-campus-domestic-campus-mci-screening-test-regulations

OBHE. (2002). *International Branch Campuses: Scale and Significance.* Briefing Note No.5 (pp. 10). London: Observatory on Borderless Higher Education.

QAA. (1999). *Code of Practice for the Assurance of Academic Quality and Standards in Higher Education. Section 2: Collaborative provision.* Gloucester: Quality Assurance Agency for Higher Education.

QAA. (2011a, 21 June). *Institutional Review: Wales, October 2010.* Retrieved from http://www.qaa.ac.uk/InstitutionReports/Reports/Pages/Inst-review-University-of-Wales-11.aspx

QAA. (2011b, 21 June). *Audit of Overseas Provision: University of Wales and TCA College, Singapore, January 2011.* Retrieved from http://www.qaa.ac.uk/InstitutionReports/Reports/Pages/overseas-University-of-Wales-11.aspx

Sexton, J. (2012). The global network university: Educating citizens of the world. In M. Stiasny & T. Gore (Eds.), *Going Global: The Landscape for Policy Makers and Practitioners in Tertiary Education* (pp. 5–12). Bingley, UK: Emerald.

Verbik, L., & Jokivirta, L. (2005a). *National Regulatory Frameworks for Transnational Higher Education: Models and Trends, Part 1.* Observatory Briefings. London: Observatory on Borderless Higher Education.

Verbik, L., & Jokivirta, L. (2005b). *National Regulatory Frameworks for Transnational Higher Education: Models and Trends, Part 2.* Observatory Briefings. London: Observatory on Borderless Higher Education.

Verbik, L., & Merkley, C. (2006). *The International Branch Campus: Models and Trends.* London: Observatory on Borderless Higher Education.

Wilmoth, D. (2006). RMIT International University Vietnam's development contribution. Case study for Master Sviluppo program.

Zhu, X., & Zhu, Y. (2011). *Capacity Building for Policies and Monitoring of Cross-Border Education in the APEC Region.* Singapore: APEC Human Resource Development Working Group.

Chapter 7

Regulation and quality assurance of foreign providers

The leading importers of cross-border education are mostly middle-income countries in which the growth in secondary-school completions and labour-market demand for graduates has outstripped the capacity of the domestic higher education system. Transnational programmes make a significant contribution to the total supply of higher education in some countries, most notably Hong Kong and Singapore. After 20 years of continued growth, by the mid 2000s fully one-third of Singapore's higher education students were enrolled in transnational education programmes (see Table 7.1).

For critics of the commercialization of higher education, transnational education is the most blatant example of the unbridled pursuit of profit. It exemplifies the separation of education from traditional academic values: classroom-based, face-to-face teaching (including pastoral and mentoring roles), by well-qualified research academics, with a commitment to community service. Further, it would seem likely that almost none of the students are disadvantaged aid-recipients (who tend to receive scholarships to study in the donor country). The worst-case picture is of low-ability students (those not accepted into regular, reputable institutions), using pre-packaged cookie-cutter foreign lecture notes, in cramped

Table 7.1 Students in Singaporean tertiary education institutions, 2005

	Number of students	Percentage
• Polytechnics	56,048	23
• Local universities (NUS, NTU, SIM)	41,628	17
• Private institutions' own programmes	26,500	11
• Institute of technical education	19,207	8
• National institute of education	2,282	1
All domestic providers	145,665	59
Transnational programmes	80,200	33
Singaporean students enrolled overseas	19,371	8
Total	*245,236*	*100*

Data sources: Lee (2005, p. 15); MoE (2006 table 15); UNESCO (2013).

office premises under the supervision of poorly qualified locals, supplemented by occasional visits by jet-lagged fly-in fly-out (FIFO) academics. The local partners are suspected to be of dubious repute: private operators, unreliable and prone to financial collapse, treating education as just any other business, and happy to rapidly shift their footloose capital and entrepreneurial cunning/skill to exploit the next money-making opportunity that arises.

The idealized counter image propounded by champions of transnational education is of high-quality education (underpinned by carefully modularized curriculum materials and pedagogically road-tested learning strategies) being delivered to where the demand is highest, saving students the cost and disruption of studying abroad, saving taxpayer funds (by shifting cost from the government to the private student), building capacity in the host country, strengthening relations between the provider and host countries, and enhancing the international reputation and competitiveness of both countries (for example, in the case of prestigious foreign campuses attracting international students to the host nation).

The potential risks for the host country are numerous. The most obvious danger is that the transnational programme may be of poor educational quality, or may be inappropriately adapted to local cultural and pedagogical requirements. There is the additional danger for consumers that the foreign operation collapses or withdraws from the host country, leaving students financially disadvantaged, with an incomplete qualification, and disruption to their educational career as they seek to find alternative options for completing their studies. More broadly, the presence of mobile foreign programmes and institutions could reduce host government prerogatives for steering the domestic system, and best utilizing higher education in the nation-building process. For example, transnational education programmes may result in an overabundance of business graduates, whereas the government seeks to boost the relative number of engineering graduates. Even a reputable and well-run transnational education programme can have negative effects on the domestic system if it draws too many – or the best and brightest – students and staff away from local institutions. There can be reputational damage to the host country if it is seen to do a poor job of regulating TNE, including filtering out dubious providers. In the case of international branch campuses, where the host has invested resources (money, land, other infrastructure) with the aim of attracting prestigious operators to their 'hub', the government can lose financially. Indeed, having a prestigious institution withdraw could in itself be grounds for reputational loss.

From a governance perspective, how can the benefits for importing countries be maximized and the negative effects be minimized? In Chapter 6 the issues are explored from the perspective of the transnational education exporting country and institution. In this chapter we are looking at matters from the perspective of the importer government. As we have also discussed above, in many cases the same country is both an importer and an exporter; that does not prevent them seeking liberal regulations for their exports and exacting stricter regulations for the import of education.

Over the past decade there have been a number of studies that have examined the extent of transnational education in particular countries or regions, and have considered the regulatory frameworks that have shaped the patterns of provision, particularly in Asia, including:

- China (Gu, 2009; Helms, 2008; Huang, 2006, 2011; McNamara, 2013; Mok & Xu, 2008; QAA, 2006; Yang, 2008);
- India (Anandakrishnan, 2011; Bhushan, 2011; P. Jayaprakash, 2011; P. K. Jayaprakash, 2010; Khadria, 2011; Ranganath & Shyamasundar, 2011; Thorat, 2011);
- Singapore (Gopinathan & Lee, 2011; Koh, 2012; Mok, 2006; Ng, 2013; Sidhu, Ho, & Yeoh, 2011; Watson & Yap, 2011);
- Malaysia (McNamara, 2013; Mok, 2012; Richards, 2012; Sirat, 2006; Tapsir & Rahman, 2012; Tham, 2013);
- Hong Kong (Maclean & Lai, 2012; Yang, 2006);
- United Arab Emirates (McNamara, 2013; Rawazik & Carroll, 2009);
- Japan (Huang, 2011; Tsurata, 2006);
- Vietnam (Welch, 2010);
- Taiwan (Song & Tai, 2006);
- Korea (Lee, 2006);
- Africa (Lane & Kinser, 2013).

Detailed national studies such as these show that the processes of registration, accreditation and quality assurance of transnational education vary widely, and may involve various ministries (education, commerce, labour, immigration) and different levels of government (municipal, provincial and national).

There are different ways of conceptualizing the regulatory approaches. In part it depends on the interests of the audience. If you are a foreign institution, you may want to know how difficult it is to enter, establish and operate in that country. This may be a comparative matter – will we direct our efforts here or there instead? If you are an importer, you will be interested in how successful the regulatory regime is, to see whether you can use it for modelling purposes: what elements can you adapt? From an academic perspective, we are interested in conceiving models for understanding what motivates the approaches and how they might develop over time.

In this chapter we look at the toolkit of actions that importing governments can use to regulate TNE, discuss the spectrum of different regulatory approaches (liberal, restrictive and in between), and propose a model for understanding the complexity of what is actually happening across countries.

There are some types of international institutions that we will not consider because they are not generally treated as foreign by host governments, such as locally established universities that are foreign-owned or foreign-backed. The last two decades have seen the emergence of large-scale cross-border investment in education. The

United Nations estimates that the total stock of foreign direct investment (FDI) in education had grown from just US$100 million in 1990 to US$10.1 billion by 2011 (UNCTAD, 2013). When one considers the list of existing branch campuses and the relatively small amounts that were invested by the parent institution, it is obvious that only a very small proportion of this foreign investment originates from higher education providers establishing a campus in another country (Lawton & Katsomitros, 2011). Much of the investment is the result of activities of large commercial conglomerates that own a stable of educational institutions in a range of countries. Some of the largest of these are Laureate International Universities (headquartered in Baltimore, USA), Apollo Group (Phoenix, USA), Kaplan (Fort Lauderdale, USA), Study Group (London), Navitas (Perth, Australia), Manipal Education and Medical Group (Bangalore, India). These and other educational multinationals typically acquire existing private education providers or sometimes establish new institutions and then seek to integrate them into a network of global services that can provide enormous economies of scale in market intelligence and student recruitment, curriculum development, assessment design, management structure, and so on. The business strategy of each is quite distinct, with some focusing on degree-level institutions, some focusing on English language and pre-university pathway programmes, and others on vocational education and training.

Despite the great shortage of supply of education in developing countries, 82 per cent of the value of all FDI in education is invested in developed economies (UNCTAD, 2013, Table 24). However, this difference in dollar values may not accurately reflect the level of activity in terms of the number of students, which is arguably a more meaningful measure. The purchase price of a private college in Hanoi providing information technology training to 1,000 students may be one-fifth of the purchase price of an equivalent institution in Sydney, though they might provide similar qualifications. Unfortunately, we have no way of knowing how many students in each country are studying in foreign-owned institutions.

In this chapter we will be examining the ways in which governments regulate institutions offering foreign educational qualifications in their territory, but this does not include foreign-owned or invested institutions which are established as a local business entity and registered as a local education provider. Curiously, many governments place far less restriction on FDI in private education than on entry of foreign education providers. For example, in India, while foreign institutions are prohibited from establishing a campus (as we will see later in this chapter) there is no limit on foreign investment in the education sector, although degree-granting power must be awarded by state and national governments (Thorat, 2011, p. 181). Ironically, it is much easier to establish a new private university backed by foreign capital than to establish a branch campus of an established university. While overseas universities are deterred, this situation will benefit the creation of the proposed Nalanda International University. The new institution, led by prominent economist Amartya Sen, will be built near the site of the ancient centre of Buddhist learning of the same name, and will be financed by foreign capital from a range of donor countries and benefactors.

We will also not be considering in any detail foreign-backed universities in this chapter. This term is used to describe a university which is a 'legally independent higher education institution of the country where it is located which is academically affiliated to one or several universities in another country (patron universities)' (Lanzendorf, 2008). This type of institution is distinct from a foreign university branch campus type, which is operated in the name of its parent university and its programmes lead to the parent institution's degrees. Like institutions that are foreign owned but locally established, these are normally treated as domestic institutions rather than foreign universities.

The 'toolkit': mechanisms for regulating transnational education

In practical terms, there is a range of measures that governments can take in relation to both campuses and programmes. There are fewer options for programmes without a local presence, as we note below.

Checking the provider's bona fides

One basic condition that governments can mandate for any mode of delivery is the requirement that the foreign institution demonstrate that it is recognized as an authorized education provider in its home jurisdiction. Incorporated into a registration process for partner-supported programmes and branch campuses, this is a means for governments to ascertain which other government is responsible for accrediting and assuring the quality of the foreign programme being imported. For programmes without a local presence, establishing the programme's bona fides in its home country is normally a prerequisite for any form of recognition the programme receives. This should result in only legitimate providers entering the market while filtering out diploma mills and low-quality providers that lack accreditation in their home country. These institutions can be attracted to transnational education because they may be more easily able to pass themselves off as a legitimate institution in places where their home system is less well-known (Garrett, 2005). The task of ascertaining which universities are recognized at home has become much easier since the International Association of Universities began compiling its List of Universities of the World which is regularly updated with information provided by authorities in each country (www.iau-aiu.net/content/list-heis). This list does not, however, include most institutions that offer sub-degree qualifications such as vocational diplomas and language courses, which are in high demand in developing countries.

Recognition of qualifications

An important tool that governments can use to influence enrolments is granting or withholding official recognition of qualifications for the purposes of employment or further study. This strategy is applicable to all forms of transnational education, but is perhaps most powerful in the case of cross-border distance education or online programmes which have no local presence. These are difficult for governments to detect, let alone to regulate. Registration for transnational programmes is normally only required if there are lectures, tutorials or examinations taking place in the host country.

Some governments, such as China, that have doubts about online degree studies refuse outright to recognize any foreign qualifications that are not earned through on campus study. Most other countries' recognition bodies treat online degrees the same as they treat qualifications earned through on campus study, as long as the qualification is recognized in the home country.

Countries that provide support for overseas study in the form of loans and tax deductions can choose to treat online programmes either as equivalent to on-campus programmes or differently. For example, Norway's State Education Loan Fund specifically excludes distance learning programmes from its funding scheme, whether they are undertaken in Norway or overseas (Lånekassen, 2013). In Australia, students can claim transnational online course fees as tax deductions in the same manner as any other course fees that are not funded by government.

Curriculum controls

Many countries require that the curriculum in the transnational programme is equivalent to that offered on the home campus, while some countries prohibit the delivery of programmes in particular fields of study (e.g. religion in China and Vietnam), or mandate the inclusion of compulsory subjects (such as Malaysian studies and the national language in Malaysia).

Some countries, including China, apply a needs test requiring applicants to demonstrate not only that there is student demand for the proposed programme but that the demand is not able to be met by other institutions.

Partnership requirements

Governments can limit the amount of equity a foreign university is able to have in a branch campus, thereby forcing them to partner with a local organization. In Malaysia, where this requirement was in place until recently, local equity partners have been Malaysian corporations in some cases, and provincial governments in others. In China, the government has usually insisted that foreign universities share ownership with Chinese university partners. Often a local equity partner is a financial necessity in any case, since universities themselves are rarely prepared to fund the cost of acquiring land and building a campus. When government support is provided to facilitate the establishment of international branch campuses (such as use of land and buildings) it is often channelled through the local partners, so that if the foreign university pulls out, the government's investment is not lost to the country.

As with branch campuses, in the case of partner-supported programmes one of the most significant requirements governments can make is the involvement of a particular type of local partner organization. For example, China and Indonesia require that foreign institutions must partner with local institutions that offer programmes at the same level (Huang, 2006; Sirozi, 2008). Here the concern is not with ownership and equity but to ensure the capability of the local institution to participate in teaching programmes at a particular level. By contrast, Malaysia and Singapore, which have been incubators of innovation in transnational education since the 1980s, allowed professional associations and private colleges that were not accredited to offer their own degrees to instead offer the degree programmes of foreign partner universities. Over two decades this has proved a very successful capacity-building strategy, and many of the local partners have outgrown their reliance on foreign universities (for a history of such partnerships see Clayton & Ziguras, 2011).

More and more host governments are implementing regulations to prevent validation by universities of programmes that they do not actually teach. For example, China requires that at least one-third of the programme is taught by staff from the awarding university and that students are enrolled with the awarding university for at least one-third of the courses in the programme. Other countries, such as Hong Kong, require that the transnational programme is equivalent to the programme taught on the home campus. India now specifically prohibits such arrangements, with its new rules stating that: 'No arrangement involving a Foreign Educational Institution granting, for a consideration, a license or permission to an Indian Educational Institution to carry out educational activity in the name of the Foreign Educational Institution shall be permitted under these regulations' (Government of India, 2013, p. 3819).

Registration requirements

The most basic form of regulation of such partnerships is to establish a registration process, allowing the ministry of education to specify and enforce a set of requirements, to publish lists of approved programmes, and to stop the operation of unapproved programmes. Requirements routinely involve stipulations about the qualifications of teaching staff, and the relative shares of teaching undertaken by local partner and awarding institution staff. The government can specify and enforce controls on tuition fees, and place restrictions on the repatriation of funds. Approvals might specify the number or proportion of local and/or international students that may be enrolled.

Staffing requirements

Staffing is a sensitive issue for governments. There are usually restrictions placed on the number of staff that can be brought in from abroad, and their qualifications. Regulatory mechanisms take the form of immigration restrictions, which often stipulate the types of foreign workers that are allowed to be brought in by a foreign enterprise, and the maximum duration of their stay. These rules usually do not differ between sectors of the economy, so employees of educational institutions are treated in a similar manner to employees in any service sector. Governments are naturally motivated by a desire to see their own citizens employed in preference to foreign nationals, whereas multinational organizations value the ability to move their workforce between branches in different countries. Salt and Wood (2013) in their study of British branch campuses found that universities had difficulty enticing staff from the home campus to relocate temporarily to the overseas branch, and had to recruit internationally to a greater extent than they had envisaged. Despite the expectations of governments and universities who might believe they are establishing a 'British' or 'Australian' campus, academic staffing tends to become very multinational very quickly. Partner institutions often also play a significant role in the staffing choices of campuses, and governments thereby have an influence on staffing by mandating particular types of local partners (Salt & Wood, 2013).

Stipulations about the nature of the provider

A government may require that the foreign university meets specific requirements, such as being a not-for-profit institution or having been in existence for a certain period of time. Since the advent of global rankings, these have been a convenient means of filtering entrants, and despite the obvious methodological shortcomings of the various ranking models, they have been attractive to some governments as a short-hand status marker. The proposed Indian regulations to allow the establishment of foreign branch campuses require that the foreign university be ranked among the top 400 in either the *Times Higher Education*, Quacquarelli Symonds or the Shanghai Jiao Tong University rankings (Ministry of Human Resource Development, 2013).

Accreditation and/or quality assurance

Host governments may exempt branch campuses from national accreditation and/or quality assurance processes on the basis that the home country is responsible, or they may choose to subject them to the same requirements that are imposed on domestic institutions. Malaysia, with one of the most well-developed regulatory frameworks for transnational education has, over time, moved from the former to the latter system. Now the Malaysian Qualifications Agency's audit teams regularly include auditors drawn from national public universities, private universities and international branch campuses. Such forms of integration can assist in the dissemination of good practice between different types of institutions, and thereby increase understanding of all participants of the standards and expectations of different sections of the higher education system.

Offering inducements

In those cases where the host nation wants to attract a prestigious provider – for example to set up a campus and thereby improve the country's hub status – it can offer a range of inducements. These may include: subsidies, low-interest loans, tax breaks, government investment, cheap land or buildings. Less tangible, but nonetheless important, the host may simply relax the normal regulatory requirements, making the undertaking less onerous for the desirable institution. The long-term sustainability of foreign programmes and campuses in many places will be determined by the degree to which they have access to the same funding schemes as local institutions, thereby improving their affordability. Qatar, for example, provides subsidies to its nationals who study in transnational programmes offered in the country.

Public promotion of transnational provision

Malaysia and Hong Kong have been particularly active in promoting transnational education to the public as a valuable component of the higher education system, earning the praise of the British Council (McNamara, 2013), whereas Singapore, as discussed in Chapter 3, is very selective, praising some elite foreign universities at every opportunity while refusing to even acknowledge the existence of many others.

The attitude of governments is liable to change over time as the sector matures. In one country we visited, the section of the ministry of education that dealt with private and foreign providers initially saw itself as playing a policing role that involved 'naming and shaming', scrutinizing the sector and publicizing the infractions of delinquent operators. A few years later, that same department – while still maintaining its critical brief – was happy to promote the sector both domestically and internationally, regarding these institutions as an important part of the nation's tapestry of education offerings.

Regulatory approaches

In this section we endeavour to discern a range of distinct approaches to regulation, and illustrate the ways in which the ideological approaches and political interests combine to shape a government's policy objectives and choice of regulatory tools. As shown above, governments do have at their disposal a wide range of measures that can be put in place to manage transnational provision. In practice, all governments pick and choose from this toolbox very selectively. Here we try to make some sense of the patterns that we see when we look across a number of importing governments' regulatory approaches.

Several studies have developed systems to classify regulatory frameworks for foreign providers. We have previously contrasted consumer protection (Hong Kong), advancing national goals (Malaysia) and protecting the local system (Australia) (McBurnie & Ziguras, 2001). Mok (2008, 2012) has also compared the regulatory regimes employed by three major transnational education importers turned exporters: Hong Kong, Malaysia and Singapore. Each of these four countries is interesting because they have relatively open, liberal policy frameworks overlaid with proactive strategic engagement by the state to boost quality and national standing. These are interesting cases, and important because they are among the most successful cases of harnessing transnational education's developmental potential anywhere in the world, but, these countries are atypical, both in their openness to foreign providers and in their integration of transnational providers into their national higher education strategy.

A much broader report by the Observatory on Borderless Higher Education (OBHE) classified the approaches of some 50 countries (Verbik & Jokivirta, 2005a, 2005b). They identify six different categories of regulatory framework: no regulations (no requirement for special permission); liberal (minimal conditions); moderately liberal (active licensing or accrediting transnational providers); very restrictive (onerous requirements); and non-recognition. They also describe movement between these categories, pointing out that quite a few countries were at that time changing their approaches. We find this approach quite useful, although Verbik and Jokivirta's use of the terms 'liberal' and 'restrictive' conflates two types of regulation – business regulation and quality assurance – that are conceptually very different. In education, as in other sectors, a process of liberalization of business regulation is often coupled with an increase in quality assurance regulation, as Braithwaite and Drahos (2000) have shown in relation to many industry sectors. Many countries that have opened their borders to transnational education have simultaneously made stringent quality demands, and these could be seen as simultaneously 'liberal' (allowing foreign entry) and 'restrictive' (squeezing out the bottom end of the market).

More recently, McNamara's (2013) study for the British Council assessed the policy environment and market conditions for transnational education in 25 host countries. Commissioned by an agency representing exporters, the study was interested in policy environments to assess 'the extent to which host country governments have implemented policies and processes to facilitate and manage inbound TNE' (p. 7). Using published guidelines and other policy documents and previous research, and supplemented with information from British and host country sources, the study scored each country on 13 indicators, shown in Table 7.2.

Table 7.2 McNamara's transnational education policy environment framework

Indicator	Scoring criteria
1. TNE strategy	• Dedicated international education body with TNE remit • Evidence of TNE host strategy • TNE incentives
2. Establishment of TNE operations	• Permission/regulations for foreign institutions to establish • Permission/regulations for establishment of TNE programmes • Clarity of establishment regulations • Academic visas or assistance with inbound faculty mobility
3. Quality assurance and accreditation	• Quality assurance of foreign institutions • Quality assurance of TNE programmes • International collaboration on quality assurance
4. Recognition of TNE	• TNE guidelines or codes of practice • Recognition of TNE qualifications • International collaboration on recognition of qualifications

Reproduced from McNamara (2013, p. 21).

This approach is more detailed than Verbik and Jokivirta's but still does not separate out business regulation from quality assurance. In fact where Verbik and Jokivirta's model considered demanding quality assurance as a form of restriction, and lack of quality assurance as more liberal, McNamara appears to rate quality assurance positively. Although the scoring methodology is not described, host countries with well-developed quality assurance regimes score more highly than those without (Table 7.3). Clearly, McNamara considers the existence of robust quality assurance measures in host countries to be to the benefit of British transnational providers.

When considered along with the World Bank's more established Doing Business ranking, the difficulty with conflating such disparate measures becomes apparent. The Doing Business ranking is very pertinent to the establishment of a branch campus, since it considers the regulatory burden involved in registering a company, buying property, opening bank accounts, and so on, all of which branch campuses are normally required to do. Some countries (such as China) score more highly in the British Council study than in the World Bank study

Table 7.3 Scoring regulatory environments for transnational providers

Country	British Council TNE Regulatory Environment Score	World Bank Doing Business Rank
Malaysia	8.0	6
Hong Kong	7.3	2
Singapore	7.2	1
UAE	6.5	23
China	5.2	96
Mauritius	5.2	20
Qatar	5.1	48
South Korea	5.1	7
Bahrain	5.0	46
Thailand	4.8	18
Vietnam	4.6	99
Nigeria	4.2	147
Pakistan	4.1	110
Botswana	4.0	56
Oman	3.9	47
Russia	3.1	92
Spain	2.8	52
Brazil	2.7	116
Mexico	2.7	53
Indonesia	2.5	120
India	1.9	134
Poland	1.8	45
Sri Lanka	1.7	85
Turkey	1.1	69
Nepal	0.8	105

Data sources: McNamara (2013, pp. 77–101); World Bank (2013).

because they have moderately restrictive business regulation but well-developed quality assurance systems. It is unfortunate that the British Council report does not score each of the four indicators separately, which would provide a clearer picture.

We have previously tried to consider the interplay of business regulation and quality assurance in practice in three of the largest host countries, Singapore, Hong Kong and Malaysia, which followed a common pattern of development with regulatory frameworks evolving to suit the conditions that existed in each stage (McBurnie & Ziguras, 2007). We conceptualized this as a four-phase model of development of programme and institution mobility:

1   Faced with a shortage of relevant, quality study options in the local tertiary system, students travel abroad to study. Transnational education is in its infancy and unregulated.
2   The capacity of the local system is built up, through a combination of public and private investment and through light-touch licensing and quality assurance which allows partnerships with foreign universities to raise institutional capacity.
3   As local capacity grows, reliance on foreign universities shifts from capacity building to building the prestige and quality of the local system. Foreign branch campuses are recruited and increasingly stringent quality assurance squeezes out the lower-status and lower-quality partner-supported programmes.
4   Having grown domestic capacity, the government looks at its options for exporting education. This may involve plans to become a 'hub' provider, attracting students from the region. The presence of prestigious foreign providers may be a key part of the drawcard. The export preparation phase involves a shake-out of providers, to ensure the quality of foreign provision and strengthening of local provision.

In these key host countries there has been over the past two decades a trend for countries to become more open to foreign providers, while making quality assurance requirements increasingly demanding. In the following section we distinguish between four regulatory approaches, by considering both business regulation (restrictive or liberal) and quality assurance – or quality filtering – regimes (minimal or comprehensive) (Table 7.4).

Table 7.4 Business regulation and quality assurance in selected countries

	Restrictive business regulation	Liberal business regulation
Minimal quality assurance	E.g. Greece, India	E.g. UK, Timor-Leste
Comprehensive quality assurance	E.g. China, Vietnam	E.g. Australia, Malaysia, Singapore, Hong Kong, Norway

Liberal regulation and minimal quality assurance

Until the last decade, transnational education was rarely within the regulatory purview of either the sending country or the receiving country, and regulatory and policy coherence remains rare. None of the 25 countries studied by the British Council has an explicit strategy for transnational education, and half have no identifiable government department with responsibility for TNE, with regulation being fragmented across education, economic and international relations units (McNamara, 2013, p. 6).

In many host countries foreign providers are not specifically restricted from offering programmes either in partnership with local institutions or through a campus of their own. Verbik and Jokivirta (2005a, 2005b) list quite a few countries as having no regulations governing foreign providers, including Austria, Czech Republic, Denmark, France, Laos, Malta, Mexico, Nigeria, Panama, Portugal, Russia, Serbia, Sri Lanka. Most countries had no regulation when transnational provision began but as McNamara (2013) notes, at some point, when the scale of transnational education reaches a critical mass governments have felt the need to regulate. When the OECD surveyed its member countries to assess the extent to which they had implemented the recommendations of the guidelines for quality provision in cross-border higher education (OECD & UNESCO, 2005), they found that a major remaining gap for governments was the establishment of a system of registration or licensing for incoming cross-border higher education providers, which was still not in place in Francophone Belgium, Czech Republic, Finland, Austria or Jordan (Vincent-Lancrin & Pfotenhauer, 2012, p. 16).

In the early days of transnational provision the scale is often negligible and does not warrant regulatory intervention. Importing-country governments often consider foreign programmes as being out of their jurisdiction, at least initially, and the responsibility of authorities in the awarding institution's country. As we have seen in Chapter 6, the exporting government may have oversight of transnational programmes, or it may not, and if not it is easy for such programmes to 'slip through the cracks' between two regulatory systems. In unregulated environments, a high level of student demand for foreign programmes can lead to rapid growth, as occurred in China, Malaysia and Singapore in the 1990s. This is often coupled with growth in private higher education generally, and in these cases the bulk of partnerships are between new domestic private education providers and foreign universities.

Large-scale transnational education has been mainly a phenomenon of cities in middle-income countries where few are able to afford overseas study but more are able to afford the significantly lower fees charged by transnational degree programmes. In some countries, such as Timor-Leste, a rapid growth in private providers is not accompanied by a growth in transnational partnerships or campuses, in large part because even transnational programme fees remain far out of reach of all but a few students. In many high-income countries, despite a lack of regulation, transnational higher education has remained insignificant because local institutions are well-established and foreign institutions are in most cases unable to access government funding that would enable them to compete with established providers. Even when they are unattractive to domestic institutions, transnational providers can use a city's location as a base to recruit international students to that location. For example, despite the UK having no effective regulation of foreign providers, London is host to at least four international branch campuses, including Limkokwing University of Creative Technology (based in Malaysia), Glion Institute of Higher Education (Switzerland), The University of Chicago Booth School of Business (United States) and Hult International Business School (United States), and there is no way of knowing which foreign programmes are offered to students based in the UK through local partner institutions. In order to be able to enrol international students from outside the EU, institutions must meet requirements of the Home Office, otherwise they are subject to no regulation (Higher Education Commission, 2013, pp. 48–49).

Collaborations between domestic private colleges and foreign universities enable new private entrants to bypass domestic regulatory frameworks which restrict the ability of unauthorized local providers to confer degrees. Private colleges that were not able to confer their own degrees could instead offer foreign degrees. Governments may appreciate the growth of such partnerships since they expand access to degree programmes without requiring the expansion of government-funded institutions. Partnerships with foreign universities may also assist in raising the standard of domestic private institutions, motivated by the foreign provider's concern with maintaining their brand reputation and/or quality assurance requirements put in place by the home country.

The lack of locally recognized accreditation and quality assurance is a problem for all private providers, who must somehow convince the public of their legitimacy, and sometimes the name of a foreign university serves this purpose. Another option for private providers is to seek accreditation from one of the national and international accreditation agencies that offer their services globally. Altbach and Knight (2007) report that US national and regional accreditors operate in more than 65 countries, alongside professional accreditation bodies such as the US Accreditation Board for Engineering and Technology and the European Quality Improvement System that accredits business programmes. These agencies do not only operate in systems which lack local accreditation systems, but they are much more important in such circumstances. Accreditation mills, companies that are unrecognized posing as legitimate accreditation agencies, also find rich pickings in such environments, offering their services both to local and transnational sub-standard providers and diploma mills (Garrett, 2005).

At some point, however, low-quality and fraudulent providers and programmes will emerge, threatening the legitimacy of the institution in question, but also the transnational education sector, and exposing the government to criticism for failing to protect the public. Unfortunate students and their families who are victims of illegitimate or failed transnational programmes may ask why they were not warned of the risks, and the appearance of diploma mills will prompt calls by legitimate transnational providers and their local partners for screening measures to reassure the public. Levy has described a similar pattern in relation to private higher education generally, which then results in 'delayed regulation' involving the development or strengthening of licensing standards and quality assurance (Levy, 2006, 2012).

Sehoole's (2008) account of South Africa's experience provides an excellent illustration of 'delayed regulation' of transnational education. In the late 1990s a large number of private providers established, many partnering with foreign educational institutions to deliver franchised programmes. Before 2001 there were around 50 foreign universities active in South Africa, most operating through partnerships with local institutions. A report by the Council on Higher Education describes a range of concerns about the quality of transnational programme delivery, including students' complaints about poor-quality programmes, private providers that were not equipped to deliver the qualifications being offered, a lack of oversight by the foreign awarding institution and awarding institutions that were considered in their home country to be of poor quality. In 2001 the government implemented a new regulatory regime that required all private and foreign institutions to seek registration with the Ministry of Education, and prohibited foreign institutions from offering degrees in South Africa unless they were registered. Fourteen foreign institutions applied for accreditation but only four were successful.

Transnational education can operate in countries in which regulatory frameworks are lacking, but it is usually risky in the short term due to the lack of quality assurance of local partners. In the longer term, operating in such environments is often unsustainable, due to both the reputational damage posed by the inevitable poor-quality providers, and by the likelihood of a subsequent restrictive government crackdown. The experience of US universities operating in Japan is a stark illustration of the riskiness of unregulated host countries. During the 1980s, many US universities established campuses in Japan even though the Ministry of Education had distanced itself from such initiatives, arguing that the US authorities alone had responsibility for governing them. The US institutions felt that, given the scale of US investment, eventually the Ministry would change its view and formally recognize the institutions as equivalent to Japanese universities. However, the Ministry continued to resist engaging with the US institutions and eventually the inability of the US universities to gain legitimacy within the Japanese system, along with poor business planning, played a significant role in the collapse of all but one, Temple University, even though at the height of interest in Japan over 100 universities had established operations or were actively exploring opportunities to do so (Chambers & Cummings, 1990).

Liberal regulation and comprehensive quality assurance

In theory a regulatory framework based on economic liberal principles would establish market conditions in which all providers, whether domestic or foreign, established or new, public or private, could operate on a level playing field. The state's role in quality assurance would be to ensure that the minimum standards that the public expect of providers are met, and that information that students and their families need to make informed choices is available to the public.

Some of the former British colonies in Asia come close to this ideal. Hong Kong, Malaysia, Singapore and Australia are open to foreign providers that meet quality requirements that are in line with those expected of domestic institutions. In Malaysia and Australia, the challenge of regulating the quality of transnational providers revealed a lack of clear expectations of domestic institutions. As a result the Malaysian Qualifications Agency was established with a mandate to ensure consistent standards across different types of institutions. In Australia the Higher Education Standards Framework articulates a set of threshold standards that are required of all providers, a process which began in 2000 in response to the efforts of a US-based diploma mill to pass itself off as an accredited Australian university (Ziguras, Reinke & McBurnie, 2003). In each country, overseas universities are required to be duly registered or accredited in their home country and meet the standards required of equivalent domestic institutions.

As we saw in the previous chapter, the British and Australian governments have been very active in transnational education policy advocacy in these countries. The British Council and consular staff work closely with ministry of education officials and representatives from British and Australian universities and local partner organizations, while encouraging collaboration between quality assurance agencies and professional associations in each country. Australia has also been active in placing transnational education on the agenda of key international bodies such as the OECD and APEC, while the UK has been very active within the EU and UNESCO. Over the past few years the British and Australian governments have worked with host governments to organize international forums at which a wide range of participants representing governments, educational institutions and quality assurance agencies showcase the long-term benefits of open regulatory environments and high-quality transnational provision. Officials and university leaders from across Asia are invited in an effort to promote similar approaches to regulation and institutional collaboration elsewhere.

However, even in these countries there are limits to the state's market neutrality, since even in these countries domestic universities are granted privileged access to public funding, to support both teaching and research. In Singapore, Malaysia and Hong Kong, during the 2000s, governments decided that the country's national standing was dependent upon having research-intensive universities as high as possible in global rankings, and each set about concentrating funding to a small number of public universities. The transnational programmes (and campuses in Malaysia's case) that had developed in these countries since the 1980s were an effective means of expanding the supply of degree-level education without making additional demands on government. The partner-supported programmes that constituted the bulk of transnational education in these countries was of peripheral significance in boosting the country's educational status, as Mok (2012) has shown in relation to Hong Kong, and as we discussed earlier in relation to Singapore, which instead invested heavily in buying-in very different transnational institutions, mostly high-status research-intensive US universities, while ignoring the existence of large-scale transnational partnerships in the government's pronouncements about Singapore's world-class system. In Adelaide too, handpicked high-status foreign universities have been lavished with public funds and official praise. In Malaysia, efforts at choosing which of its universities to invest in to climb the global rankings never considered Monash and Nottingham universities as candidates, even though each has a large well-established campus in the country and is much higher in the rankings than any Malaysian university. At this point, the national university, like the national airline, becomes a 'flag bearer', and governments find it difficult to see past the nationalistic symbolism to the utility of research. The branch campuses in Malaysia do have access to some public research funds, but must work much harder for much less funding than their colleagues in public universities. Likewise, researchers at the two branch campuses in Australia, Carnegie Mellon University and University College London, are not eligible to apply for the country's main sources of research funding, the Australian Research Council and National Health and Medical Research Council grants.

Restrictive regulation and minimal quality assurance

Socialist countries managed to effectively outlaw transnational provision along with all other forms of non-state provision of higher education, but it appears that only North Korea and Cuba continue such prohibitions today. More common is to refuse to recognize any foreign educational institutions and programmes operating within a country's borders and the qualifications they issue as a matter of principle regardless of the quality of the education provided. Nevertheless, the institutions may in some cases be able to operate as commercial enterprises but outside the jurisdiction or recognition of educational authorities, thereby being prevented from operating as legitimate educational institutions in the eyes of the state. Branch campuses tend to be more heavily restricted than partner-supported programmes. McNamara (2013) found that in some of the 25 countries studied there is no legal provision for the establishment of international branch campuses (India, Nepal, Sri Lanka and Turkey) while in others their legality is unclear (Indonesia and Thailand) (p. 7). This differs from the approach considered above in that the government is clearly opposed to the foreign qualifications and in most cases advises students not to study with unrecognized providers. By refusing to engage with such institutions the same problems with quality and fake providers may emerge, but because the government has not condoned the operations it is able to point to these problems as further reasons to support the non-recognition of such institutions. The long-running dramas that are still playing out today in Greece and India provide good examples of this approach.

In Greece, private colleges have been in existence alongside public universities for over a century. American accredited colleges that were established in the early days of Greek independence were joined after accession to the EU by colleges offering British degree programmes. However, the 1975 Greek Constitution states that education is free and may only be provided by the state. On this basis successive governments have refused to recognize the degrees offered by these colleges, both the degrees issued by the US accredited colleges and the European degrees issued through transnational partner-supported programmes (for a more detailed account see McBurnie & Ziguras, 2007).

The major protagonists in Greece have been the European Commission on the one hand, and on the other, Greek universities and polytechnics and their unions. The EC argues that Greece must recognize European professional qualifications wherever they are issued and must allow non-government education providers to operate. From Brussels, frequent requests and several European Court rulings have ordered Greece to adhere to European directives related to professional mobility and competition policy. From Athens, spokespersons for public providers and unions maintain three types of arguments for the prohibition of private and transnational education. (Because of the practice of electing university leaders and the considerable influence of elected staff and students representatives in university management, the political views of the institutions, the staff unions and students associations are very closely aligned.) Their primary point of contention is a fundamental question of the role of the state. They continue a traditional socialist ideological opposition to any organization but the state providing education, and anyone but the state funding that education. Their second line of argument stems from a nationalist ideological obsession with the sovereignty of the Greek Constitution and disdain for foreign actors including British universities, US accreditation bodies and European government. A third line of argument is naked self-interest. The public institutions do not wish to compete with private and foreign providers either for students or for government funds, and are prepared to use any means available to them to protect the public monopoly.

Frequently, claims about the poor quality of non-government providers are made. For example the spokesperson for the academic union told a newspaper that 'The worst Greek university has better infrastructure and staff than the best private college in Athens' (Kitsantonis, 2011). Anyone who has visited a range of public universities and private colleges in Greece, as we have, knows that this is obviously untrue, but the accuracy of the observation is clearly not the point. In the hyperbolic political culture of Greek higher education reforms the unreality of many such fantasies about quality have not dented the Left's ability to mobilize mass protests and strike actions. For decades, any effort to introduce quality assurance measures for private and transnational providers has been resisted by the public institutions, which have no interest in ensuring the continuing existence of such providers, let alone their quality.

In 2008 a conservative government passed a law establishing a process that would lead to recognition of private colleges. The process would involve a panel of academics working with Ministry of Education and Religious Affairs staff to review the applications of private colleges. Many of the academics nominated to the panel by their universities staged public resignations to demonstrate their

opposition to the exercise in principle (Marseilles, 2009). One of the key requirements of the registration process was that colleges had to provide a bank guarantee
of €500,000 for each campus they operate. After two years, 30 of the 40 colleges
that applied were recognized. Now at least there is a minimal quality assurance
process in place, but one that appears focused on commercial factors and other
inputs rather than the quality of education provided.

The European Commission is not satisfied with this process, arguing that
the requirement to provide a large bank deposit breaches EU laws on freedom to offer and receive services and that the requirements for qualifications
for staff teaching in foreign degree programmes constitute an undue intervention by the Greek state in relation to a service provided by another EU
member (Kitsantonis, 2011). The unions representing academics in universities and polytechnics were not happy either, and when the recognition of 30
colleges was later announced immediately threatened to continue their legal
actions to prevent recognition, both in the Greek courts and the courts of
the European countries in which the colleges' partner universities are located,
and to appeal to the governing boards of the partner universities themselves
(Λακασας, 2010). The Ministry of Education and Religious Affairs, now with
a new policing role over the private sector, has moved to close down unregis-
tered colleges, prohibit others from using the term 'university' in their name
and enforce consumer protection laws relating to misleading advertising.

In a parallel process a Greek court decision finally granted European professional qualifications earned at private colleges the same status as those earned in
Greek universities (Labi, 2010). This finally accepts the outcomes of a key European directive on portability of professional qualifications, and respects a European
Court order for Greece to comply or face a penalty of €975,000 (Kitsantonis,
2011). However, the government and public education institutions still do not
recognize the foreign degrees earned through private colleges as being equivalent
to Greek public university degrees. The battle to rectify this has now been taken
up by the tripartite committee organizing the Greek government bailout led by
the European Commission with the European Central Bank and the International
Monetary Fund (*Kathimerini*, 2012).

Like Greece, India also has no process for registration of foreign providers and
existing transnational education that operates with an unclear legal status. Some
of the arguments put forward in the long and heated debate in India concerning
foreign providers bears remarkable similarity, despite differences in scale (India's
population is over 100 times that of Greece) and complexity (since India's higher
education landscape is much more diverse). However, unlike Greece, where a
liberalization campaign has been imposed from outside the country, in India the
impetus to regulate foreign programmes is not concerned primarily with liberalization and is not imposed from outside the country.

Two Bills were approved by Cabinet for submission to Parliament, one in 2007
and another in 2010, but neither was ratified. The Bills did, however generate a considerable amount of debate in India, not so much about the merits of

different forms of regulation but rather, as in Greece, focusing on whether or not foreign providers should be welcomed at all. One of the key motivations of efforts to introduce a regulatory framework is the view that the lack of regulation has fostered poor quality and unscrupulous practices. The 'Statement of Objects and Reasons' included with 'The Foreign Educational Institutions (Regulation of Entry and Operations) Bill 2010' expressed these concerns:

> A number of Foreign Educational Institutions have been operating in the country and some of them may be resorting to various malpractices to allure and attract students. There is no comprehensive and effective policy for regulation on the operations of all the foreign educational institutions in the country. Due to lack of policy or regulatory regime it has been very difficult to make meaningful assessment of the operations of the foreign educational institutions and absence of such meaningful assessment has given rise to chances of adoption of various unfair practices besides commercialisation. . . . The enactment of a legislation regulating entry and operation of all the foreign educational institutions is necessary to maintain the standards of higher education within the country as well to protect the interest of the students and in public interest.
>
> (Parliament of India, 2010, p. 10)

This is hardly a ringing endorsement of transnational education, but rather an acceptance that an active regulatory approach to foreign providers is preferable to passive non-recognition. The draft legislation reflects the very vocal opposition to the entry of foreign providers in India voiced by the academic community, Left political parties and unions. These groups are opposed to the commercialization of education and characterize international providers as more commercially motivated than domestic providers. There is also a concern that foreign institutions will be able to outcompete domestic institutions for profitable programmes, while leaving domestic institutions to offer those unprofitable programmes that are nevertheless essential for social and economic development (Bhushan, 2006).

While private education in Greece remains relatively peripheral, in India it has grown on a massive scale, not because of state policies but despite them. Kapur and Mehta (2004) argue that a 'de facto privatization of Indian higher education is occurring as a result of the exit of Indian elites from public institutions, to both private sector institutions within the country as well as those abroad' (p. 3). While on the one hand, the judiciary has enforced a prohibition on public universities charging fees to students, on the other, private providers have been quick to fill the void, since the private funding available to higher education far exceeds the available public funds. However, because the regulatory environment is so restrictive of private higher education, the private institutions are dependent upon the entrepreneurial abilities of supportive politicians and a connection with a state university through which the degree is issued. Kapur and Mehta observe that rather than serving the interests of India's middle classes, the current state of poor regulation of mass private education reflects a culture of rent-seeking on behalf of vested interests. As we will see in the description below, the emergent regulatory framework governing foreign providers is entirely consistent with the long history of Indian *dirigisme*, which continues to find strong expression in higher education. Kapur and Mehta (2004) argue that 'Much of what goes in the name of education policy is a product of the one overriding commitment of the education bureaucracy, namely state control in as many ways as possible' (p. 15). Public universities, they observe, remain tightly integrated into networks of power and patronage in politics and the bureaucracy at the state and national level, and any outside competition is fiercely resisted.

In 2013, without requiring new legislation to be passed by Parliament, new regulations governing transnational partnerships were put into effect and forthcoming regulations governing branch campuses were announced (Government of India, 2013; Lawton, 2013; Ministry of Human Resource Development, 2013). Foreign campuses are to be subject to a range of eligibility conditions (Ministry of Human Resource Development, 2013). First, they must be 'ranked among the top 400 universities of the world as per the ranking published by Times Higher Education, Quacquarelli Symonds (QS) or the Academic Ranking of World Universities (ARWU) by Shanghai Jiao Tong University'. Such status thresholds have been a common feature of previous proposals, and appear to be widely supported both because they limit the number of new entrants and because it is believed that revenue seeking institutions will be kept out. A panel appointed by the Indian government to recommend options for reform of the higher education sector – chaired by leading educationist and eminent physicist Yash Pal elaborated nicely some of the thinking behind the such limitations:

> But giving an open license to all and sundry carrying a foreign ownership tag to function like universities in India, most of them not even known in their own countries, would only help them earn profit for their parent institutions located outside or accrue profit to the shareholders. If the best of foreign universities, say amongst the top 200 in the world, want to come here and work, they should be welcomed.
>
> (Pal, 2009, p. 40)

Much discussion has focused on whether or not the world's top universities will rush to establish in India, but there has been less focus on what types of institutions will be prevented from entering. The regulations would appear to prevent the entry of niche institutions that may be very good in their field but not among the world's top 400 universities, and low-cost career-focused providers which are not high status but essential to broaden access to international programmes. Other restrictions included in the proposed regulations include that foreign universities must also be not-for-profit legal entities, have been in existence for at least 20 years, and must lodge a bank deposit of around US$4 million that will be forfeited if the institution is found to have breached any of the regulations. All of these regulations appear designed to ensure that only a small number of well-funded elite institutions are able to establish campuses. The only measures that focus on the quality of the education provided are the standard stipulations that the institution must be accredited in its home country or by an international accreditation agency, and their programmes must be of quality comparable to those offered to students in its main campus. Their degrees would be recognized in the same manner as degrees from the university's home country. As Bhushan has noted, the proposed regulatory framework for campuses has the objective of allaying fears, and 'Nowhere is it mentioned that foreign education providers are supposed to improve the quality of Indian higher education through academic exchange or through the spirit of competition' (Bhushan, 2011, p. 168).

Regulations released in 2013 governing partner-supported programmes establish for the first time an approval process that existing and new collaborations must undergo (Government of India, 2013). At face value these seem much less onerous and may lead to a rapid expansion in partner-supported programmes now that their legality has been clarified. Foreign institutions must be partnered with an Indian government institution, or an Indian private institution that has been awarding degrees and postgraduate diplomas for at least five years. Both institutions must be appropriately accredited. They must apply to the University Grants Commission (UGC) for approval, specifying the facilities, faculty, fees, curriculum and 'requisite funds for operations for a minimum of three years'; however, the regulations do not specify the standards required in each of these categories (Government of India, 2013, p. 3818). The licensing of Indian education institutions to issue awards on behalf of foreign education institutions is explicitly prohibited. In cases where the UGC finds that a partnership has breached the conditions they can take action against the Indian institution and may 'blacklist' the foreign provider, thereby preventing them from offering any other programmes in India.

This regulation provides a clear legal framework for the first time for partner-supported programmes, but like the branch campus regulation, it does actually not make access any easier. The regulations state that providers must abide by the requirements of Indian regulatory agencies, and one such agency, the All India Council for Technical Education (AICTE) has had regulations in place since 2003 governing transnational collaborations although until now without the legal framework to enforce these (Bhushan, 2006). The AICTE has jurisdiction over technical institutions and engineering, technical and management programmes offered by universities. It appears that programmes in these fields will need to meet AICTE requirements as well as the requirements of the new UGC regulations. This is not straightforward, however, because many inconsistencies remain. The AICTE guidelines require that students admitted to collaborations and twinning programmes (as opposed to branch campuses) 'should spend at least one semester of the course work of the Programme in the Foreign University/Institution in its parent Country' whereas the new regulations allow for the whole programme to be delivered in India (AICTE, 2013b, p. 2).

Many transnational programmes have applied for AICTE approval but few have been approved (Anandakrishnan, 2011, p. 195). By late 2013 only nine foreign universities had been approved to run programmes in India, between them being approved to recruit 1,268 students in India in the academic year 2013/14 in these fields (AICTE, 2013a). Interestingly, there is around the same number of foreign universities included in AICTE list of unapproved institutions (AICTE, 2013c). Now that the regulations have been published, presumably the UGC and AICTE will be able to take steps to close these non-approved programmes. But there are many more that have so far escaped AICTE's attention and may now be under threat of closure. While it is difficult to know how many programmes currently exist, Agarwal (2008) estimates, based on several studies, that there are around 15,000 students enrolled in around 150 foreign programmes, mostly in collaboration with an Indian partner institution and in professional and technical education fields (pp. 90–91). It remains to be seen whether implementation of the new regulations leads to a forced closure of the majority of existing transnational programmes, as occurred in South Africa, or leads to an expansion of higher quality programmes as the legal basis for the operation and recognition of programmes is clarified.

In Greece and India, domestic institutions are fearful of having to compete with foreign providers to lure domestic students, but in some countries domestic institutions are also concerned about transnational providers competing with them for international students. One could imagine this being a concern in key destinations such as London or Kuala Lumpur which are both attractive to transnational providers for that reason.

Restrictive regulation and comprehensive quality assurance

Some countries that continue to restrict the entry of foreign providers have adopted quality assurance measures along the lines of those proposed in Greece and India. As we have seen, restrictive regulation on its own in the absence of quality assurance can lead to a wide range of providers of highly variable quality entering the market despite the government's best intentions. Some countries therefore combine restrictive entry requirements with quality assurance in order to both regulate the scale and quality of provision. Sometimes the development of quality assurance requirements accompanies a liberalization of business regulation.

China presents a good example of this approach, seeking to recruit high-status foreign institutions while being able to bar the entry of institutions that are deemed to be of low quality or status or which pose a competitive challenge to domestic institutions. For example, the Chinese Ministry of Education has recently decided to more actively vet foreign programme applications, announcing in April 2007 that if a proposed programme is 'already popular and concentrated among those Chinese institutions, or if its proposed tuition and other charges are significantly higher than the cost, the proposal will not be accepted or approved'.

China has no ideological commitment to openness and internationalization, rather it allows in foreign education providers on the same basis as it allows in foreign corporations and capital – foreign capital should be here as long as it is useful to us. There are also concerns about the potential for cultural imperialism. Gu, for example, stresses that China should engage with foreign influences but maintain control over their impacts. He provides the following policy advice:

> When running Sino-foreign cooperative institutions and programs, it is necessary for the Chinese partners to make the courses or programs offered relevant to the Chinese context. This can be achieved by identifying Chinese as the primary medium of instruction, developing curricula that reflect China's culture and reality, auditing imported textbooks, requiring Chinese faculty members to participate in the entire course of education, having an insight into the motivations of foreign partners, and maintaining a dominant role in the course of delivery ... . The key to cultural security lies in the enhancement of individual and collective cultural self-awareness in the process of cultural contacts.
>
> (Gu, 2009, p. 641)

In April 2007, the government published the *Notification of the Ministry of Education on Further Regulating Chinese-Foreign Co-operation in Running Schools*, which expressed the authorities' views concerning the progress and problems with foreign cooperation in practice. The government criticized cooperative arrangements on various grounds, including non-compliance with government requirements, undue focus on financial matters, political insensitivity, inappropriate advertising and the need to improve quality assurance.

The regulations are open to interpretation by the authorities. Depending on whether or not the proposed cooperative partnership is welcomed, the regulations can be interpreted and applied favourably or unfavourably. In this light, a British report suggests that:

> if you take the trouble to establish good relations with officials and make sure they understand why you are there and what you are trying to achieve in China, then you can often get interpretations that are effectively permissive of what you want to do .... So when I see the phrase 'yuan-z shang' (in principle), I know that there may be a possibility of doing it.
>
> (Halper, 2007, p. 17)

Good relations and a reputable Chinese partner mean that there is room for further discussion with Chinese authorities; in this sense, the regulations are indeed flexible, as intended by the general (and sometimes vague) terms in which they are expressed.

Conclusion

The importer state has a combination of powers and constraints. At the most basic level, it has the power to allow the foreign provider in and to deny access. Along the way, as discussed above, there are a range of regulatory tools at the government's disposal to shape the nature of the relationship and the way the provider can operate. At the same time the government has domestic and international constraints. Domestically, governments must overcome opposition from local institutions to allowing foreign competitors to enter the national systems. Often a compromise is reached in which foreign providers are allowed to operate but do not have access to the same funding and status as domestic providers. International constraints include adherence to the provisions of trade agreements and the prospect of damaging the country's international reputation by being too heavy handed or unreasonable. Fundamentally, though, governments tend to take on domestic opposition to foreign providers when they believe that the benefits to the nation – capacity building, international student recruitment, demonstration effects and enhancing the country's educational profile – justify the political and regulatory energy required.

The OECD's *Guidelines for Quality Provision in Cross-Border Higher Education* (OECD & UNESCO 2005) established some very clear advice for governments to ensure that their students and other stakeholders were able to access cross-border higher education while being protected from degree and diploma mills. In reviewing the implementation of these amongst OECD members states, Vincent-Lancrin and Pfotenhauer (2012, p. 16) ask:

1   whether governments have established or encouraged a comprehensive, fair and transparent system of registration or licensure for cross-border higher education;
2   whether comprehensive capacity for quality assurance and accreditation of cross-border provision has been created;
3   whether governments consult and coordinate amongst the various competent bodies for quality assurance and accreditation, both nationally and internationally;
4   whether governments provide accurate, reliable and easily accessible information on the criteria, standards and consequences of registration, licensure, quality assurance and accreditation of cross-border higher education;
5   whether governments participate in the UNESCO regional conventions on the recognition of qualifications and have established national information centres.

This list of expectations is as useful now as it was when it was developed in 2005. If such policies are so clearly beneficial, however, why have they not been universally adopted?

Economic liberals argue that there is a need for governments to think about the education sector like most other sectors of the economy, establishing rules for the operation of the sector so that consumers (students) and providers (the educational institutions) are able to make their own decisions within that sector, and governments basically set the rules rather than running the system; that's a big leap but that's what's required and that's the direction we're heading in. Liberalization is not yet reflected in the General Agreement on Trade in Services. There's a huge gap between what governments are doing in practice and what they're prepared to commit to in a legally binding agreement. We suggest that governments are not entirely confident about the effectiveness of the regulatory framework they're introducing. They want to be able to keep their options open, to backtrack, to introduce new regulations, to possibly introduce discriminatory regulations against foreign providers if they need to.

Rather than committing to a set of trade rules or some other externally mandated criteria, a government can choose to maintain its prerogatives by simply not spelling out the rules. Then they have the flexibility to deal with matters as they arise. An anecdotal illustration: some 20 years ago one of the authors was asked by his institution to find out about the regulations of a particular country where it was already teaching several courses with local partners. In the mists of time, things had seemed to proceed on conversations and handshakes, and this made the new Vice Chancellor nervous in case problems arose. He wanted transparency. The responsible person in the host country education ministry informed us that we were currently in good standing with the authorities, and that we would certainly be informed if that situation changed; there was no need to 'become legalistic'.

Justifiably or not, education has a particular resonance that most other aspects of the economy do not – it is redolent of nationalism, cultural development, self-actualization, ethics, hopes for the future of one's children and so on. That makes it harder for many governments to treat it with hard-nosed economic rationalism, even if they want to. A quick political calculation will often suggest that too much tampering with the present system runs the risk of alienating the domestic public, particularly if the beneficiaries are seen to be foreign countries or foreign commercial providers.

References

Agarwal, P. (2008). India in the context of international student circulation: Status and prospects. In H. de Wit, P. Agaral, M. E. Said, M. T. Sehoole & M. Sirozi (Eds.), *The Dynamics of International Student Circulation in a Global Context* (pp. 83–112). Rotterdam and Taipei: Sense.

AICTE. (2013a). Foreign collaborations. Retrieved from www.aicte-india.org/misappforeigncoll.htm

AICTE. (2013b). Foreign university/collaborations. Retrieved from www.aicte-india.org/foreignuniversities.htm

AICTE. (2013c). Unapproved institutions. Retrieved from www.aicte-india.org/misunapprovedinstitutions.htm

Altbach, P. G., & Knight, J. (2007). The internationalization of higher education: Motivations and realities. *Journal of Studies in International Education*, *11*(3–4), 290–305. doi: 10.1177/1028315307303542.

Anandakrishnan, M. (2011). Quality assurance mechanisms for technological disciplines in the context of transnational education in India. In A. Stella & S. Bhushan (Eds.), *Quality Assurance of Transnational Higher Education: The Experiences of Australia and India* (pp. 191–200). Australian Universites Quality Agency and the National University of Educational Planning and Administration.

Bhushan, S. (2006). *Foreign Education Providers in India: Mapping the Extent and Regulation*. London: Observatory on Borderless Higher Education.

Bhushan, S. (2011). Overview of the Indian scenario. In A. Stella & S. Bhushan (Eds.), *Quality Assurance of Transnational Higher Education: The Experiences of Australia and India* (pp. 159–171). Australian Universites Quality Agency and the National University of Educational Planning and Administration.

Braithwaite, J., & Drahos, P. (2000). *Global Business Regulation*. Cambridge: Cambridge University Press.

Chambers, G. S., & Cummings, W. K. (1990). *Profiting from Education: Japan-United States International Educational Ventures in the 1980s*. New York: Institute on International Education.

Clayton, D., & Ziguras, C. (2011). Transnational education: Delivering quality Australian programs offshore. In D. Davis & B. Mackintosh (Eds.), *Making a Difference: Australian International Education* (pp. 302–330). Sydney: UNSW Press.

Garrett, R. (2005). *Fraudulent, Sub-standard, Ambiguous: The Alternative Borderless Higher Education*. London: Observatory on Borderless Higher Education.

Gopinathan, S., & Lee, M. H. (2011). Challenging and co-opting globalisation: Singapore's strategies in higher education. *Journal of Higher Education Policy and Management*, *33*(3), 287–299. doi: 10.1080/1360080x.2011.565001.

Government of India. (2013). University Grants Commission (promotion and maintenance of standards of academic collaboration between Indian and Foreign educational institutions). *Gazette of India* (3816).

Gu, J. (2009). Transnational education: Current developments and policy implications. *Frontiers of Education in China*, *4*(4), 624–649. doi: 10.1007/s11516-009-0033-y.

Halper, A. (2007). Navigating the legalities. In A. Fazackerley (Ed.), *British Universities in China: The Reality Beyond the Rhetoric. An Agora Discussion Paper*. London: Agora: The Forum for Culture and Education.

Helms, R. M. (2008). *Transnational Education in China: Key Challenges, Critical Issues, and Strategies for Success*. London: Observatory on Borderless Higher Education.

Higher Education Commission. (2013). *Regulating Higher Education: Protecting Students, Encouraging Innovation, Enhancing Excellence*. London: Higher Education Commission.

Huang, F. (2006). Transnational higher education in mainland China: A focus on foreign degree-conferring programs. In F. Huang (Ed.), *Transnational Higher Education in Asia and the Pacific Region* (pp. 21–34). Hiroshima: Research Institute for Higher Education Hiroshima University.

Huang, F. (2011). Transnational higher education in Japan and China: A comparative study. In D. W. Chapman, W. K. Cummings & G. A. Postiglione (Eds.), *Crossing Borders in East Asian Higher Education* (Vol. 27, pp. 265–282): Dordrecht, Netherlands: Springer.

Jayaprakash, P. (2011). *Transnational Education in India: A Stakeholder Focused Analysis of the Foreign Educational Institutions Bill*. Norderstedt, Germany: Lambert Academic Publishing.

Jayaprakash, P. K. (2010). Transnational education in India: Premises of the Foreign Educational Institutions Bill (2010). Erasmus Mundus Master's Thesis, University of Oslo.

Kapur, D., & Mehta, P. B. (2004). *Indian Higher Education Reform: From Half-Baked Socialism to Half-Baked Capitalism*. Boston, MA: Center for International Development at Harvard University.

Kathimerini. (2012, 9 July). Troika urges full recognition of private college degrees. Retrieved from www.ekathimerini.com

Khadria, B. (2011). Some policy perspectives on transnational education. In A. Stella & S. Bhushan (Eds.), *Quality Assurance of Transnational Higher Education: The Experiences of Australia and India* (pp. 201–214). Australian Universites Quality Agency and the National University of Educational Planning and Administration.

Kitsantonis, N. (2011, 10 April). E.U. presses Greece on private colleges. *New York Times*. Retrieved from www.nytimes.com/2011/04/11/world/europe/11iht-educLede11.html

Koh, A. (2012). Tactics of interventions: Student mobility and human capital building in Singapore. *Higher Education Policy*, 25(2), 191–206. doi: 10.1057/hep.2012.5.

Labi, A. (2010, 11 April). Greek court paves way for recognition of degrees from private colleges. *Chronicle of Higher Education*. Retrieved from http://chronicle.com/blogs/ticker/greek-court-paves-way-for-recognition-of-degrees-from-private-colleges/22458

Lane, J. E., & Kinser, K. (2013). Cross-border higher education in Africa: Collaboration and competition. *International Perspectives on Education and Society, 21, The Development of Higher Education in Africa: Prospects and Challenges*, 99–126. doi: 10.1108/s1479-3679(2013)0000021007.

Lånekassen. (2013). Godkjenning av utdanning i utlandet [Recognition of education abroad]. Retrieved from www.lanekassen.no/nb-NO/Hovedmeny/Stipend-og-lan/Utland/Utdanninger/Godkjenning-av-utdanning-i-utlandet

Lanzendorf, U. (2008). *Foreign-Backed Universities: A Status Report on International Academic Affiliation*. London: Observatory on Borderless Higher Education.

Lawton, W. (2013). Foreign universities in India: Bypassing parliament. *Borderless Report* (October).

Lawton, W., & Katsomitros, A. (2011). *International Branch Campuses: Data and Developments*. London: Observatory on Borderless Higher Education.

Lee, S. J. (2005). Educational upgrading through private educational institutions. *Singapore Statistics Newsletter* (September), 15–17.

Lee, M.-H. (2006). Transnational higher education of Korea: The task and prospects. In F. Huang (Ed.), *Transnational Higher Education in Asia and the Pacific Region* (pp. 91–108). Hiroshima: Research Institute for Higher Education Hiroshima University.

Levy, D. C. (2006). The unanticipated explosion: Private higher education's global surge. *Comparative Education Review, 50*(2), 217–240.

Levy, D. C. (2012). The decline of private higher education. *Higher Education Policy, 26*(1), 25–42. doi: 10.1057/hep.2012.26.

Maclean, R., & Lai, A. (2012). Policy and practice possibilities for Hong Kong to develop into an education hub: Issues and challenges. In M. Stiasny & T. Gore (Eds.), *Going Global: The Landscape for Policy Makers and Practitioners in Tertiary Education* (pp. 145–156). Bingley, UK: Emerald.

Marseilles, M. (2009). Greece: Licensing of private colleges postponed. Retrieved 13 September 2009 from www.universityworldnews.com/article.php?story=20090911233827114

McBurnie, G., & Ziguras, C. (2001). The regulation of transnational higher education in Southeast Asia: Case studies of Hong Kong, Malaysia and Australia. *Higher Education, 42*(1), 85–105.

McBurnie, G., & Ziguras, C. (2007). *Transnational Education: Current Issues and Future Trends in Offshore Higher Education*. London: RoutledgeFalmer.

McNamara, J. (2013). *The Shape of Things to Come: The Evolution of Transnational Education: Data, Definitions, Opportunities and Impacts Analysis*. London: British Council.

MoE. (2006). *2006 Education Statistics Digest*. Singapore: Ministry of Education.

Ministry of Human Resource Development. (2013). Opening of campuses by foreign universities. Retrieved from http://pib.nic.in/newsite/PrintRelease.aspx?relid=99225

Mok, K. H. (2006). The quest for a regional hub of higher education: Transnational higher education and changing governance in Singapore. In F. Huang (Ed.), *Transnational Higher Education in Asia and the Pacific Region* (pp. 127–150). Hiroshima: Research Institute for Higher Education Hiroshima University.

Mok, K. H. (2008). Varieties of regulatory regimes in Asia: the liberalization of the higher education market and changing governance in Hong Kong, Singapore and Malaysia. *The Pacific Review, 21*(2), 147–170. doi:10.1080/09512740801990220.

Mok, K. H. (2012). International benchmarking with the best: The varied role of the state in the quest for regional education hubs in Malaysia and Hong Kong. In G. Steiner-Khamsi & F. Waldow (Eds.), *World Yearbook of Education 2012: Policy Borrowing and Lending in Education* (pp. 167–190). London and New York: Routledge.

Mok, K. H., & Xu, X. (2008). When China opens to the world: A study of transnational higher education in Zhejiang, China. *Asia Pacific Education Review, 9*(4), 393–408.

Ng, P. T. (2013). The global war for talent: responses and challenges in the Singapore higher education system. *Journal of Higher Education Policy and Management, 35*(3), 280–292. doi: 10.1080/1360080x.2013.786859.

OECD & UNESCO. (2005). *Guidelines for Quality Provision in Cross-Border Higher Education*. Paris: United Nations Educational, Scientific and Cultural Organization and the Organisation for Economic Co-operation and Development.

Pal, Y. (2009). *Report of The Committee to Advise on Renovation and Rejuvenation of Higher Education*. New Delhi: Ministry of Human Resource Development.

Parliament of India (2010). *The Foreign Educational Institutions (Regulation of Entry and Operations) Bill, 2010*. Bill No. 57 of 2010 C.F.R.

QAA. (2006). *UK Higher Education in China: An Overview of the Quality Assurance Arrangements*. Mansfield, UK: The Quality Assurance Agency for Higher Education.

Ranganath, H. A., & Shyamasundar, M. S. (2011). Quality assurance of transnational higher education in India. In A. Stella & S. Bhushan (Eds.), *Quality Assurance of Transnational Higher Education: The Experiences of Australia and India* (pp. 183–189). Australian Universites Quality Agency and the National University of Educational Planning and Administration.

Rawazik, W., & Carroll, M. (2009). Complexity in quality assurance in a rapidly growing free economic environment: A UAE case study. *Quality in Higher Education*, 15(1), 79–83.

Richards, C. (2012). The emergence of the Malaysian education hub policy: Higher education internationalisation from a non-western, developing country perspective. In M. Stiasny & T. Gore (Eds.), *Going Global: The Landscape for Policy Makers and Practitioners in Tertiary Education* (pp. 157–168). Bingley, UK: Emerald.

Salt, J., & Wood, P. (2013). Staffing UK university campuses overseas: Lessons from MNE practice. *Journal of Studies in International Education*. doi: 10.1177/1028315313483773.

Sehoole, M. T. (2008). South Africa and the dynamics of international student circulation. In H. de Wit, P. Agaral, M. E. Said, M. T. Sehoole & M. Sirozi (Eds.), *The Dynamics of International Student Circulation in a Global Context* (pp. 141–165). Rotterdam and Taipei: Sense.

Sidhu, R., Ho, K. C., & Yeoh, B. (2011). Emerging education hubs: The case of Singapore. *Higher Education*, 61(1), 23–40. doi: 10.1007/s10734-010-9323-9.

Sirat, M. (2006). Transnational higher education in Malaysia: Balancing benefits and concerns through regulations. In F. Huang (Ed.), *Transnational Higher Education in Asia and the Pacific Region* (pp. 109–126). Hiroshima: Research Institute for Higher Education Hiroshima University.

Sirozi, M. (2008). Indonesian experiences in the global dynamics of international students' circulation. In H. de Wit, P. Agaral, M. E. Said, M. T. Sehoole & M. Sirozi (Eds.), *The Dynamics of International Student Circulation in a Global Context* (pp. 113–140). Rotterdam and Taipei: Sense.

Song, M.-M., & Tai, H.-H. (2006). Transnational higher education in Taiwan. In F. Huang (Ed.), *Transnational Higher Education in Asia and the Pacific Region* (pp. 151–169). Hiroshima: Research Institute for Higher Education Hiroshima University.

Tapsir, S. H., & Rahman, M. A. A. (2012). The impact of transnational higher education in Malaysia. In M. Stiasny & T. Gore (Eds.), *Going Global: The Landscape for Policy Makers and Practitioners in Tertiary Education* (pp. 169–178). Bingley, UK: Emerald.

Tham, S. Y. (2013). Internationalizing higher education in Malaysia: Government policies and university's response. *Journal of Studies in International Education*. doi: 10.1177/1028315313476954.

Thorat, S. K. (2011). The regulatory and facilitative aspects of transnational education in India. In A. Stella & S. Bhushan (Eds.), *Quality Assurance of Transnational Higher Education: The Experiences of Australia and India* (pp. 173–182). Australian Universites Quality Agency and the National University of Educational Planning and Administration.

Tsurata, Y. (2006). Transnational higher education in Japan. In F. Huang (Ed.), *Transnational Higher Education in Asia and the Pacific Region* (pp. 59–90). Hiroshima: Research Institute for Higher Education Hiroshima University.

UNCTAD. (2013). *World Investment Report 2013: Global Value Chains and Trade for Development*. New York and Geneva: United Nations Conference on Trade and Development.

UNESCO. (2013). Data centre. Retrieved 21 October 2013 from www.uis.unesco.org

Verbik, L., & Jokivirta, L. (2005a). *National Regulatory Frameworks for Transnational Higher Education: Models and Trends, Part 1.* Observatory Briefings. London: Observatory on Borderless Higher Education.

Verbik, L., & Jokivirta, L. (2005b). *National Regulatory Frameworks for Transnational Higher Education: Models and Trends, Part 2.* Observatory Briefings. London: Observatory on Borderless Higher Education.

Vincent-Lancrin, S., & Pfotenhauer, S. (2012). *Guidelines for Quality Provision in Cross-Border Higher Education: Where Do We Stand?* Paris: OECD.

Watson, G., & Yap, S. (2011). A changing landscape: Malaysia, Singapore and the Asian education hubs of the future. Paper presented at the AIEC.

Welch, A. R. (2010). Internationalisation of Vietnamese higher education: Retrospect and prospect. In G. Harman, M. Hayden & T. N. Pham (Eds.), *Reforming Higher Education in Vietnam: Challenges and Priorities.* Dordrecht, Netherlands: Springer.

World Bank. (2013). *Doing Business 2014: Understanding Regulation for Small and Medium-Size Enterprises.* Washington, DC: International Bank for Reconstruction and Development/The World Bank.

Yang, R. (2006). Transnational higher education in Hong Kong: An analysis. In F. Huang (Ed.), *Transnational Higher Education in Asia and the Pacific Region* (pp. 35–58). Hiroshima: Research Institute for Higher Education Hiroshima University.

Yang, R. (2008). Transnational higher education in China: Contexts, characteristics and concerns. *Australian Journal of Education, 52*(3), 272–286.

Ziguras, C., Reinke, L., & McBurnie, G. (2003). 'Hardly neutral players': Australia's role in liberalizing trade in education services. *Globalisation, Societies and Education, 1*(3), 359–374.

Λακασας, Α. (2010, 29 July). Οι άδειες κολεγίων στα δικαστήρια [College approvals in the courts]. Η Καθημερινή [*Kathimerini*]. Retrieved from http://news.kathimerini.gr/4dcgi/_w_articles_ell_2_29/07/2010_409645

Conclusion

We have seen in the various chapters of this book how increasing mobility of students and programmes poses new regulatory challenges for governments. While governments have been focused on improving national higher education systems – grappling with the most effective ways of raising participation rates, reducing inequalities in access, aligning graduate outcomes with the workforce needs of the future, and so on – their efforts are complicated by the ever greater permeability of those national systems. It is tempting, and surprisingly common, to ignore the international 'leakage' between systems. A glance at the official description of higher education on any country's ministry of education website will normally portray a hermetically sealed national system, with national institutions serving national students. Those students and providers who have either entered or departed that national system are usually overlooked. In this book we have focused on those states that have been at the forefront of developing innovative modes of governance of cross-border educational flows, but the truth is that most states have devoted little time and energy to such challenges. We expect this situation to change over time as effective regulatory measures become more widely adopted and normalized.

Our preference has been to analyse these novel approaches, and unpack their benefits and risks. Where there have been clear ideologically driven disputes driving differences in approaches we have tried to foreground them, but it seems to us that such clarity in policymaking on these issues is rare. The dominance of user-pays market liberalism in the UK and Australia is well documented here and elsewhere, as is the nationalist protectionism that has driven policy in India and Greece. But in many ways the motivations of different political actors in these cases are more complex than the clichéd depiction of them suggests. In most countries, though, the regulatory approaches to cross-border higher education lack any type of coherence. This is partly because potential policy problems we have outlined in this book concern a wide range of government agencies that rarely coordinate well, especially on issues like these that are not of major electoral significance. We are conscious that in Chapter 1 we have outlined three ideological approaches to cross-border higher education which then appear infrequently in subsequent chapters, like a feature film in which the stars make only cameo appearances. In each of the chapters we trust that readers will be able to identify the influence of one of these 'policy prescriptions' or another, even though the extent to which governments are actually swayed by these is difficult to know in a broad-ranging study such as this one. What we would like to do in this concluding chapter is to imagine what the impact might be of taking seriously these prescriptions to the regulation of cross-border degree mobility, student migration, and transnational programmes and institutions. We will endeavour to bring together the issues discussed through the book by constructing scenarios that illustrate what we believe might occur if governments were to wholeheartedly adopt a free-market approach, or concern themselves only with achieving equity and protection of the vulnerable, or adopt policies that are purely designed to harness cross-border higher education to boost national competitiveness. For the second of these we take a slightly different approach here compared with Chapter 1, and instead of considering the implications of various diverse critiques of commercialism, here we focus on how one might respond to inequalities in access.

In the brief summaries that follow we sketch the main features of each approach, and point to some of the examples discussed in the book which could provide models for each of these approaches. We do not, however, go into any detail here about the technical difficulties involved, or obvious tensions between different types of objectives.

Mobile degree student scenarios

Liberalizing the global education degree market

In a purer global education market, states would intervene much less in the business of exporting education. Governments would not provide export subsidies to their institutions and would not fix the prices they charge. Providers would be prevented from 'dumping' education on global markets at below the cost of production. Those states that currently fund incoming students and set prices, such as Germany, France, Japan and China, would adopt the market model currently employed in Anglophone countries. Licensing regimes for institutions should not discriminate against private or sub-degree providers, and instead should allow a wide variety of providers to compete, with variable levels of quality and price. Where governments act as the purchaser of education for their citizens, they would treat domestic and foreign providers equivalently, as some Northern European states have done, so that students who travel abroad to undertake degrees would be entitled to the same level of funding support as they would at home.

Maximizing equity in degree student mobility

There are several steps that both host countries and students' home countries could take that would redress current inequalities in access to foreign degree study. The cost of tuition fees and living expenses in host countries is a major impediment, and there are several ways governments could address this. Host governments could redress this by providing funded places for all students whether international or domestic, as Germany and France do currently, or at least providing the same level of government subsidy in countries like the UK where students pay part of the cost of their studies. Another approach could be to use means testing to determine eligibility for scholarships or fee discounts, so student contributions are progressive in that the more affluent contribute more to the cost of running an institution than the poor. Extending the rights enjoyed by local students to international students would also assist less affluent students. Eliminating restrictions on work rights for international students, for example, would allow those who need to finance their studies by working, as many local students do. Providing international students with access to healthcare systems on the same basis as local students would also reduce costs. All these measures involve extending support to students on the basis of need rather than nationality.

Governments in students' home countries could also take steps to reduce inequalities in access. There is probably little they can do to reduce the outflow of affluent students, but they could broaden access by providing scholarships or means-tested funding to those students who cannot otherwise afford to study abroad. Such schemes are increasingly common in middle-income countries, using various combinations of merit-based and needs-based eligibility. A bigger impact would be achieved by making existing government funding internationally portable. Governments in education-importing countries might extract concessions or preferential treatment from particular host governments or even individual providers. This can be effective when the sending government has the ability to influence where students study, as China's JSJ can, or where governments tie their loans and funding to preferred destinations. Scholarship funding bodies, in China, Saudi Arabia and Mexico for example, already do this, but such approaches could also be extended to support fee-paying students. From host governments they might seek for their mobile students more generous work rights, access to healthcare or other public services, streamlined student visa issuance, or more generous treatment of accompanying spouses and children. From institutions they might seek discounted fees, subsidized accommodation, intensive and proactive pastoral care especially tailored to their students' requirements, discounted language preparatory programmes, additional tailored academic support services.

Maximizing national competitiveness through student mobility

Self-funded students clearly make a contribution to the expansion of higher education systems in host countries and governments can support institutions in recruiting fee-paying students by allowing them to teach in English and to keep the income such students generate, as well as implementing effective national promotion, licensing of institutions and student visa processing. Regulation of providers and students needs to focus on ensuring quality education outcomes and to avoid reputational damage that can result from educational values being compromised by commercial imperatives. The recruitment of international students can also play a significant role in internationalizing one's higher education institutions, which governments can support by encouraging the recruitment of foreign academics and the development of internationally focused programmes. Most international degree students return to their home countries to build careers, and the ongoing relationships with those overseas alumni are perhaps the most important contribution to national competitiveness that student mobility can make. As well as maximizing the flow of self-funded students, it often makes strategic sense for governments to fund students from particular countries. China has begun to support thousands of incoming students from developing countries in which it has strategic and commercial interests, in much the same way as the United States has done for decades.

Governments of students' home countries can use overseas education providers to supplement local provision, particularly in areas of critical importance to national competitiveness. Norway used this approach for several decades, judging that it was more cost-effective to fund students to study overseas than to expand local provision. In less affluent middle-income economies, where the majority of international students hail from, the cost of providing education locally is usually much lower than sending students abroad, but there is limited capacity. For this reason most governments have prioritized funding their nationals' doctoral studies abroad in the expectation that these students will build an internationally competitive education sector upon their return. The loan schemes used in Colombia and Mexico provide an effective model for governments to support a much larger number of students, and by careful setting of eligibility requirements and remission of debt, it is possible to steer students towards fields of study and subsequent employment that are judged most critical in fostering competitiveness. Because students tend to maintain ongoing relationships with the places in which they studied, encouraging students to undertake degrees in particular countries may also be strategically useful, either because that country is more advanced and expertise can thus be imported, or because the country is a major trading partner.

Student migration scenarios

Liberalizing the global market for students turned migrants

Market liberals tend to stress the benefits that arise from the unimpeded choices made by individual actors. In the case of international student migration they would advocate that home country governments not coerce students to return but rather trust that students are the best judge of where their skills are most productively employed. Those who remain abroad may at some point in the future decide to return to their home country, but the decision should be theirs.

Regarding the host country policies, governments should facilitate the free movement of labour. Just as institutions should be enabled to compete globally for students, so should employers be able to access the international market for labour. Governments should allow former international students the opportunity to seek employment through such schemes as automatic postgraduate work rights of the kind the several Anglophone exporters have adopted. When former students find employment they should be granted work visas without fuss, as they can in Germany or Singapore.

Maximizing equity in student migration

From the perspective of the student's home country there are two serious inequalities – the unequal access to the means to emigrate, and unequal outcomes of those who emigrate and those who stay behind. The first of these challenges is mostly a question of who is able to study overseas, and the measures we discussed above in relation to outbound mobility are equally pertinent here. The second challenge is trickier. As we saw in Chapter 5, efforts by governments to entice former students to return in order to better contribute to the home country are costly and usually effective only on a small scale. Taxing citizens who reside abroad, as the USA does, is a means of redistributing income back to the home country but may prove difficult to implement. The most effective measure we have seen is loans programmes that reward returning students by writing off part of their debt but require students who do not return to pay back the full cost of the support they have received. Such schemes have the benefit of both broadening access to migration and encouraging return.

The experiences of the UK and Australia demonstrate how host governments can broaden access to student migration. Less affluent students seek less costly means to enter the workforce, and enrol in shorter programmes that provide entry to the workforce and residency rights. Governments could extend post-study work rights and permanent residency for students who complete sub-degree or short postgraduate qualifications and provide opportunities for students to work during their studies. These students need to be protected from unscrupulous education providers, employers and landlords, but should be given as much opportunity to migrate as more affluent students who are able to fund more expensive programmes of several years' duration.

Maximizing national competitiveness through student migration

For governments of students' home countries, non-returning international students could limit the country's competitiveness. Schemes that recruit targeted individuals, such as academics and researchers, who are able to make a significant impact in the home country, have been recruited back successfully in China, albeit on a very small scale considering the size of the country. A more effective strategy is to support the development of international education locally, so that fewer students need to leave the country in order to obtain the types of qualifications they desire, as Malaysia and Singapore have done very successfully. Effective diaspora engagement strategies may be the best way for governments to harness their overseas graduates in order to support national development. For this reason many governments are sponsoring a wide range of opportunities for ongoing engagement of former international students in the life of the nation while living abroad, from dual citizenship to professional associations to summer schools for their children.

Host governments are in an enviable position, being able to pick and choose which former international students are offered the opportunity to remain after completing their studies. Effective means of selecting residents from this pool of graduates include post-study work rights so that employers may then sponsor those that they seek to retain, and points systems that select for those qualifications and skills that are known to be in short supply. They might provide further inducements such as scholarships with generous post-study residency rights to the most sought-after doctoral students. The scale of demand for migration to high-income countries can make these schemes very difficult to manage. As immigration programmes prioritize particular qualifications or skills, motivated students will respond and the scale of applications can easily vastly exceed the migration intake or the available positions in the workforce in that field, resulting in underemployed graduate-migrants. Governments need to regulate carefully to avoid collusion between poor-quality colleges, unethical migration agents and dubious employers, who may together fashion pathways designed to meet the requirements of the visa application processes but result in new permanent residents whose qualifications have no credibility with employers.

Transnational provision scenarios

Liberalizing the global transnational education market

More than other topics considered in this book, free trade advocates have devoted much energy to promoting open markets for transnational education providers. They hold that governments in importing countries should allow foreign institutions (and locally owned private institutions as well) to establish without any restriction on their programmes, fees or size and they should be treated no less favourably than domestic institutions. The mix of institutions and programmes should therefore be determined by student demand and provider responsiveness rather than governmental fiat. Successful institutions will grow while others will decline, but overall the quality of the system will improve. For exporting countries, institutions should be able to operate independently of government and invest in operations beyond their borders if they choose. Government's role is to ensure that quality assurance measures are in place for offshore provision as they are at home.

Maximizing equity in the provision of transnational higher education

There is often much concern expressed by education providers in importing countries about the negative effects foreign entrants have on existing institutions. Because there is not a level playing field (that is, foreign providers often have an established reputation and access to resources that local providers lack), the government must limit the scale of foreign provision and provide preferential treatment for local institutions. If they do not, affluent students will bypass meritocratic selection systems that have been established for local institutions and instead buy their way into prestigious foreign providers. Governments in China, Greece, Indonesia, Japan and many others have imposed a range of measures to restrict foreign providers on equity grounds. The range of measures they have employed include limiting both the number and size of providers, enforcing price controls to keep their fees low, denying access to government-funded places, and refusing to recognize their qualifications.

A very different approach to inequitable access is to encourage transnational provision as a means of expanding access, as Malaysia and Singapore have done, freeing up space in local institutions. Where there is large-scale transnational education it is usually the case that the most affluent students will continue to prefer to study in elite local universities or to study overseas. Rather than limiting access to public funds, making means-tested support available to less affluent students to attend foreign institutions can serve to reduce inequalities in access. Governments in exporting countries can support their institutions to broaden access abroad by encouraging not only elite branch campus developments but also vocational educational and training programmes and low-cost large-scale partnerships that expand educational and employment opportunities for large numbers of students.

Maximizing national competitiveness through transnational education

Welcoming foreign programmes and campuses can be a way for governments to support the rapid development of education and training to meet development needs where local institutions are not able to quickly respond to labour market demands. Transnational provision can play a significant role in assisting the development of the local system, through a combination of public and private investment and institutional partnerships. As local provision grows, reliance on foreign providers can shift from capacity building to building the prestige and quality of the local system. Host governments should apply stringent quality standards to both foreign and domestic providers. Transnational institutions can also attract students from abroad, increasing the scale of a country's education system and expanding the pool of graduating students who may then be able to be recruited by employers. The best response to concerns about staff being drawn away from the domestic system is to allow transnational providers to recruit staff from overseas, which assists in expanding local capacity overall.

For exporting countries, offshore programmes and campuses allow institutions to significantly broaden their reach, enrolling students who are not able to study in the home country due to the cost, family responsibilities or the need to continue working. While the graduates of these programmes do not have the same level of attachment to the exporting nation as students who have studied in the home country, by encouraging inter-campus mobility and alumni engagement those students too can constitute an alumni diaspora. Similarly, there is the perceived effect of enhanced international reputation for the successful exporter, and reputational damage if a country's offerings are seen to be substandard or prone to collapse or sudden withdrawal.

Concluding remarks

This exercise in proposing hypothetical scenarios based on very clear philosophical principles has been useful in showing us how in practice the approaches the governments have so far adopted have instead been pragmatic compromises. It is clear that we are far from the emergence of an unfettered borderless education market. States are actually increasingly involved in regulating flows, but are motivated by a range of concerns that are rarely coherently articulated let alone implemented with a whole-of-government approach. This book has looked at broad-ranging policy objectives and the toolkit of measures employed within a number of countries that are heavily involved in cross-border higher education. There are undoubtedly other approaches that we have not touched on and other motivations that we have overlooked, and it is clear that in such a rapidly changing field the next decade will produce as many experiments in governance as the past decade has. We hope that this study can contribute to that process of experimentation, refinement and analysis in ways that benefit the next generation of students, both those who pursue studies in foreign institutions and their peers who stay closer to home.

Index

Altbach, P. 11–5, 18, 26, 27, 50, 100, 161
Asia Pacific Economic Cooperation organization (APEC) xviii, xx, 6–10, 143, 163
Australia: and trade liberalization 4–8, 10, 12, 20–1; and mobile students xxiii, 25, 27–8, 30–2, 35–7, 40–5, 55–9, 61, 63–4, 66, 68, 70–6; and migration xxii, xxv, 81–95, 102, 104–5, 113, 115, 118, 121, 183; and transnational provision 128–30, 133–44, 153, 159, 163–4

brain drain *see* migration
branch campus xx, xxvi, 2–4, 13–14, 18–9, 31, 45, 54–5, 72, 107, 129–33, 138, 141, 149–169, 185–6; *see also* transnational education

Canada xix, 12, 25, 28–30, 35, 37, 40, 58, 61, 64, 81, 83–4, 88, 90, 99, 118, 131
capacity building xxvi, 2, 5, 8–10, 13, 18–9, 52, 56, 62, 100, 104, 108, 117, 122, 129, 148–9, 154, 159, 172, 185–6
Chile 60–2
China: and mobile students 26, 28, 33–4, 36–7, 40, 46, 52–4, 58, 60, 63, 67–9, 71–2, 75–6, 180–2; and migration 88, 90–1, 100, 105–6, 108, 113–14, 117–8, 122, 183; and transnational provision 8, 129–31, 133, 138, 140, 150, 153–4, 158–60, 170–1, 185
Colombia 62, 112, 131, 182

competition x, xxiv, xxv, 3, 6, 10, 11, 35, 37, 40–1, 65, 81, 85–6, 92, 122, 165, 168–9
competitiveness 17–21
consumer protection 45, 50, 68, 76, 132, 156, 166
credit mobility 13, 25, 29–32, 57, 59, 76
culture x, 4, 32, 45, 75, 87, 104, 120, 165, 168, 171
curriculum xvi, xxvi, 6, 16, 19, 26, 31, 59, 133, 135, 139, 149, 151, 153, 169

distance education 3, 128, 132, 135–6, 138, 153

exchange (semester and year) *see* credit mobility
exporting countries xxvi, 6–7, 11, 15–7, 20–1, 25–47, 70, 71, 81–96, 100, 128–144, 160, 180, 184–6

fees *see* tuition fees
funding 7, 10, 13, 17, 25–8, 34, 36–8, 41, 42, 44, 50, 56–68, 75, 76–7, 104, 105, 112, 114, 153, 156, 161, 163–5, 167, 172, 180–2; *see also* tuition fees
France 27–8, 36–7, 40, 42, 54, 58, 81, 130, 160, 180–1

General Agreement on Trade in Services (GATS) xviii, 1–7, 12–21, 62–7
Germany 27–8, 34, 36–7, 40, 42, 81, 83, 129, 131, 180–1, 183
globalization xv–xix, 1–21, 25, 31, 119